ISLAM TODAY

ISLAM TODAY

S R Ali

MD Publications Pvt Ltd
New Delhi
www.mdppl.com

Published by :

MD Publications Pvt Ltd
"MD House", 11, Darya Ganj,
New Delhi - 110 002
Phone : +91-11-45355555
E-mail : contact@mdppl.com
Website: www.mdppl.com

ISBN: 978-81-7533-273-7

Published and Printed by Mr. Pranav Gupta on behalf of **MD Publications Pvt Ltd** at Mohit Enterprises, Delhi.

PREFACE

The word *Islam* is a homograph, having multiple meanings, and a triliteral of the word salam, which directly translates as *peace*. Other meanings include submission or the total surrender of oneself to God (see Islam (term)). An adherent of Islam is a Muslim, meaning "one who submits (to God)". The word *Muslim* is the participle of the same verb of which *Islâm* is the infinitive. Muslims regard Islam as the completed and universal version of an original monotheistic faith revealed to peoples before, including to Adam, Abraham, Moses, Jesus, and other prophets. Islamic tradition holds that previous messages have changed and the revelations were distorted.

The Muslim world is changing. Three years after the atrocity of 9/11, it may be in the early stages of a reformation, albeit with a small "r". From Morocco to Indonesia, people are trying to develop a more contemporary and humane interpretation of Islam, and some countries are undergoing major transformations. Much of the attention is focused on reformulating the sharia, the centuries-old body of Islamic law deeply embedded in a medieval psychology. The sharia is state law in many Muslim countries such as Saudi Arabia, Iran, Pakistan and the Sudan. For many conservative and radical Muslims, the sharia is Islam: it cannot be changed, and must be imposed in exactly the shape it was first formulated in the ninth century. Since 9/11, there has been a seismic shift in this perception. More and more Muslims now perceive Islamic law to be dangerously obsolete. Muslims worldwide are acknowledging the need for fundamental change in their perception of Islam. They are making conscious efforts to move away from medieval notions of Islamic law and to implement the vision of justice, equality and beauty that is rooted in the Koran. If such changes continue, the future will not repeat the recent past.

The present struggle, more or less in all Muslim countries, is that the people are not prepared to go along with the rulers in the direction in which they are trying to take them; and the rulers are not prepared to lead the people in the direction in which they desire to move. This has resulted in a perpetual conflict in all the Muslim countries of the world.

The miserably slow peace of progress in the Muslim countries shows how heavily they have had to pay for the perpetual conflict resulting from their rulers' attempts to foist alien values upon them. None of the Muslim countries have been able to make any remarkable progress in any sphere. The people in power have striven all along to de-Islamize the people whereas the people have been keenly desirous of a return to Islam. The story has been repeated, more or less, in the other Muslim countries that have achieved freedom during recent decades. A nation can develop and progress only when there is complete harmony between the conscience of the people and the policies of the government. It is only for such ideals, principles and policies as accord with their own sentiments and aspirations that a people can be expected to stake their all.

I am very grateful to Mr. Pranav Gupta, Director of MD Publications Pvt Ltd, New Delhi, for his kind cooperation and support for this book.

S R Ali

CONTENTS

1

History of Islam

The First Phase: The Ideal Period

In the first phase of our history, a single individual was chosen by God and appointed to reconstruct the life of mankind on the basis of faith in the unity of Godhead, belief in the life hereafter, and obedience to the teachings of the prophets. For thirteen long years that individual preached this message in Mecca, and he was more than a preacher: he was an embodiment of the type of individual that Islam sought to produce. By his behavior and conduct, his deeds and words, his treatment of others and his attitude towards men, he showed what kind of character and moral excellence Islam sought to promote and how a believer in Islam should conduct himself in the rough and tumble of life. The Prophet of Islam was a perfect embodiment of the principles that he preached and the precepts that he enjoined.

The Prophet's message and his personal example soon began to influence people, and within a few years he was joined by a large number of persons. All these converts to Islam accepted the Prophet's teachings earnestly after having fully comprehended its meaning and significance; not one of them responded to his call without understanding it in all its ramifications. And since they had adopted Islam through conscious understanding, all of them molded their lives on the pattern enjoined by the Prophet. The life of each one of the converts to Islam in Mecca during the first thirteen years underwent the transformation and revolution that Islam seeks to bring about in the lives of all men. Not only this. They also actively struggled against all the forces, internal as well as external that stood against the revolution. In the process they readily made the greatest conceivable sacrifices for the cause and happily suffered all imaginable hardships, for they treasured the new values of life above everything else and were not prepared to abandon them at any cost. What is more striking, they did not content themselves with their personal adoption of the Islamic creed and all that it stood for: they were also determined to establish the Islamic way of life and ensure its supremacy in the world. And they staked their lives to ensure that they would never again be governed by any other way of life.

Within thirteen years the Prophet was able to gather around him a small but devoted group of courageous and selfless people; and then he migrated along with these people to Medina, where he set up in the first instance a small city-state. The area of that state did not exceed that of a small township of the present day, its population was merely six to seven thousand. But soon this tiny state became a challenge to the whole of Arabia.

Its founder and chief, the Prophet of Islam began to establish a new social order which was the very antithesis of the pre-Islamic social system of the Arabs. And within a few years he succeeded in setting up a model Islamic society and state. The social order was a perfect manifestation of the Islamic ideals of human civilization and culture, of morality and private ethics, of social justice and economic equity, of brotherhood and fraternity, of solidarity and cohesion. The teachings of Islam no longer remained mere theoretical expressions; they became a living reality in individual and social life. Now one could see with the eyes under one's brows what type of man Islam wants to produce and what type of society and economy it wants to establish and what blessings all this brings to human life.

Within eight brief years, this small State, covering a few square miles and embracing a few thousand souls came to dominate the whole of the Arabian Peninsula extending over more than a million square miles. And it was not merely a political change: it brought about a total and radical transformation of the life of the community in all its aspects. Their view of life, their values, their morals, and their mode of living, all underwent a revolutionary change. Both the spirit and form of their civilization and culture underwent a radical transformation which eventually changed the course of human history. The community as well as its individual members adopted a new mode of thinking, a new kind of conduct and behavior and a new aim and mission of life which they had never known during the several thousand years of their previous history. For centuries before the advent of Islam, the Arabs had been split into countless political groups and factions, and their political life had been plagued by confusion; mutual hostility of tribal chieftains and blood wars. Islam made a clean sweep of this bloody confusion and established a unified and orderly political system.

This was no mean achievement in itself; but Islam accomplished something much more difficult in bringing about an intellectual, moral and Cultural Revolution. It is indeed a pity that a biased historiography has misrepresented this great change as the outcome of a series of wars and expeditions, and many Western orientalists have all along been shouting from the housetops that Islam was spread by the sword. The truth is that the total number of persons killed on both sides in the wars fought during the days of the Prophet did not exceed one thousand and two hundred. Anyone with a grain of sense should find it easy to see that such a great revolution could not possibly have been wrought by the sword.

The Real Cause of Success

In fact the real reason for the success of that great and unique revolution was very different from what detractors of Islam have made it out to be. During the earlier years when the Prophet preached Islam in Mecca, only a small number of people could comprehend its meaning and significance. It was understood and appreciated only by those who were gifted with rare powers of intellect and comprehension, who could rise above the deep-rooted prejudices of the days of ignorance, who could recognize and accept the truth, who could follow it in practice and who possessed the moral courage to stake their lives for the sake of the ideals they had adopted.

Later, with the Prophet's migration to Medina, the situation changed radically. With the help of a small group of devoted followers gifted with these qualities and imbued with this spirit, the Prophet succeeded in establishing an Islamic social order in Medina. As the head of a free Islamic state be began to introduce and implement the entire Islamic scheme of reconstruction and reform and thus provided a concrete and striking manifestation of the moral, social and political ideals of the new Faith. People could now see for themselves the peace and order, the virtue and righteousness, the honesty and integrity, the equity and justice, the fraternity and equality that an Islamic society could establish.

They could see how it could resolve economic difficulties and problems and purify and ennoble the lives of men. No one, except those who refused to see, could shut his eyes to these glaring realities, which stood in such sharp contrast to the dismal state of affairs before the advent of Islam, when the hand of each was against all and society was reeking with all manner of corruption and immorality. Even those who had at one time pitted themselves against the Prophet and staked their lives in a bid to crush the new faith in the cradle began to see the light. Such stalwarts as Khalid bin Walid, Akrimah bin Abu Jehl and Amr bin Aas were converted to the new religion. Even people like Abu Sufyan and cannibalistic Hind ultimately recognized that Islam, which had brought about such radical and revolutionary changes, in Arab society, was the true religion. The Islamic social order that the Prophet had established was an irrefutable evidence of the inherent soundness of faith and doctrines upon which it was founded.

Thanks to this great revolution the Prophet succeeded in creating the new community with a new code of public morality and a new pattern of individual character. Their collective life was governed entirely by the principles and precepts of Islam. Their beliefs and thoughts were purely Islamic. Their religion was not vitiated by the worship of any deity other than Allah.

Their individual and collective morality had been purged of the evils of the days of ignorance and caste in the mould of Islamic ethics. The civilization and culture of that society were perfectly in accord with the spirit of Islam, and the State was governed exclusively by the laws of Islam. The life of the community was completely devoted to the cause of Islam and every one of its members was prepared to die for the sake of his faith, for the ideals he now lived by. The community pledged to bear the standard of God and uphold His cause in the world.

This became the collective ideal of the community. And it was generally believed that the very purpose of the establishment of the Islamic State was to enforce the principles of Islam in the territories under its sway and to strive to spread the Faith to other parts of the world. The propagation of Islam was the mission of the new community. The State it had succeeded in setting up was a living embodiment of the principles and ideals of Islam and was also the standard bearer of the Faith in the world.

The formation of the first Muslim community and the establishment of the first Islamic state were followed, during the period of the rightly guided Caliphate, by a phenomenal expansion of Islam which may well be described as an explosion. Within the span of a few years the tide of Islamic expansion had overwhelmed a vast part of the globe extending from Turkistan and Afghanistan to Northern Africa. This wonderful phenomenon is bound to set any intelligent student of history thinking about its causes. It should be easy to see that it could not be attributed to physical power or material superiority.

The people of Arabia were not endowed with any extraordinary physical or material strength, and their land lacked even ordinary natural resources. Indeed, with the exception of the recently discovered oil, Arabia is still miserably poor in resources. Its population does not exceed ten million even now; during the rightly guided Caliphate it must have been merely a fraction of what it is today. The causes of the phenomenon must therefore be sought in factors other than material.

It is obvious that the power that led Islam to triumph was the character and conduct of its votaries as reflected in the behavior of each one of them in peace and war, in the administration of conquered lands and in the treatment of the vanquished enemies. It lay in their unflinching faith and spotless character. When power was tempered with justice, authority imbued with virtue, and leadership crowned with morality, a new historic force was released - a force that conquered not merely lands but hearts and souls. This is how the miracle was accomplished.

The subjects of the Iranian and Roman Empires, which Islam overran and vanquished, could not have shut their eyes to the radical difference between the character and conduct of their old and new rulers. Under the old regime, they could not have imagined in their wildest dreams the governors and other dignitaries of state living and moving about like ordinary mortals, always accessible even to the humblest of men, ever ready to hear the grievances of those in distress. When under the Islamic regime they saw such rulers, all, except those blinded by rank prejudice, were compelled to recognize the moral superiority of the new rulers and of their religion.

Like the governors and other administrators, the conquering armies of Islam showed exemplary behavior. As they would pass through a conquered city, thousands of women, attractively made up, would line up on the balconies to see the soldiers' march past; and not one of them would raise his eyes to catch a glimpse of beauty on exhibition. Indeed, a whole army would sometimes march through a city without becoming aware of the inviting presence of pretty women on the balconies.

This was something that the peoples of these lands had never seen or heard: what they had seen and heard was that no woman's honor was safe at the hands of a conquering army. In the circumstances, it was but natural that the battalions of the new conquerors should win the hearts of the vanquished peoples.

Scrupulous regard for the honor of women was but one of the many unique features of the character and conduct of the new conquerors; strict honesty in financial and other dealings with the conquered was another. For instance, whenever, a Muslim army was forced by enemy pressure to withdraw from any part of a conquered territory, it would refund all the taxes collected from the people to meet the cost of administration, because it was no longer in a position to discharge the responsibilities of administration and of protecting their lives and properties. This was again a complete departure from the precedent set by the earlier conquerors and rulers, who, far from refunding collected levies, would rob and plunder as much as they could before evacuating an occupied territory. The peoples of those lands could not have expected any conqueror to be honest in political dealings or administrative matters; what they actually experienced now was saintly character and exemplary conduct in every aspect of life. It was virtue incarnate, and they couldn't but be overwhelmed by it.

This then was the real power and strength which enabled the earlier Muslims to conquer a large part of the world. There is no doubt that they achieved much more through their excellent character and exemplary conduct than they did by the force of arms. Each one of them had embraced and adopted Islam on the basis of a full understanding and appreciation of the creed, and had molded his character and personality in harmony with the spirit of the Faith.

Therefore, in all aspects of their lives and in all spheres of their conduct, they acted faithfully in accordance with the tenets and injunctions of Islam; no temptation could make them flinch or swerve from their path, no oppression could force them to budge an inch from their stand, nor could any power, however great and terror striking, stand in their way.

The people whom they conquered and ruled were not their political slaves but their admirers and their followers. They embraced the conquerors' religion, accepted their culture and even adopted their language. And down to the present day these conquered peoples regard their Muslim conquerors as their heroes and exemplars; on the other hand they are not willing to identify themselves with their non-Muslim fellow countrymen or ancestors. Could such a radical and total change in the lives and thoughts of men have possibly been brought about by the force of arms?

That was the first phase of the history of Islam. This is sot the occasion to discuss the details of that stage of our history. What needs to be emphasized in the context of the present discussion is the fact that Islam achieved such spectacular success in the first phase of its history because its votaries had consciously and earnestly accepted its principles and doctrines, which were fully reflected in the life and character of individuals and the conduct of the community and because a State determined to stake its all on establishing the rule of God on earth had come into being. These were the causes that gave Islam in the very first phase of' its history a momentum that have survived for nearly fourteen hundred years and promises to last for ever. Even today, when the Muslims are in a state of cultural degeneration almost all over the world, they 'bear the imprint of the glorious fast stage of their history.

However corrupt or degenerate a Muslim may be today, he still cherishes, in his heart of hearts, the ideal of Islamic society that was established by the Prophet and maintained and consolidated by the rightly guided Caliphs. He can never completely forget that ideal which continues to illumine the world. Every Muslim is still fascinated by that ideal and desires to see it realized once again. During the many long centuries since the end of the early Caliphate, Islam has been constantly spreading, and there is no part of the world where the light of the Faith has not reached. All this expansion and progress has been in spite of the.fact that there has been no dearth amongst the Muslims of tyrannical rulers, dissolute nobles or immoral commoners.

We have long since ceased to be an ideal nation that could serve as a source of inspiration to the rest of mankind. If Islam has been spreading in the world in spite of the sorry state of the Muslims, it is because they are still enamoured of Islam in its pristine purity, as it was preached and practiced by the Prophet, his first four Caliphs and his Companions. It is that Islam which people still regard as the tree Faith and which they desire to follow. Moreover, the little virtue that one still finds in the character and conduct of Muslims is a faint reflection of the great qualities that their ancestors had developed during the earlier decades of Islam. The imprint of glorious the beginning of Islam upon the life of the community has no doubt faded a great deal with the passage of time, but it has not vanished, and its influence abides. Whatever dynamism, we find today in Islam is entirely due to the great movement that Islam generated during the initial years of its historic career.

The Second Phase: Kingship and its Cultural Consequences

Let us now proceed to discuss the second phase of our history. This phase started with a rapid expansion of Islam over a vast part of the globe. The number of conversions to Islam during the period was so large and its speed so fast that their education and training became a serious problem and a difficult task. Despite the fact that persons of exemplary conduct existed and they were indeed the embodiment of Islamic teachings and the charm of their personality, their moral excellence and their flawless character, deeds and behaviour attracted everyone who came in contact with them to the extent that even the Quran is witness when it declares that the call was so irresistible that whole flocks of people were swept into it. But it was not physi-cally possible to induce in these millions of converts the same radical transformation which the earlier Muslims had gone through.

Consequently, the proportion of Muslims who fully understood the principled of Islam and faithfully followed them in life began to decline. On the other hand, there was a rapid increase in the proportion of Muslims who had earnestly embraced Islam but did not fully understand it and were therefore unable to mould their lives completely in conformity with the principles and precepts of the Faith. This state of affairs eventually brought about a political upheaval which swept away the institution of caliphate and established kingship.

Causes of the Success of Kingship

Different writers and thinkers have attributed the substitution of kingship for the Caliphate to various causes. To me it seems the change was due to the fact that the number of Muslims with a full and proper understanding of the principles of Islam had declined rapidly with the passage of' time; so had the proportion of Muslims whose character and conduct were in perfect conformity with the tenets and precepts of the Faith. On the other hand, the number of Muslims who did not properly understand the principles increased so enormously that it soon became impossible to save Muslim society from the harmful effects of their ignorance, deficient understanding and moral weaknesses. Consequently, the Caliphate gave way to kingship, and this phase of our history extended over several centuries. It is not possible for me in the course of this brief address to discuss in detail all the influences at work during that period of our history and analyze various elements and factors involved.

Disruption of Leadership

The first and the most harmful result of the establishment of kingship was that the leadership of Muslim Millat split into two sections. During the days of the Prophet and the Right guided Caliphs the leadership of the Muslim community was centered at one place. All affairs of life spiritual, moral, intellectual, cultural, political or philosophical were held and directed by a common authority. The political affairs of the community, the dispensation of justice, the administration of the State, the conduct of war all were being organized and directed from a common center. And the very persons, who controlled all these varied activities, were also the spiritual, moral and intellectual leaders of the community. The entire leadership of the Ummah was centred at the place. But the advent of kingship resulted in a rift in this leadership while political control remained in the hands of the rulers, in the spiritual, moral and intellectual spheres, leadership passed to the theologians, the jurists and the Sufis. The jurists became the religious, moral and spiritual leaders and guides of the Muslims, and the kings assumed the political leadership of the community. This bifurcation of leadership was inherently pernicious and was in any event bound to have disastrous consequences for the community. What made it worse was that, political power, following the logic of its nature, sought to extend itself beyond the political sphere and to control and direct the life of the community in all the fields religious, moral, intellectual etc. The religious scholars, the jurists and the Sufis, for their part, were not prepared to tolerate any interference in ethical or religious matters that might be repugnant to the spirit or principles of Islam and tend to corrupt the religious or moral life of the people. This conflict between the political and religious leaderships resulted in mutual estrangement and hostility, which has continued down to the present day.

Kingship no doubt brought a host of evils in its wake, but even during that period, the Muslims did much better than other nations in corresponding portions of their history. Indeed the Muslims produced a larger number of good, God tearing kings than did any other community. But, while one must give these virtuous kings all the praise that is due to them, there is little doubt that, on the whole, the natural and necessary consequences of the system of kingship were detrimental to the interests of Islam and the Muslims. One very harmful effect of the system was that the Muslim kingdoms shirked their duties as the upholders of the cause of Islam and confined themselves, more or less, to the conquest of new lands and the realization of tribute from the conquered peoples. Their failure ultimately resulted in conditions that have caused grave and lasting harm to Muslims in a large part of the world. For instance, take this sub continent. Many of you here must have migrated to Pakistan from territories which were under the sway of Muslims for a long as eight hundred years-for instance, Delhi and the surrounding areas, East Punjab, U.P. and the Deccan. If the Muslim rulers of these territories during the Middle Ages had done their duty to Islam, and taken it upon themselves to spread and propagate the Faith, you would not have been forced today to abandon your hearths and homes.

To the limited extent that Islam did spread during the centuries of Muslim rule in India it was due to the efforts of the theologians and the Sufis. The rulers not only made no contribution towards the spread of Islam, their behavior and conduct generally tended to thwart the expansion of the creed. By their.tyrannical rule and oppressive policies, by their bullying and high handedness, by the their dissolute living and otherwise immoral conduct, most of the kings and lesser potentates tended to alienate people from Islam rather than make the Faith popular; only a few of them could boast of character and conduct that would induce non-Muslims to join the ranks of Islam. These few exceptions no doubt deserve all praise, but it is obvious that, on the whole, kingship caused grave harm to the cause of Islam.

Lack of Proper Education

The spread and expansion of Islam in these parts of the world was due almost entirely to the example and endeavors of the ulema, the Sufis and other men of virtue and character. Their efforts, however, had some very obvious limitations. They could at best influence people with their deeds and words, show them the right path and exhort them to follow it. They could not possibly ensure the proper education and training of the hundreds and thousands of people who were embracing Islam. This was the business of the rulers, who had little interest in the matter. If they had only cooperated with the preachers of Islam, and made suitable arrangement for the education of those whom the preachers were drawing into the fold of Islam by their voluntary efforts, things would have shaped quite differently. As it was, the endeavors of the preachers were assisted and sustained only by the philanthropists; who set up religious trusts and established schools. Obviously, this could not be an effective substitute for government action, without which it was not possible to liberate the converts from the shackles of ignorance and superstition and develop them into true Muslims.

The harmful effects of this grave deficiency in the education of Muslims during Muslim rule in India have persisted down to this day. The bulk of the Muslims of this country are still soaked in archaic superstition and shaked by rites and customs inherited from their pre-Islamic past. Their knowledge of Islam is poor and defective and their life is vitiated by persisting influences 'of Hinduism and Buddhism and various other influences rooted in their unislamic past. In other words our past still dogs our steps and vitiates our present.

Growth of Parochial Pride and Prejudice

Another evil that developed amongst the Muslims during that period was the growth of racial, tribal and national pride and prejudice. The malady had its origin as far back as the Omayyad regime and grew rapidly thereafter; later it continued to erupt and spread from time to time like an epidemic, and destroyed various Muslim empires in different parts of the world.

It was this deadly malady that brought about the ruin of the Omayyad Empire, vitiated the life of the Arab tribes, destroyed the Omayyads in Spain and ultimately caused the annihilation of the Muslims in that land. Nearer home, it was responsible for the destruction of the Mughal Empire and of the Muslim States in Deccan. God and his Prophet had urged the Muslims to unite through their common belief in the Islamic creed, and to be brethren unto one another. Unfortunately the Muslims generally tended to forget and ignore the injunction and to relapse into racial, ethnic and regional prejudices.

This prejudice, which proved the bane of the Muslims everywhere in the world, is inherent in the system of kingship. During the period of kingship in the history of Islam, the kings themselves exploited to the full the racial and other prejudices, among their people. The Omayyads, for example, were challenged and ultimately destroyed by the Abbasids, who instigated the Persians against the Arabs with a view to promoting their own interests and replacing the Omayyad Kingship with their own.

Racial and national prejudices not only played havoc with the old Muslim empires, they are still corrupting and poisoning the life of the people of Pakistan. Not long ago, the Muslims of the sub-continent united in the name of Islam and rallying around its banner achieved a singular triumph in the establishment of Pakistan. But no sooner had the victory been achieved than the old racial and ethnic prides and prejudices began to reemerge and reassert themselves: we again began to think in terms of race and language and region, as Pathans or Punjabis, Bengalis or Sindhis. This, if the history of Islam is any guide, is an evil portent for the nation.

Selfishness

Another malady that had its origin during the period of kingship, and continued to spread thereafter was the erosion of the Muslim's loyalty to Islam and the Millat and its ultimate replacement by loyalty to the self and the clan or family. Islam had originally abolished all loyalties based upon race, language or nationality, and replaced them with a single, absolute loyalty to God, His Prophet and the Faith. It was on the basis of this supreme loyalty that Islam sought to build the character of the individual. But during the period of kingship this loyalty soon began to weaken, and since it was the foundation of public morality and private character, its weakening naturally resulted in the growth of selfishness and self-promotion. In the absence of ideals and higher loyalties, people are not willing to make any sacrifices and everyone is interested merely in feathering his own nest or promoting the interests of his family or clan. This was what happened in Muslim society during the era of kingship.

It became a mercenary society in which the services of mercenary soldiers or administrators were available to anyone and material comfort assumed paramount importance in the life of the individual as well as the community. The Muslims provided mercenary soldiers on a large scale for the armies of different non-Muslim and States principalities.

For instance, the Marathas who were among the deadliest enemies of Islam in India, had a large number of Muslims in their armed forces. Later, Muslims joined the British forces in larger numbers and helped the invaders to conquer the land. In fact, the British did not have to bring in a large army from overseas: they could find within the country both the soldiers that they needed to conquer it and the civil servants that they needed to run the administration.

None of the local mercenaries seemed to ponder for a moment whom they.were conquering the land for, or whom they were administering it for. The reason was that the Muslims had ceased to have any loyalty higher than their loyalty to themselves or their families or clans-a loyalty which must in the final analysis turn human beings into soulless and heartless mercenaries.

In course of time, this pernicious process affected the entire Muslim world, ultimately destroying all the Muslim States from the Philippines to Morocco and paying the way for the Western domination. This domination was by no means an accidental development: it was the result of deep rooted historical causes which I cannot discuss in detail here.

The Third Phase: Slavery and its Aftermath

In this sub-continent as well as in other Muslim countries the alien rulers subjected the people to all kinds of oppression and inequity. They destroyed the old Muslim empires, deprived the Muslims of their rich lands, took over their religious trusts and trifled with their lives, honor and property. But far more deadly for the Muslims than any of these inequities was the destruction of the old educational system and its replacement by a new system of education based upon entirely different moral values and cultural norms. Through this new intellectual instrument they sought to alienate the future generations of Muslims from their past and ensure that they would treat themselves with contempt, feel ashamed of their own history and traditions, disdain their own culture as out of date and retrogressive, and reject their own distinctive system of life as impracticable. On the positive side, the new education sought to inculcate in the future generations of Muslims the belief that all knowledge, culture and morality belonged to the West and that the ideal conception of humanity was that of the West.

This was indeed the worst of the countless crimes that the alien masters perpetrated upon the Muslims of this land. The old system of education had enabled us to maintain our links with our past and keep ourselves acquainted with our religion; it had served to keep the community anchored to its traditions and culture. The new system of education supplanted the old and made it practically worthless from the economic point of view. All Muslims who aspired for progress and success in life abandoned the old system of education and adopted its alien substitute. This great change in the educational system had deep and far reaching effects on the life of the community under the force of circumstances nearly all the effective elements in society those that were relatively well off and were also intelligent and educated, ambitious and active, and endowed with the qualities of leadership turned to the new system of education, which tended to alienate them from, and make them disdainful of, their own religion, culture and history.

Transfer of Leadership

With the introduction of the new system of education, the alien rulers restricted the avenues of progress to those educated under that system. This was a deliberate policy aimed at forcing the Muslims to abandon their children to the new system of education and allow it to alienate them from their religion and culture. All the Western powers pursued this policy on a large scale in all the Muslim countries that passed under their sway. A natural corollary of this policy was that the more a Muslim could alienate himself from his past and detach himself from his cultural moorings, the easier would he find it to rise to the higher positions in the administration. This policy was, of course, never reduced to a regular rule nor, indeed, was it necessary to make it a part of the administrative formulary. It was just followed as a unwritten rule calculated to bring into the highest positions in society and administration, Muslims who only owed a formal allegiance to Islam and were practically non-Muslims in their character, conduct and everyday life. Consequently, within a short period, such Muslims captured all the effective positions in the administration and in social and economic life that were open to members of the Muslim community.

Movements of Liberation

The study of Western literature and history stimulated the urge for political freedom in a large section of the young men educated under the new system, and sooner or later the urge Sowed into organized movements for liberation in all the Muslim Countries. Naturally enough the leadership of this movement passed into the hands of those who had been educated under the new system, who could understand, and make themselves understand, in the language of the rulers, and knew how to deal with the ruling nation. The logic of the situation demanded this kind of leadership and left no.alternative for the community. The products of the old religious schools were not fit to lead the Muslims at that juncture; the community therefore had to accept the leadership of the new educated class.

The new leaders of the community were by no means genuinely devoted to Islam, but nearly all of them appealed to the religious sentiments and susceptibilities of the Muslims, for that were the only way to secure their allegiance and support. In every country, the new leaders appealed to the Muslims in the Faith. They proclaimed that they were fighting a war between Islam and unbelief and called upon the Muslims to join them, to devote all their energies to the: struggle and, if necessary, lay down their lives to ensure the supremacy of Islam.

This trick was played upon the Muslims in every Muslim country. The latest instance in point is Algeria. In Algeria as elsewhere in the Muslim world Islam was exploited to the full in the struggle for liberation. Algerian leaders have confessed to me that unless they told their people that they were engaged in a war between Islam and Kufr (unbelief), not a single soul would come forward to join the struggle. In short, it was in the name of Islam that the people were called, it was in the name of Islam that they responded to the call and rallied to the banner and it was from Islam that they derived the super human courage to go through the ordeals to which they were daily subjected during the struggle for freedom.

Similarly, when the Greeks invaded Asia Minor after the First World War, Mustafa Kemal exploited Islam to the full. He would go into the rank and file of the armed forces with the Holy Book in his hand and warn them if they did not join him in the war against the Greeks, the Qur'an would soon be eliminated from Turkey. It was this appeal in the name of Islam that aroused the Turks and induced them to measure swords with the Greeks in spite of the shortage of arms on the Turkish side and the overwhelming support and aid of the Western Allies on the Greek side. Fighting under the banner of Islam, the Turks eventually triumphed over the much more powerful aggressors and booted them out of Turkey.

It was practically the same story in every Muslim country struggling for freedom. The leaders were, on the whole, virtually ignorant of Islam and indifferent to it. They had no will to enforce the writ of Islam in the land, or even to mould their own lives in accordance with its principles. They had grown under a new civilization and culture and their values, tastes and inclinations had changed radically. But the common Muslim people were compelled to entrust their leadership to such elements, who in turn appealed to the religious sentiments of the Muslims and exploited then as best as they could. Where ever the Muslims have won a battle of national liberation, the appeal to Islam has played a decisive role in the outcome.

The Fourth Phase: After Freedom

We now pass on to the fourth phase of our history, during which almost all the Muslim lands liberated themselves from foreign political domination.

A New Tragedy

Unfortunately, however, political power and economic control have passed in all these countries into the hands of those who have little knowledge of their religion and less pride in their cultural traditions. Indeed, most of them treat all the traditions of the Muslim nation with contempt and think that the Muslims will be unable to make any progress in life and to achieve an honorable position in the comity of nations if they adopt the Islamic way of life and stick to Islamic principles and values. To them, the only road to redemption and progress lies through wholesale adoption of Western ideas, theories and values. This is indeed their considered opinion; and it could hardly be otherwise, for, their education and training was designed to produce precisely this kind of attitude and approach. The alien rulers deliberately fostered and strengthened such elements and pitched them in key positions in all departments of life. This happened morn or less in all the Muslim countries. The wars of liberation were fought in the name of Islam, but after the people had won the hard way, through untold sufferings and sacrifices, Islam was practically thrown overboard.

The latest instance in point is that of Algeria. After its Muslim population had succeeded in liberating its homeland through super-human sacrifices and at the cost of hundreds of thousands of lives, the leaders suddenly proclaimed that Algeria would be a secular, socialist state. Turkey, Pakistan, Tunisia and Egypt have witnessed more or less similar phenomena during the past few decades, take Tunisia, for instance. The Muslim bulk of its population were called to battle in the name of Islam, and it was for the sake of the Faith that they challenged French rule and ultimately overthrew it through a struggle in which they had to make very heavy sacrifices. But soon after the war had been won, President Bourguiba told the Muslims that their fasting in the month of Ramadan adversely affected production. Mr. Bourguiba thus tried to undermine the faith of the Muslims of Tunisia much in the same way as the Soviet Union. The contention that fasting hampers production is obviously aimed at abolishing the institution of fasting, for nearly all the relatively young and able bodied members of a community are engaged in production, and the old and the sick are anyhow exempted from fasting.

Much to the chagrin of the groups that wield power in the Muslim lands today, the truly religious elements have survived everywhere. They know the principles and doctrines of Islam and the injunctions of God and His Prophet. They know what Islamic culture and civilization really mean. Unfortunately, however, these people lack the education and training necessary for effective governance and efficient administration in the present conditions.

These elements share the sentiments and aspirations of the common Muslims, who are confident that, if voted to power they will not seek to undermine Islam, and foist an un-Islamic way of life upon them. But on the other hand the people fear that these elements will not be able to lead the nation, run the affairs of state, take care of the administration, organize the dispensation of justice, manage the finances of the country and conduct its foreign relations. And the people have good reasons for their misgivings and fears about the religious elements' abilities and capacities in these spheres.

The Real Difficulty

The average Muslim is bewildered and stands miserably divided between his inherent loyalty to Islam and lack of confidence in the practical abilities of the elements that stand for the establishment of the Islamic way of life. It is true that the bulk of the people in any Muslim land have little knowledge of their religion, that they are morally weak and their conduct and habits are generally repugnant to the principles of Islam.

Nevertheless, as I have pointed out earlier, the extraordinary force of the original Islamic movement is not yet completely spent, and the spark that survives is still capable of kindling the flame of an Islamic revival. For instance, you may ask even the most corrupt and depraved Muslim whether he regards drinking, adultery, gambling or bribery as permissible or proper for a Muslim. There can be no doubt about the answers, which will clearly prove that the values of the common Muslim have not changed at all in spite of his moral decline and degeneration. These values have gone into his blood and become a part of his very being. Or, ask an average Muslim what he thinks of a dance by a semi nude woman: he will undoubtedly refuse to agree that it is in accord with the spirit of Islamic culture. The average Muslim is no doubt ignorant; he hardly understands the Qur'an and knows practically nothing of the Hadith. Nevertheless his thoughts and beliefs still reflect in some degree the moral notions and cultural concepts that have survived down the generations in the world of Islam. In spite of his ignorance and moral degeneration, the average Muslim still tends naturally to look at things in the light of his communal traditions and to form his opinions accordingly.

Almost all Muslims all over the world have some basic notions about Islam and its values, which, however vague, are essentially correct. In Pakistan as well as in Turkey, in Iran as well as in Egypt and Algeria, Muslims believe more or less in the same common Islamic values. And it is not possible to persuade any large body of Muslims, anywhere in the world that the values of the modern West have anything in common with Islamic values.

Moreover, although the average Muslim may not have any considerable knowledge of Islam, there is no doubt that ho is enamoured of it. Recent developments in the world of Islam have proved it beyond a shadow of doubt that Muslims can be aroused and inspired and induced to make sacrifices only in the name of Islam; no other call can appeal to them.

A Muslim can lay down his life only if he is sure that he is doing it for the sake of Allah and will be rewarded for it with a place in heaven. A Muslim who is not inspired by this belief will not be persuaded to lay down his life and will indeed be the most cowardly of men.

Unfortunately, however, political leadership and state power has, in all the Muslim countries, passed into the hands of elements who, in opposition to the manifest sentiments and aspirations of the people, seek to set national life in a direction contrary to the Islamic way of life. If conditions are otherwise favorable, they seek to achieve their objective openly under the banner of secularism as they did in Turkey under Mustafa Kemal. Elsewhere, they continue to pay lip service to Islam and try to foist Western values and culture upon the people in the name of Islam. But fortunately, it is not possible for them to mislead the bulk of the Muslims in any country. However ignorant or degenerate a Muslim people may be, they cannot be persuaded to accept any manifestly unIslamic belief, idea or practice as Islamic.

In Turkey and the Soviet Union, attempts to de Islamize the Muslims were accompanied by such violence and cruelty as we in this country would find it difficult even to imagine. In Turkey, for instance, thousands of people were killed only because they were not prepared to change their headgear. Since the Western hat introduced by the new rulers was not available within the country, condemned stocks were imported from Europe. Thus this great 'reform' was introduced at the point of the bayonet, and the rulers went so far as to impose martial law to enforce the desired change. But in spite of all this oppression, we find that the average Turk is as good a Muslim today as he ever was. This has established conclusively that the Turks cannot by any means be made to abjure Islam and accept any way of life repugnant to it.

The Present Struggle

The present struggle, more or less in all Muslim countries,, is that the people are not prepared to go along with the rulers in the direction in which they are trying to take them; and the rulers are not prepared to lead the people in the direction in which they desire to move. This has resulted in a perpetual conflict in all the Muslim countries of the world. And this is 'Islam Today'.

In all the Muslim countries, we witness organized attempts to de-Islamize the people. Education has been designed as to eliminate Islamic values, vitiate the morals of the new generation and alienate it from its culture and traditions. Attempts are also being made to promote amongst the masses new cultural values that are bound to corrupt their morals. Western thought and disciplines are being introduced and encouraged. All that these policies and efforts can achieve is to reduce the Muslims to a characterless people; they cannot, even at their best, succeed in persuading the Muslims to give up Islam and deliberately accept a secular state.

The miserably slow peace of progress in the Muslim countries shows how heavily they have had to pay for the perpetual conflict resulting from their rulers' attempts to foist alien values upon them. None of the Muslim countries have been able to make any remarkable progress in any sphere. Turkey, for instance, has been a free state since 1924, but can it boast of any great progress in industry or trade? During the same period, Japan has made amazing progress in practically all fields of life and now stands amongst the moat advanced nations of the world.

Obviously the reason for Turkey's failure to progress lies in the internal conflict to which she has been subjected by her secularist rulers. The people in power have striven all along to de-Islamize the people whereas the people have been keenly desirous of a return to Islam. The story has been repeated, more or less, in the other Muslim countries that have achieved freedom during recent decades. It should be clear to us that no nation can become really strong or achieve any great progress in any field if it is involved in a perpetual conflict between the conscience of the people and the policies of the rulers. Even if such a nation is compelled to tolerate its rulers, it can not be expected to give them its wholehearted cooperation; and the people's non-cooperation and resentment might become a source of danger to the state itself. A nation can develop and progress only when there is complete harmony between the conscience of the people and the policies of the government. It is only for such ideals, principles and policies as accord with their own sentiments and aspirations that a people can be expected to stake their all.

In trying to set up and maintain more or less secular system of society and government, the rulers of various Muslim countries are motivated solely by self-interest. They know fully well what the people want. They know it from more or.less direct experience that their people fought and won the battle of freedom in the name of Islam. They are also fully conscious of their people's deep and abiding association with Islam and all that it stands for. But, on the other hand, the rulers have acquired a vested interest in the perpetuation of the Western way of life. They have accepted Western culture themselves and made their children's future dependent upon the continuance of the Western way of life. Self-interest, therefore, prevents them from following the Islamic way of life. They are determined to retain power in their hands and are not prepared to adopt the Islamic way of life; therefore, they are trying to de-Islamize the people. This is the logic of their policies.

About the Future

The future of the whole world of Islam will depend upon the attitude that the Muslims ultimately adopt towards Islam. If, unfortunately, the present hypocritical attitudes and anti-Islamic policies persist, I am afraid that the newly liberated Muslim nations will not be able to preserve their freedom for a long time: sooner or later, they must relapse into slavery and into a state even worse than their present condition. The threatened disaster can be averted only through a faithful and total adoption of the Islamic way of life. The Muslim nations can again become a force in the world and leaders of mankind if those who rule them today come to their senses even now; if, under a genuine system of democracy, the people are allowed to choose their own rulers, and if truly Islamic systems of government, economic organization and, education are established. The Muslims command a vast part of the globe, stretching from Indonesia to Morocco and endowed with great manpower and enormous resources. If thin whole bloc unites under the banner of Islam, and earnestly adopts and rigorously follows the Islamic way of life, no power will be able stand in its way and stop its march on the road to progress.

Is Islam Practicable Today?

At the beginning of this discourse, namely, whether Islam can achieve supremacy in the modern world, whether the other communities of mankind can be expected to embrace Islam, and how, and whether, Islam is a practicable creed in the present age ?

We should be clear that we cannot expect the rest of mankind to offer to embrace Islam without any effort on our part. Indeed, no community ever made any such offer during any period of the history of Islam. Ever the Prophet of Islam did not receive any spontaneous response when he first called mankind to the path of Islam. Great movements that seek to revolutionize human society and the ways of men can succeed only if they have behind them a powerful personality who is determined to break the resistance of fossilized tradition and to change the shape of things and the course of the events. Take Communism, for instance. It sought to bring about radical changes to make a clean sweep of private property and bring all wealth under state control. And yet, when some powerful persons set themselves to the task and resolved to achieve the end at all cost, they succeeded. There is therefore no reason why an Islamic revolution should not be successful in the present age.

Similarly, the question whether Islam is a practicable creed in the present-day world is clearly absurd. Islam has always banned a practicable religion and will remain practicable for all times to come. The point is whether there is any nation in the world today that is prepared to adopt the Islamic way of life totally and without any reservations. The starting point of the history of Islam as a world force was the acceptance by the whole Arab nation of the social, economic, political and cultural system of Islam sad its willingness to mould individual character and communal life in harmony with the principles of the new Faith. That nation not only rallied round the banner of Islam but also resolved to carry that banner into the outside world, to dedicate itself to the cause of Islam and to die for it if necessary.

Similarly, if any community of men today adopts Islam in it: entirety, organizes its life and conduct fully in accordance with Islamic principles, and dedicates itself totally to the cause, there is no reason why the rest of mankind should not be persuaded to embrace and adopt Islam today. It is, of course, impossible to achieve anything merely though discourses and discussion and pugilistic writings, indeed, even to convince others that Islam is still practicable. But if we can establish in time and space a system of life truly embodying the ideals, principles and doctrines of Islam, all right-minded people are bound to be attracted by it and, in course of time, to accept it.

2

Reflections on Islam and Modern Life

Islam and Modern Thought

Few subjects arouse more passion and debate among Muslims today than the encounter between Islam and modern thought. The subject is of course vast and embraces fields ranging from politics to sacred art, subjects whose debate often causes volcanic eruptions of emotions and passions and vituperations which hardly lead to an objective analysis of causes and a clear vision of the problems involved. Nor is this debate which consumes so much of the energies of Muslims and students of Islam helped by the lack of clear definition of the terms of the debate and an insight into the actual forces involved. The whole discussion is also paralyzed by a psychological sense of inferiority and a sense of enfeeblement before the modern world which prevents most modernized Muslims from making a critical appraisal of the situation and of stating the truth irrespective of the fact whether it is fashionable and acceptable to current opinion or not. Let us then begin be defining what we mean by modern thought.

It is amazing how many hues and shades of meaning have been given to the terms "modern" ranging from contemporary to simply "innovative", "creative", or in tune with the march of time. The question of principles and in fact the truth itself is hardly ever taken into consideration when modernism is discussed. One hardly ever asks whether this or that idea or form or institution conforms to some aspect of the truth.

The only question is whether it is modern or not. The lack of clarity, precision and sharpness of both mental and artistic contours, which characterizes the modern world itself, seem to plague the contemporary Muslim's understanding of modernism whether he wishes to adopt its tenets or even to react against it. The influence of modernism seems to have dimmed that lucidity and blurred the crystalline transparency which distinguishes traditional Islam in both its intellectual and artistic manifestations.

When we use the term "modern", we mean neither contemporary nor up-to-date nor successful in the conquest and domination of the natural world. Rather, for us "modern" means that which is cut off from the transcendent, from the immutable principles which in reality govern all things and which are made known to man through revelation in its most universal sense.

Modernism is thus contrasted with tradition (al-din); the latter implies all that which is of Divine Origin along with its manifestations and deployments on the human plane while the former by contrast implies all that is merely human and now ever more increasingly subhuman, and all that is divorced and cut off from the Divine Source. Obviously, tradition has always accompanied and in fact characterized human existence whereas modernism is a very recent phenomenon.

As long as man has lived on earth, he has buried his dead and believed in the after life and the world of the Spirit. During the "hundreds of thousands" of years of human life on earth, he has been traditional in outlook and has not "evolved" as far as his relation with God and nature seen as the creation and theophany of God are concerned. Compared to this long history during which man has continuously celebrated the Divine and performed his function as God's vicegerent (khalifah) on earth, the period of the domination of modernism stretching from the Renaissance in Western Europe in the 15th century to the present day appears as no more than the blinking of an eye. Yet, it is during this fleeting moment that we live; hence the apparent dominance of the power of modernism before which so many Muslims retreat in helplessness or which they join with a superficial sense of happiness that accompanies the seduction of the world.

A word must also be said about the term "thought" as it appears in the expression modern thought. The term thought as used in this context is itself modern rather than traditional. The Arabic term fikr or the Persian and ishah, which are used as its equivalence, hardly appear with the same meaning in traditional texts.

In fact what would correspond to the traditional understanding of the term would be more the French pensee as used by a Pascal, a term which can be better rendered as meditation rather than thought. Both fikr and ishah are in fact related to meditation and contemplation rather than to a purely human and therefore non-divine mental activity which the term thought usually evokes.

If then we nevertheless use the term thought, it is because we are addressing an audience nurtured on all that this term implies and are using a medium and language in which it is not possible, without being somewhat contrite, to employ another term with the same range of meaning embracing many forms of mental activity but devoid of the limitation in the vertical sense that the term "thought" possesses in contemporary parlance.

All these forms of mental activity which together comprise modern thought and which range from science to philosophy, psychology and even certain aspects of religion itself, possess certain common characteristics and traits which must be recognized and studied before the Islamic response to modern thought can be provided. Perhaps the first basic trait of modern thought to be noted is its anthropomorphic nature. How can a form of thought which negates any principle higher than man be but anthropomorphic? It might of course be objected that modern science is certainly not anthropomorphic but that rather it is the pre-modern sciences which must be considered as man-centered. Despite appearances, however, this assertion is mere illusion if one examines closely the epistemological factor involved.

It is true that modern science depicts a universe in which man as spirit, mind and even, psyche has no place and the Universe thus appears as "inhuman" and not related to the human state. But it must not be forgotten that although modern man has created a science which excludes the reality of man from the general picture of the Universe, the criteria and instruments of knowledge which determine this science are merely and purely human. It is the human reason and the human senses which determine modern science. The knowledge of even the farthest galaxies is held in the human mind. This scientific world from which man has been abstracted is, therefore, nevertheless based on an anthropomorphic foundation as far as the subjective pole of knowledge, the subject who knows and determines what science is, is concerned.

In contrast, the traditional sciences were profoundly non anthropomorphic in the sense that for them the locus and container of knowledge was not the human mind but ultimately the Divine intellect. True science was not based on purely human reason but on the Intellect which belongs to the supra-human level of reality yet illuminates the human mind. If medieval cosmologies placed man at the center of things it is not because they were humanistic in the Renaissance sense of the term according to which terrestrial and fallen man was the measure of all things but it was to enable man to gain a vision of the cosmos as a crypt through which he must travel and which he must transcend. And certainly one cannot begin a journey from anywhere except where one is.

Modern Thought

If the characteristic of anthropomorphism is thus to be found in modern science, it is to be seen in an even more obvious fashion in other forms and aspects of modern thought whether it be psychology, anthropology or philosophy. Modern thought, of which philosophy is in a sense the father and progenitor, became profoundly anthropomorphic the moment man was made the criterion of reality. When Descartes uttered "I think, therefore I am" (cogito ergo sum), he placed his individual awareness of his own limited self as the criterion of existence for certainly the "I" in Descartes assertion was not meant to be the Divine "I" who through Hallaj exclaimed "I am the Truth" (ana'l-Haqq), the Divine "I" which according to traditional doctrines alone has the right to say "I".

Until Descartes, it was Pure Being, the Being of God which determined human existence and the various levels of reality. But with Cartesian rationalism individual human existence became the criterion of reality and also the truth. In the mainstream of Western thought, and excluding certain peripheral developments ontology gave way to epistemology, epistemology to logic; and finally by way of reaction logic became confronted with those anti-rational "philosophies" so prevalent today.

What happened in the post-medieval period in the West was that higher levels of reality became eliminated on both the subjective and the objective domains. There was nothing higher in man than his reason and nothing higher in the objective world than what that reason could comprehend with the help of the normal human senses. This was of course bound to happen if one remembers the well-known principle of ad equation (the ad equation of St. Thomas Aquinas) according to which to know anything there must be an instrument of knowledge adequate and conforming to the nature of that which is to be known. And since modern man refused to accept a principle higher than him, obviously all that issued from his mind and thought could not but be anthropomorphic.

A second trait of modernism, closely related to anthropomorphism, is the lack of principles which characterizes the modern world. Human nature is too unstable, changing and turbulent to be able to serve as the principle for something. That is why a mode of thinking which is not able to transcend the human level and which remains anthropomorphic cannot but be devoid of principles. In the realm of the life of action, namely the domain of morality (although morality cannot be reduced simply to action) and, from another point of view, politics and economics, everyone senses this lack of principles. But one might object that principles do exist as far as the sciences are concerned. Here again, however, it must be asserted that neither empiricism nor validification through induction nor yet reliance upon the data of the senses as confirmed by reason can serve as principles in the metaphysical sense. They are all valid in their own level as is the science created by them. But they are divorced from immutable principles as is modern science which has discovered many things on a certain level of reality but because of its divorce from higher principles has brought about disequilibrium through its very discoveries and inventions. Only mathematics among the modern sciences may be said to possess certain principles in the metaphysical sense.

The reason is that mathematics remains, despite everything, a Platonic science and its laws discovered by the human mind continue to reflect metaphysical principles as reason itself cannot but display the fact that it is a reflection, even if a dim one, of the Intellect. The discoveries of the other sciences, to the extent that they conform to some aspect of the nature of reality, of course possess a symbolic and metaphysical significance, but that does not mean that these sciences are attached to metaphysical principles and integrated into a higher form of knowledge. Such integration could take place but as a matter of fact it has not. Modern science, therefore, and its generalizations like other fruits of that way of thinking and acting which we have associated with modernism, suffer from the lack of principles which characterize the modern world, a lack which is felt to an even greater degree as the history of the modern world unfolds.

It might be asked what other means of knowledge were available to other civilizations before the modern period. The answer is quite clear at least for those Muslims who know the intellectual life of Islam: revelation and intellectual intuition or vision (dhawq, kashf or shuhud). The Muslim intellectual saw revelation as the primary source of knowledge not only as the means to learn the laws of morality concerned with the active life. He was also aware of the possibility for man to purify himself until the "eye of the heart" ('ayn al-qalb), residing at the center of his being, would open and enable him to gain the direct vision of the supernal realities.

Finally he accepted the power of reason to know, but this reason was always attached to and derived sustenance from revelation on the one hand and intellectual intuition on the other. The few in the Islamic world who would cut this cord of reliance and declare the independence of reason from both revelation and intuition were never accepted into the mainstream of Islamic thought. They remained marginal figures while in a reverse fashion in the post-medieval West those who sought to sustain and uphold the reliance of reason upon revelation and the Intellect remained on the margin while the mainstream of modern Western thought rejected both revelation and intellectual intuition as means of knowledge. In modern times even philosophers of religion and theologians rarely defend the Bible as a source of a sapiental knowledge which could determine and integrate scientia in the manner of a St. Bonaventure. The few who look upon the Bible for intellectual guidance are usually limited by such shallow literal interpretations of the Holy Book that in their feuds with modern sciences the rationalistic camp comes out almost inevitably as the victor.

Features of Modernism

When one ponders over these and other salient features of modernism, one comes to the conclusion that in order to understand modernism and its manifestations, it is essential to comprehend the conception of man which underlies it. One must seek to discover how modern man conceives of himself and his destiny, how he views the anthropos vis-à-vis God and the world. Moreover, it is essential to understand what constitutes the soul and mind of men and women whose thoughts and ideas have molded and continue to mold the modern world.

For surely if such men as Ghazzali and Rumi or for that matter an Erigena or Eckhardt were the occupants of the chairs of philosophy in leading universities in the West another kind of philosophy would issue forth in this part of the world. A man thinks according to what he is, or as Aristotle said, knowledge depends upon the mode of the knower. A study of the modern concept of man as being "free" of Heaven, complete master of his own destiny, earth-bound but also master of the earth, oblivious to all eschatological realities which he has replaced with some future state of perfection in profane historical time, indifferent if not totally opposed to the world of the Spirit and its demands and lacking a sense of the sacred will reveal how futile have been and are the efforts of those modernistic

Muslim "reformers" who have sought to harmonize Islam and modernism in the sense that we have defined it. If we turn even a cursory glance at the Islamic conception of man, at the homo islamicus, we shall discover, the impossibility of harmonizing this conception with that of modern man.

The homo islamicus is at once the slave of God (al-'abd) and His vicegerent on earth (khalifatallah fi'l ard). He is not an animal which happens to speak and think but possesses a soul and spirit created by God. The homo Islamicus contains within himself the plant and animal natures as he is the crown of creation (ashraf al-makhluqat) but he has not evolved from the lower forms of life. Man has always been man. The Islamic conception of man envisages that man is a being who lives on earth and has earthly needs but he is not only earthly and his needs are not limited to the terrestrial.

He rules over the earth but not in his own right, rather as God's vicegerent before all creatures. He therefore also bears responsibility for the created order before the Creator and is the channel of grace for God's creatures. The homo islamicus possesses the power of reason, of ratio which divides and analyzes, but his mental faculties are not limited to reason. He also possesses the possibility of inward knowledge, the knowledge of his own inner being which is in fact the key to the knowledge of God according to the famous prophetic hadith "He who knows himself knoweth His Lord" (man 'arafa nafsahu faqad 'arafa rabbahu).

He is aware of the fact that his consciousness does not have an "external, material cause but that it comes from God and is too profound to be affected by the accident of death.

The homo islamicus thus remains aware of the eschatological realities, of the fact that although he lives on this earth, he is here as a traveller far away from his original abode. He is aware that his guide for this journey is the message which issues from his home of origin the Origin, and this message is none other than revelation to which he remains bound not only in its aspect of law as embodied in the Shari'ah but also in its aspect of truth and knowledge (Haqiqah). He is also aware that man's faculties are not bound and limited to the senses and reason but that to the extent that he is able to regain the fullness of his being and bring to actuality all the possibilities God has placed within him, man's mind and reason can become illuminated by the light of the spiritual and intelligible world to which the Holy Quran refers as the invisible ('alam al-ghayb).

Obviously such a conception of man differs profoundly from that of modern man who sees himself as a purely earthly creature, master of nature, but responsible to no one but himself and no amount of wishy-washy apologetics can harmonize the two.

The Islamic conception of man removes the possibility of a Promethean revolt against Heaven and brings God into the minutest aspect of human life. Its effect is therefore the creation of a civilization, an art, a philosophy or a whole manner of thinking and seeing things which is completely non-anthropomorphic but theo-centric and which stands opposed to anthropomorphism which is such a salient feature of modernism.

Nothing can be more shocking to authentic Muslim sensibilities than the Titanic and Promethean "religious" art of the late Renaissance and the Baroque which stands directly opposed to the completely non-anthropomorphic art of Islam. Man in Islam thinks and makes in his function of homo sapien and homo faber as the 'abd of God and not as a creature who has rebelled against Heaven. His function remains not the glorification of himself but of his Lord and his greatest aim is to become "nothing", to undergo the experience of fana' which would enable him to become the mirror in which God contemplates the reflections of His own Names and Qualities and the channel through which the theophanies of His Names and Qualities are reflected in the world.

Of course what characterizes the Islamic conception of man has profound similarities with the conception of man in other traditions including Christianity and we would be the last to deny this point. But modernism is not Christianity or any other tradition and it is the confrontation of Islam with modern thought that we have in mind and not its comparison with Christianity. Otherwise what could be closer to the Islamic teaching that man is created to seek perfection and final spiritual beatitude through intellectual and spiritual growth, that man is man only when he seeks perfection (talib al-kamal) and attempts to go beyond himself than the scholastic saying Homo non prorie humanus sed superhumanus est (which means that to be properly human man must be more than human).

The characteristics of modern thought discussed earlier, namely its anthropomorphic and by extension secular nature, the lack of principles in various branches of modern thought and the reductionism which is related to it and which is most evident in the realm of the sciences are obviously in total opposition to the tenets of Islamic thought, as the modern conception of man, from whom issue these thought patterns is opposed to the Islamic conception of man. This opposition is clear enough not to need further elucidation here. There is one characteristic of modern thought, however, which needs to be discussed in greater detail as a result of its pervasive nature in the modern world and its lethal effect upon the religious thought and life of those Muslims who have been affected by it, namely, the theory of evolution.

In the West no modern theory or idea has been as detrimental to religion as the theory of evolution which instead of being taken as a hypothesis in biology, zoology, or paleontology, parades around as if it were a proven scientific fact. Furthermore, it has become a fashion of thinking embracing fields as far apart as astrophysics and the history of art. Nor has the effect of this manner of thinking been any less negative on Muslims affected by it than it has been on Christians.

Usually modernized Muslims have tried to come to terms with evolution through all kinds of unbelievable interpretations of the Holy Quran forgetting that there is no way possible to harmonize the conception of man (Adam) to whom God taught all the "names" and whom He placed on earth as His khalifah and the evolutionist conception which sees man as "ascended" from the ape.

It is strange that except for a few fundamentalist Muslim thinkers who have rejected the theory of evolution on purely religious grounds, few Muslims have bothered to see its logical absurdity and all the scientific evidence brought against it by such men as L. Bounoure and D. Dewar despite the ecstatic claims of its general acceptance by various standard dictionaries and encyclopedias. In fact, as it has been stated so justly by E. F. Schumacher, "evolutionism is not science; it is science fiction, even a kind of hoax." Some Western critics of evolution have gone so far as to claim that its proponents suffer from psychological disequilibrium while recently a whole array of arguments drawn from information theory have been brought against it.

It is not our aim here to analyze and refute in detail the theory of evolution, although such a refutation by Muslim thinkers is essential from scientific as well as metaphysical, logical and religious points of view as it has been already carried out in the Occident.

What is important to note here is that the evolutionary point of view which refuses to see permanence anywhere, for which the greater somehow "evolves" from the "lesser" and which is totally blind to the higher states of being and the archetypal realities which determine the forms of this world is but a result of that loss of principles alluded to above. Evolutionism is but a desperate attempt to fill the vacuum created by man's attempt to cut the hands of God from His creation and to negate any principle above the merely human which then falls of necessity to the level of the sub-human.

Once the Transcendent Principle is forgotten, the world becomes a circle without a center and this experience of the loss of the center remains an existential reality for anyone who accepts the theses of modernism, whether he is a Christian or a Muslim.

Utopianism

Closely allied to the idea of evolution is that of progress and utopianism which both philosophically and politically have shaken the Western world to its roots during the past two centuries and are now affecting the Islamic world profoundly? The idea of unilateral progress has fortunately ceased to be taken seriously by many noted thinkers in the West today and is gradually being rejected in the Islamic world as an "idol of the mind" before which the earlier generation of modernized Muslims prostrated without any hesitation. But the utopianism which is closely related to the idea of progress bears further scrutiny and study as a result of the devastating effect it has had and continues to have on a large segment of the modernized Muslim "intelligentsia".

Utopianism is defined by the Oxford English Dictionary as follows: "impossible ideal schemes for the amelioration of perfection of social conditions".

Although the origin of this term goes back to the well-known treatise of Sir Thomas More entitled Utopia and written in 1516 in Latin, the term utopianism as employed today has certain implications ante-dating the 16th century although the term itself derives from More's famous work. The Christian doctrine of the incarnation, combined with a sense of idealism which characterizes Christianity was of course present before modern times.

Utopianism grafted itself upon the caricature of these characteristics and whether in the form of the humanitarian socialism or such figures as St. Simon, Charles Fourier or Robert Owen or the political socialism of Marx and Engels, led to a conception of history which is a real parody of the Augustinian City of God.

The utopianism of the last centuries, which is one of the important features of modernism, combined with various forms of Messianism led and still lead to deep social and political upheavals whose goals and methods cannot but remain completely alien to the ethos and aims of Islam. Utopianism seeks to establish a perfect social order through purely human means. It disregards the presence of evil in the world in the theological sense and aims at doing without God, as if it were possible to create an order based on goodness but removed from the source of all goodness.

Islam has also had its descriptions of the perfect stage or society in works as those of al-Farabi describing the madinat al-fadilah or the texts of Shaykh Shihab al-Din Suhrawardi referring to the land of perfection which is called in Persian na kuja-abad, literally the land of nowhere, utopia. But then, it was always remembered that this land of perfection is nowhere that is beyond the earthly abode and therefore identified with the eighth clime above the seven geographic ones.

The realism present in the Islamic perspective combined with the strong emphasis of the Holy Quran upon the gradual loss of perfection of the Islamic community as it moves away from the origin of revelation prevented the kind of utopianism present in modern European philosophy from growing upon the soil of Islamic thought.

Moreover, the Muslim remained always aware that if there is to be a perfect state, it could only come into being through Divine help. Hence, although the idea of the cyclic renewal of Islam through a "renewer" (mujaddid) has been always alive as has the wave of Mahdi'sm which sees in the Mahdi the force sent by God to return Islam to its perfection, Islam has never faced within itself that type of secular utopianism which underlies so much of the politico-social aspects of modern thought. It is therefore essential to be aware of the profound distinction between modern utopianism and Islamic teachings concerning the mujaddid or renewer of Islamic society or the Mahdi himself.

It is also basic to distinguish between the traditional figure of the mujaddid and the modern reformers who usually, as a result of their feeble reaction to modern thought, have hardly brought about the renewal of Islam. There is finally one more characteristic of modern thought which is essential to mention and which is related to all that has been stated above. This characteristic is the loss of the sense of the sacred. Modern man can practically be defined as that type of man who has lost the sense of the sacred and modern thought is conspicuous in its lack of awareness of the sacred. Nor could it be otherwise seeing that modern humanism is inseparable from secularism. But nothing could be further from the Islamic perspective in which there does not even exists such a concept as the profane or secular, for in Islam, as already mentioned, the One penetrates into the very depths of the world of multiplicity and leaves no domain outside the domain of tradition.

This is to be seen not only in the intellectual aspects of Islam but also in a blinding fashion in Islamic art. The Islamic tradition can never accept a thought pattern which is devoid of the perfume of the sacred and which replaces the Divine Order by one of a purely human origin and inspiration. The confrontation of Islam with modern thought cannot take place on a serious level if the primacy of the sacred in the perspective of Islam and its lack in modern thought is not taken into consideration. Islam cannot even carry out a dialogue with the secular by placing it in a position of legitimacy. It can only take the secular for what it is, namely the negation and denial of the sacred which ultimately alone is while the profane or secular only appears to be.

In conclusion, it is necessary to mention that the reductionism which is one of the characteristics of modern thought has itself affected Islam in its confrontation with modernism. One of the effects of modernism upon Islam has been to reduce Islam in the minds of many to only one of its dimensions, namely the Shari'ah, and to divest it of those intellectual weapons which alone withstand the assault of modern thought upon the citadel of Islam.

The Shari'ah is of course basic to the Islamic tradition; it is the ground upon which the religion is based. But the intellectual challenges posed by modernism in the form of evolutionism, rationalism, existentialism, agnosticism and the like can only be answered intellectually and not jurisdically nor by ignoring or disregarding them and expecting some kind of magical wedding between the Shari'ah and modern science and technology.

The successful encounter of Islam with modern thought can only come about when modern thought is fully understood in both its roots and ramifications and the whole of the Islamic tradition brought to bear upon the solution of the enormous problems which modernism poses for Islam. At the center of this undertaking lies the revival of that wisdom, that hikmah or Haqiqah, which lies at the heart of the Islamic revelation and which will remain valid as long as men remain men and bear witness to Him according to their theomorphic nature and their state of servitude before the Lord ('ubudiyyah), the state which is the raison d'etre of human existence.

3

Theorizing Islam

Islamic Politics

Islam is based on intelligence and intelligence is light as expressed in the hadith, inna'l-'aqla nurun (verily intelligence is light). The characteristic expression of Islam is the courtyard of an Alhambra whose forms are so many crystallizations of light and whose spaces are defined by the rays of that light which symbolizes, in this world, the Divine Intellect. It must be remembered that even during relatively short period of five centuries; the Muslim world has remained for the most part traditional and did not feel the full impact of modernism until a century ago.

In the modern world more cases of loss of religious faith are to be traced to the theory of evolution as their immediate cause than to anything else.... for the more logically minded, there is no option but to choose between the two, that is, between the doctrine of the fall of man and the 'doctrine' of the rise of man, and to reject altogether the one not chosen.

One might also explain the rapid spread of the theory of evolution as a pseudo-religion in the West by saying that to some extent at last it came to fill a vacuum already created by a weakening of faith. But as far as Islam is concerned, its effect has been to corrode and weaken an already existing faith as it was for those Christians who still possessed strong religious faith when the theory of evolution spread in the late 19th century and in fact up to this day.

Twenty years and eight months later, a similarly unimaginable confrontation between Middle Eastern political reality and American complacency exploded at the World Trade Center and the Pentagon. Two calamitous incidents twenty years apart hinging to some degree on currents in Islamic politics: What understanding did we achieve during that 20 year interval?

It would be an exaggeration, but only a slight one, to say that at a policy level we learned nothing. After an initial couple of years during which scholars tried to deny any significant connection between the Iranian revolution and Islamic religious reassertion, a torrent of studies of Islamic movements and political currents gushed from academic and journalistic presses around the world.

The nearly complete ignorance of contemporary Islamic political-religious phenomena that had marked the decades from the end of World War II to the fall of the Shah gave way to an abundance of observations and theories. There is little to indicate, however, that any government policy horses chose to drink from the fresh scholarly water poured in their trough. On September 11, 2001, therefore, while a substantial number of analysts in the scholarly world could honestly claim that they had seen and understood the handwriting on the wall, even if the message had not included the date, place, and time of the actual attacks, very few people in the policy community could make the same claim.

The knowledge that accumulated between 1981 and 2001 never intersected the world of policy because it was never integrated into an overall vision of Middle Eastern/ Islamic politics of sufficient persuasiveness to unseat the long-standing assumptions that had guided most policy decisions since World War II. It has long been a commonplace that U.S. policies over that period reflected a calculation of national interest that had three components: security for the state of Israel, maintenance of a steady flow of petroleum at reasonable prices and denial of opportunities for the Soviet Union to secure footholds in the region. In addition, several theoretical assumptions derived from modernization theory channeled the ways in which policy makers sought to ensure these national interests:

1. In the process of modernization, economic development normally precedes democratization, which can go awry if it is not based on mass education, and a solid and prosperous middle class.
2. The process of modernization is necessarily accompanied by a growth of secularism and a retreat of religion from the public stage to the arena of private observance.
3. Strong guidance- preferably by academy-trained military officers, western-educated technocrats, or monarchs willing to collaborate with western powers- is needed to channel resources efficiently and rein in immature or demagogic advocates of democratisation.

These several assumptions, which were well articulated by the scholars who laid the theoretical foundation for the field of Middle East studies in the late 1950s, resulted in a fairly consistent and bipartisan policy outlook for half a century. Moreover, they seemed to work.

Instability in the early postwar decades gave way in the 1970s to authoritarian regimes, some military and some monarchical that sought to develop their economies, educate their young people along modern and often secular lines, and exclude from the political arena anyone who advocated placing communism or Islam at the center of political life. The United States agonized over Israel's unexpected vulnerability in the Ramadan war of 1973, suffered through the oil crisis that came out of the war, and worried continuously about Soviet expansion. Islamic politics, however, never reached the threshold of visibility on the worry list, despite the fact that the writings of Sayyid Qutb, Ayatollah Khomeini, and many others were achieving broad circulation and stimulating their readers to dream about different social and political orders.

The decade from the Iranian Revolution to the collapse of Soviet power saw widely varying estimates of the role of Islam in the world. Devotees of modernization tried to dismiss the new religious phenomena as inter-generational angst, lopsided modernization, or a passing phase. Theorists wedded to the inseparability of revolution and liberalization sought to account for the Iranian anomaly, in some instances by associating it theoretically with fascism.

Cold Warriors began to think of international Islamic militancy, directed from Tehran, as a new wine pouring into the aging bottles of international communism. Islam specialists devoted themselves to creating various mutually incompatible classification schemes by which specific Muslim writers or groups might be divided into: modernists, reformists, revisionists, fundamentalists, radicals, moderates, reactionaries, progressives, what have you.

That none of these schemes for fitting new Islamic phenomena into old theoretical frameworks succeeded in creating a new basis for policy formulation is hardly surprising. On the one hand, the hold of the preexisting models was so tenacious that analysts were reluctant to abandon them and strike out into uncharted territory. On the other, the scholars who claimed to have a grasp of the new phenomena did not share the same grip. In contrast to the various currents of modernization theory, Realism in international relations theory, Cold War deterrence theory, or the notion of the rentier state in economics, no voice rose above the clangor of conflicting estimates of Islam with the sort of simple, cogent, persuasive analysis needed by policy makers who might be considering an abandonment, or even a partial abandonment, of policies that were heading in the wrong direction.

The failure of theory culminated in the aftermath of the Gulf War of 1991. Academic specialists invited to a conference at the Pentagon in November, 1990 to speculate on the prospects for the Middle East five years after the resolution of the Iraq crisis, whether by war or by diplomacy, had little to contribute beyond a consensus that "the Arab street" would be incensed by any attack on Iraq. The only appraisal of the postwar situation that quickly came to pass came from a State Department official who said that after the war, the Arab states would sit down at the negotiating table with Israel. In keeping with the basic triad of American interests, the State Department looked at a scenario of war against Iraq and asked: How can this improve Israel's security? The possible consequences for Iraq, for Iran, for Saudi Arabia and the Gulf states, areas where subsequent events would demonstrate the saliency of Islamic perspectives, were not seriously discussed.

So now that we have been given a second and brutally effective wake-up call, whom does the United States turn to for sorely needed new ideas? To begin with, there is no reason to suppose that the old theories will wither away. Reassertions of the primacy of the Israeli-Palestinian dispute come from both camps, though with different twists. Energy professionals fear for the future of affordable gasoline if relations with Saudi Arabia worsen because of a perception that many current problems have deep roots there. Cold War acolytes muster international coalitions to fight overt and covert wars of many years' duration against worldwide enemies. Modernization mavens, metamorphosed into globalization gurus, measure internet access, youth unemployment, and international debt loads and warn that unbalanced and stagnant economies make democracy a dicey proposition.

But where is the new voice in the choir, the one that offers a persuasive analysis of contemporary religious-political currents in the Islamic world? Does it sing lead? Does it harmonize? Or is it not heard at all? So far, and to our peril, it seems to be singing to itself. Islam gets star billing in the tragedy we are witnessing. It deserves to play an equivalent role in our thinking about how to resolve the tragedy. Any outline of a theory of Islamic politics must cover some bases:

1. *The nature of authority in the contemporary Islamic world:* The process of modernization as carried out by nineteenth century reformists, European colonizers, and independent monarchist and secular nationalist regimes subvert or co-opt traditional Muslim authorities and uproot their essentially conservative hold on the Muslim public. How did printing in the late nineteenth century and electronic media in the late twentieth century foster changes in the means of asserting authority and the credentials of those putting themselves forward as authorities? How have these changes entered the political arena: As sources of new thinking? As buttresses of old thinking? As forces supporting participatory government? As forces supporting violence? As forces supporting totalitarianism?
2. *The ways in which the Islamic community has responded to parallel crises in past centuries:* Since Islam is a religion with a past that long precedes imperialism, the nation-state, and the invention of modernity, how have previous breakdowns in authority and perceptions of external attack been resolved? Does the structure of the religion at either the dogmatic or the sociological level offer clues to understanding the parameters within which contemporary Muslim communities will address their current dilemmas?
3. *The potential and probable impact of participatory government on the role of Islam in thought and society:*

While Islam is an old religion, current attempts to wed it with participatory government are new. Do those attempts, looked at in comparison with the history of other democratization experiences, warrant optimism and support? If the range of feasible political choices is limited to authoritarian government or participatory government strongly influenced by advocates of Islamic politics, which promises more in terms of future desirable developments?

4. *The relationship between Muslim societies and the United States:* The United States continues to play a dominant role in world affairs for the foreseeable future, is there a posture that the United States should adopt toward Islam that recognizes its historic and continuing centrality in the lives of believers? Does such a posture imply specific policies, and is maintenance of that posture of such significance that it should stand on equal footing with other calculations of American national interest?

This list, which might well extended by others, serves the purpose of demonstrating the degree to which "bringing Islam in" will require a profound rethinking of a half century of social science theories. Simply admitting the continuing salience of religious belief as a touchstone of public behavior calls into question the equation of modernity with secularization that took form during the Enlightenment and has ever since underlain a good proportion of scholarly theorizing.

To go beyond such an admission and grant proponents of an "Islam policy" a seat at the table with Arabs and Israelis demanding priority for their parochial feud, energy advocates fearful of instability in the Persian Gulf, and globalization cheerleaders seeking to place all policy eggs in the economic basket would require a major rupture in the ways we are accustomed to looking at the world. This rupture will only occur when it is recognized that the seeming foreign policy successes of the second half of the twentieth century planted the seeds of our current crisis.

There is much to be said for retaining and refining the theories that guided our policies during that half century—they did, after all, achieve some worthwhile goals—but to put them up for reconsideration without factoring in a systematic and theoretically articulated understanding of Islam, and possibly, by extension, some other religions, risks planting more seeds and reaping yet more poisonous harvests.

Islam and the Challenge of Democracy

A Muslim jurist writing a few centuries ago on the subject of Islam and government would have commenced his treatise by distinguishing three types of political systems. The first he would have described as a natural system—like a primitive state of nature, an uncivilized, anarchic world where the most powerful tyrannize the rest. Instead of law there would be custom; instead of government there would be tribal elders who would be obeyed only as long as they remained the strongest.

The jurist would then describe a second system, ruled by a prince or king whose word is the law. Because the law is fixed by the arbitrary will of the ruler and the people obey out of necessity or compulsion, this system, too, is tyrannical and illegitimate.

The third and best system would have been the caliphate, based on Shari'ah law—the body of Muslim religious law founded on the Qur'an and the conduct and statements of the Prophet. Shari'ah law, according to Muslim jurists, fulfills the criteria of justice and legitimacy and binds governed and governor alike. Because it is based on the rule of law and thus deprives human beings of arbitrary authority over other human beings, the caliphate system was considered superior to any other.

In espousing the rule of law and limited government, classical Muslim scholars embraced core elements of modern democratic practice. Limited government and the rule of law, however, are only two elements of the system of government with the most compelling claim to legitimacy today. Democracy's moral power lies in the idea that the citizens of a nation are the sovereign, and—in modern representative democracies—they express their sovereign will by electing representatives. In a democracy, the people are the source of the law and the law in turn is to ensure fundamental rights that protect the well-being and interests of the individual members of the sovereign.

For Islam, democracy poses a formidable challenge. Muslim jurists argued that law made by a sovereign monarch is illegitimate because it substitutes human authority for God's sovereignty. But law made by sovereign citizens faces the same problem of legitimacy. In Islam, God is the only sovereign and ultimate source of legitimate law. How, then, can a democratic conception of the people's authority be reconciled with an Islamic understanding of God's authority?

Answering this question is extraordinarily important but also extraordinarily difficult, for both political and conceptual reasons. On the political side, it must be said at the outset that democracy faces a number of practical hurdles in Islamic countries—authoritarian political traditions, a history of colonial and imperial rule, and state domination of economy and society. But philosophical and doctrinal questions are important, and I propose to focus on them here as the beginning of a discussion of the possibilities for democracy in the Islamic world.

A central conceptual problem is that modern democracy evolved over centuries within the distinctive context of post-Reformation, market-oriented Christian Europe. Does it make sense to look for points of contact in a remarkably different context? My answer begins from the premise that democracy and Islam are defined in the first instance by their underlying moral values and the attitudinal commitments of their adherents—not by the ways that those values and commitments have been applied.

If we focus on those fundamental moral values, I believe, we will see that the tradition of Islamic political thought contains both interpretive and practical possibilities that can be developed into a democratic system. To be sure, these doctrinal potentialities may remain unrealized: without will power, inspired vision, and moral commitment there can be no democracy in Islam. But Muslims, for whom Islam is the authoritative frame of reference, can come to the conviction that democracy is an ethical good, and that the pursuit of this good does not require abandoning Islam.

Democracy and Divine Sovereignty

Although Muslim jurists debated political systems, the Qur'an itself did not specify a particular form of government. But it did identify a set of social and political values that are central to a Muslim polity. Three values are of particular importance: pursuing justice through social cooperation and mutual assistance, establishing a non-autocratic, consultative method of governance; and institutionalizing mercy and compassion in social interactions. So, all else equal, Muslims today ought to endorse the form of government that is most effective in helping them promote these values.

The Case for Democracy

Several considerations suggest that democracy—and especially a constitutional democracy that protects basic individual rights—is that form. My central argument (others will emerge later) is that democracy—by assigning equal rights of speech, association, and suffrage to all—offers the greatest potential for promoting justice and protecting human dignity, without making God responsible for human injustice or the degradation of human beings by one another. A fundamental Qur'anic idea is that God vested all of humanity with a kind of divinity by making all human beings the viceroys of God on this earth: "Remember, when your Lord said to the angels: 'I have to place a vicegerent on earth,' they said: 'Will you place one there who will create disorder and shed blood, while we intone Your litanies and sanctify Your name?' And God said: 'I know what you do not know'".

In particular, human beings are responsible, as God's vicegerents, for making the world more just. By assigning equal political rights to all adults, democracy expresses that special status of human beings in God's creation and enables them to discharge that responsibility. Of course God's vicegerent does not share God's perfection of judgment and will. A constitutional democracy, then, acknowledges the errors of judgment, temptations, and vices associated with human fallibility by enshrining some basic moral standards in a constitutional document—moral standards that express the dignity of individuals. To be sure, democracy does not ensure justice. But it does establish a basis for pursuing justice and thus for fulfilling a fundamental responsibility assigned by God to each of us.

Of course, in a representative democracy some individuals have greater authority than others. But a democratic system makes those authorities accountable to all and thus resists the tendency of the powerful to render them immune from judgment. This requirement of accountability is consistent with the imperative of justice in Islam. If a political system has no institutional mechanisms to call the unjust to account, then the system is itself unjust, regardless of whether injustice is actually committed or not. If the criminal law does not assign punishment for rape, then it is unjust, quite apart from whether that crime is ever committed or not. It is a moral good in and of itself that a democracy, through the institutions of the vote, separation and division of power, and guarantee of pluralism at least offers the possibility of redress.

We have a provisional case for democracy, then, founded on a fundamental Islamic idea about the special status of human beings in God's creation. It is provisional because we have not yet considered the great challenge to that case: how can the higher law of Shari'ah, founded on God's sovereignty, be reconciled with the democratic idea that the people, as the sovereign, can be free to flout Shari'ah law?

God as the Sovereign

Early in Islamic history the issue of God's political dominion (hakimiyyat Allah) was raised by a group known as the Haruriyya (later known as the Khawarij) when they rebelled against the fourth Rightly Guided Caliph 'Ali Ibn Abi Talib. Initially, the supporters of 'Ali, the Haruriyya turned against him when he agreed to arbitrate his personal political dispute with competing political faction led by a man named Mu'awiya.

'Ali himself had agreed to the arbitration on condition that the arbitrators be bound by the Qur'an and give full consideration to the supremacy of the Shari'ah. But the Khawarij—pious, puritanical, and fanatical—believed that God's law clearly supported 'Ali. So they rejected arbitration as inherently unlawful and, in effect, a challenge to God's sovereignty. According to the Khawarij, 'Ali's behavior showed that he was willing to compromise God's supremacy by transferring decision making to human actors. They declared 'Ali a traitor to God, and after efforts to reach a peaceful resolution failed they assassinated him. After 'Ali's death, Mu'awiya seized power and established himself as the first caliph of the Umayyad Dynasty.

Anecdotal reports about the debates between 'Ali and the Khawarij reflect an unmistakable tension about the meaning of legality and the implications of the rule of law. In one such report members of the Khawarij accused 'Ali of accepting the judgment and dominion (hakimiyya) of human beings instead of abiding by the dominion of God's law. Upon hearing of this accusation, 'Ali called upon the people to gather around him and brought a large copy of the Qur'an. 'Ali touched the Qur'an while instructing it to speak to the people and inform them about God's law. Surprised, the people gathered around 'Ali exclaimed, "What are you doing? The Qur'an cannot speak, for it is not a human being!" Upon hearing this, 'Ali exclaimed that this was exactly his point. The Qur'an, 'Ali explained, is but ink and paper and it does not speak for itself. Instead, it is human beings who give effect to it according to their limited personal judgments and opinions.

Such stories are subject to multiple interpretations, but this one points most importantly to the dogmatic superficiality of proclamations of God's sovereignty that sanctify human determinations. Notably, the Khawarij's rallying cry of "dominion belongs to God" or "the Qur'an is the judge" (la hukma illa li'llah or al-hukmu li'l-Qur'an) is nearly identical to the slogans invoked by contemporary fundamentalist groups.But considering the historical context, the Khawarij's sloganeering was initially a call for the symbolism of legality and the supremacy of law that descended into an unequivocal radicalized demand for fixed lines of demarcation between what is lawful and unlawful.

To a believer, God is all-powerful and the ultimate owner of the heavens and earth. But when it comes to the laws in a political system, arguments claiming that God is the sole legislator endorse a fatal fiction that is indefensible from the point of view of Islamic theology. Such arguments pretend that (some) human agents have perfect access to God's will, and that human beings could become the perfect executors of the divine will without inserting their own human judgements and inclinations in the process.

Moreover, claims about God's sovereignty assume that the divine legislative will seeks to regulate all human interactions, that Shari'ah is a complete moral code that prescribes for every eventuality. But perhaps God does not seek to regulate all human affairs, and instead leaves human beings considerable latitude in regulating their own affairs as long as they observe certain minimal standards of moral conduct, including the preservation and promotion of human dignity and well-being.

In the Qur'anic discourse, God commanded creation to honor human beings because of the miracle of the human intellect—an expression of the abilities of the divine. Arguably, the fact that God honored the miracle of the human intellect and the human being as a symbol of divinity is sufficient to justify a moral commitment to protecting and preserving the integrity and dignity of that symbol of divinity. But—and this is 'Ali's central point—God's sovereignty provides no escape from the burdens of human agency.

When human beings search for ways to approximate God's beauty and justice, then, they do not deny God's sovereignty; they honor it. It is honored as well in the attempt to safeguard the moral values that reflect the attributes of the divine. If we say that the only legitimate source of law is the divine text and that human experience and intellect are irrelevant to the pursuit of the divine will, then divine sovereignty will always stand as an instrument of authoritarianism and an obstacle to democracy. But that authoritarian view denigrates God's sovereignty.

I will further develop this argument below, but to make the case more compelling and accessible, I need first to lay a broader foundation for Islamic political and legal doctrines.

Government and Law

Many Muslim fundamentalists and Western orientalists contend, God's dominion or sovereignty means that God is the sole legislator, and then one would expect that a caliph or Muslim ruler would be treated as God's agent or representative.

If God is the only sovereign within a political system, then the ruler ought to be appointed by the divine sovereign, serve at His pleasure, and implement His will. But just as the meaning and implications of God's sovereignty was the subject of an intense debate in pre-modern Islam, so were the powers of the ruler and the place of law in circumscribing those powers. And some lines of argument in the debate resonate with modern democratic ideas.

Ruler and Ruled

It is well established, at least in Sunni Islam, that the Prophet died without naming a successor to lead the Muslim community. The Prophet intentionally left the choice of leadership to the Muslim nation as a whole. A statement attributed to the Rightly Guided Caliph Abu Bakr asserts, "God has left people to manage their own affairs so that they will choose a leader who will serve their interests.

The word khalifa (caliph), the title given to the Muslim leader, literally means successor or deputy. Early on Muslims debated whether it was appropriate to name the leader the Caliph of God (khalifat Allah), but most scholars preferred the designation Caliph of the Prophet of God (khalifat rasul Allah).

But the Caliph—whether the Prophet's successor or God's deputy—did not enjoy the authority of either the Prophet or God whose powers of legislation, revelation, absolution, and punishment cannot be delegated to any other. But how much of the Prophet's authority does the Caliph enjoy? And to whom does the Caliph answer?

If the Caliph's primary obligation is to implement divine law, then arguably the Caliph answers only to God. So long as the Caliph's actions are plausible interpretations of God's mandates, then such interpretations must be accepted and the Caliph has fulfilled his duties to the people. Only God can assess the Caliph's intentions, and—most Sunni jurists argued—a ruler is not removable from power unless he commits a clear, visible, and major infraction against God (i.e., a major sin).

Muslim jurists did not, however, completely sever the connection between ruler and people. In Sunni theory the Caliphate must be based on a contract ('aqd) between the Caliph and ahl al-hall wa al-'aqd (the people who have the power of contract) who give their bay'a (allegiance or consent to the Caliph): the Caliph is to receive the bay'a in return for his promise to discharge the terms of the contract. The terms of the contract were not extensively discussed in Islamic sources.

Typically, jurists would include the obligation to apply God's law and to protect Muslims and the territory of Islam; in return the ruler was promised the people's support and obedience. The assumption has been that Shari'ah law defines the terms of the contract.

Who are the people that have the power to choose and remove the ruler? The Mu'tazili scholar Abu Bakr al-Asam (d. 200/816) argued that the public at large must have this power: there must be a general consensus over the ruler and each person must individually give his consent. The vast majority of Muslim jurists argued more pragmatically that ahl al-hall wa al- aqd are those who possess the necessary shawka (power or strength) to insure the obedience or, in the alternative, the consent of the public.

The idea of the consent of the governed, despite its democratic resonance, ought not to be equated with conceptions of delegated powers or government by the people. Consent in pre-modern Muslim discourses appears to be the equivalent of acquiescence. Underlying these discussions is a certain amount of distrust towards the laity (al-'amma): "They [the laity] tend to float with every ebb and flow, and maybe [the laity] will be more content with choosing [to the Caliphate] the wrong-doers instead of the righteous [rulers]. . . This type of attitude was widespread among Muslim jurists, and considering the historical period in which they wrote—well before any experience with mass democracy or broad literacy—it is not surprising. As a result many of the concepts employed in political discourses suggest an idea of representative government but never fully endorse it. In the dominant paradigm both ruler and ruled are God's agents (khulafa' Allah) in implementing the divine law.

The Rule of Law

As noted above, an essential characteristic of a legitimate Islamic government is that it is subject to and limited by Shari'ah law. Although this concept does offer support for the rule of law, we must distinguish between the supremacy of law and the supremacy of a set of legal rules. The two are quite distinct, and both are suggested in the Islamic legal tradition. Once again, Islamic political thought contains a range of interpretive possibilities. And once again, some of those possibilities resonate more strongly with democratic principles.

In asserting the supremacy of Shari'ah, Muslim scholars typically were arguing that its positive commandments, such as punishment for adultery or the drinking of alcohol, ought to be honored by the government. But a government that declares its intention to abide by all the positive commandments of Shari'ah may nevertheless manipulate the rules in order to obtain desired results. Under the pretense of guarding public modesty the government could pass arbitrary laws forbidding many forms of public assembly; under the guise of protection of orthodoxy it could pass arbitrary laws to punish creative expression; under the guise of protecting individuals from slander, it could suppress many forms of political and social criticism; and a government could imprison or execute political dissenters, claiming that they are sowing fitnah (discord and social turmoil).

Arguably, all these governmental actions are Shari'ah-compliant unless there is a clear sense of the limits imposed upon the ability of the government to service and promote even the Shari'ah.

But the rule of law need not be taken to mean that government is bound by a codebook of specific regulations. Instead, it might be interpreted as requiring a government bound by processes of making and interpreting laws, and even more importantly as requiring that those processes themselves be bound by fundamental moral commitments—in particular to human dignity and freedom.

We find some evidence for this alternative conception of the rule of law in the pre-modern juristic literature. Jurists discussed the limits to be placed on the lawmaking power of the state, in part under the rubric of public interest (al-masalih al-mursalah) and blocking the means to illegality (sadd al-dhari'ah). Both jurisprudential concepts enabled the state to extend its law making powers in order to fulfill a good or avoid an evil. For instance, pursuant to the principle of blocking the means, the lawmaker could claim that behavior that is lawful ought to be considered unlawful because it leads to the commission of illegal acts.

In essence, both public interest and blocking the means made law more flexible and adaptive. Of course, they could be employed to expand the law not only in the service of the public good but at the expense of individual autonomy as well. In particular, blocking the means to evil, founded on the idea of preventive or precautionary measures (al-ihtiyat), could be exploited to expand the power of the state under the guise of protecting the Shari'ah. This type of dynamic can be avoided in part by adopting procedural guarantees, but more importantly by understanding that the rule of law is as ensuring the dignity and freedoms of human beings, which the Shari'ah can be utilized to justify but not to undermine.

An important dimension to the challenge of establishing the rule of law is the complex relationship between Shari'ah law, as articulated by jurists, and the administrative practices of the state or expediency laws (al-ahkam al-siyasiyyah).

While in the first two centuries of Islam it was possible to find jurists citing the practices of the state as a normative precedent, this became increasingly rare. By the fourth/tenth century Muslim jurists had established themselves as the only legitimate authority empowered to expound the law of God. The practice of the state was not considered illegitimate, but only the Muslim jurists could settle the law. The state was expected to enforce divine laws, not to determine their content.

Still, as the enforcer of divine laws the state was granted broad discretion over matters of public interest (known as the field of al-siyasah al-Shar'iyyah). State regulations were lawful and enforceable as long as they did not contravene the divine law, as expounded by the jurists, or constitute an abusive use of discretion (al-ta'assuf fi masa'il al-khiyar).

For this reason jurisprudential works meticulously documented the determinations of jurists but did not document state regulations, which were documented by state functionaries in works on the administrative practices of the state. In the dictum of Muslim jurists, Shari'ah is considered the foundation of law and politics is its protector. (Similarly, Muslim jurists often would assert that religion is the foundation and the political authorities are its protector.) This paradigm, however, leaves unresolved the core problem of how to clearly delineate the limits of government power. To what extent can the government extend the reach of its laws under the guise of guarding or properly fulfilling purposes of Shari'ah?

Concerns about the reach of the government's power under Shari'ah have antecedents in Islamic history and so, by the standards of the modern age, this is not an entirely novel issue. But such concerns are nearly absent from the framework of contemporary Islamists. To date, Islamist models, whether in Iran, Saudi Arabia, or Pakistan, have endowed the state with legislative power over the divine law. For instance, the claim of precautionary measures (blocking the means) is used today in Saudi Arabia to justify a wide range of restrictive laws against women, including the prohibition against driving cars. This is a relatively novel invention in Islamic state practices and in many instances amounts to the use of Shari'ah to undermine Shari'ah.

Traditionally, Muslim jurists insisted that the rulers ought to consult with the jurists on all matters related to law, but the jurists themselves never demanded the right to rule the Islamic state directly and in fact, until recently neither Sunni nor Shi'i jurists ever assumed direct rule in the political sphere. Throughout Islamic history the jurists ('ulama) performed a wide range of economic, political, and administrative functions but most importantly acted as negotiative mediators between the ruling classes and the laity. As Afaf Marsot states, "[The 'ulama] were the purveyors of Islam, the guardians of its tradition, the depository of ancestral wisdom, and the moral tutors of the population." While they legitimated and often explained the rulers to the ruled, the jurists also used their moral weight to thwart tyrannous measures and at times led or legitimated rebellions against the ruling classes. Modernity, however, has turned the 'ulama from "vociferous spokesmen of the masses" into salaried state functionaries who play a primarily conservative, legitimist role for the ruling regimes in the Islamic world. The disintegration of the role of the 'ulama and their co-optation by the modern praetorian state, with its hybrid practices of secularism, have opened the door for the state to become the maker and enforcer of the divine law; in so doing the state has acquired formidable power that has further ingrained the practice of authoritarianism in various Islamic states.

Consultative Government

The Qur'an instructs the Prophet to consult regularly with Muslims on all significant matters and indicates that a society that conducts its affairs through some form of deliberative process is considered praiseworthy in the eyes of God (3:159; 42:38). There are many historical reports suggesting that the Prophet consulted regularly with his Companions regarding the affairs of the state. In addition, shortly after the death of the Prophet the concept of shura (consultative deliberations) had become a symbol signifying participatory politics and legitimacy.

The failure to enforce or adhere to shura became a common theme invoked in narratives of oppression and rebellion. For example, it is reported that the Prophet's cousin 'Ali reproached Umar b. al-Khattab, the second caliph, and Abu Bakr, the first caliph, for not respecting the shura by nominating Abu Bakr to the caliphate in the absence of the Prophet's family. And the opposition to 'Uthman b. 'Affan (r. 23–35/644–656), the third Rightly Guided Caliph, accused him of destroying the rule of shura because of his alleged nepotistic and autocratic policies.

Although the precise meaning of shura in these historical narratives is unclear, the concept most certainly did not refer merely to a ruler's solicitation of opinions from notables in society; it signified, more broadly, resistance to autocracy, government by force, or oppression. This is consistent with the juristic hostility towards despotism (al-istibdad) and whimsical and autocratic governance (al-hukm bi'l hawa wa al-tasallut). Even when Muslim jurists prohibited rebellions against despotic rulers, they tolerated despotism as a necessary evil, not as a desirable good.

After the third/ninth century the concept of shura took more concrete institutional shape in the discourses of Muslim jurists. Shura became the formal act of consulting ahl al-shura (the people of consultation), who according to the juristic sources are the same group of people who constitute ahl al-'aqd (the people who choose the ruler). Sunni jurists debated whether the results of the consultative process are binding (shura mulzima) or non-binding (ghayr mulzima). If the shura is binding then the ruler must abide by the determinations made by ahl al-shura.

The majority of jurists, however, concluded that the determinations of ahl al-shura are advisory and not compulsory. But, rather inconsistently, many jurists asserted that after consultation the ruler must follow the opinion that is most consistent with the Qur'an, Sunnah, and the consensus of jurists. Al-Ghazali expressed the general consensus when he said that "despotic, non-consultative, decision-making, even if from a wise and learned person is objectionable and unacceptable."

Modern reformists have seized upon the ideal of a consultative government as a way of arguing for the basic compatibility between Islam and democracy. But even if the ethic of shura is expanded into a broader concept of a participatory government, concerns about majority tyranny underscore that the moral commitments informing the lawmaking process are as important as the process itself. So even if shura is transformed into an instrument of participatory representation, it must itself be limited by a scheme of private and individual rights that serve an overriding moral goal such as justice. In other words, shura must be valued not because of the results it produces but because it represents a moral value in itself. As a result, regardless of the value of specific dissenting views, dissent would be tolerated because doing so is seen as a basic part of the mandate of justice.

The Islamic tradition of legal-political thought, then, suggests ideas of representation, consultation, and legal process. But the precise content of those ideas remains contested and provides no direct link between Islam and democracy. To understand the democratic possibilities of Islam we must look more deeply into the role of human beings in God's creation and the central importance of justice in human life assigned by the Qur'an.

Justice and Mercy

Justice plays a central role in the Qur'anic discourse: it is an obligation we owe to God, and also to one another. In addition, the imperative of justice is tied to the obligations of enjoining the good and forbidding the evil, and the necessity of bearing witness on God's behalf. Although the Qur'an does not define the constituent elements of justice, it emphasizes the ability to achieve justice as a unique human charge and necessity—an obligation that falls on all of us in our capacity as vicegerents. In essence the Qur'an requires a commitment to a moral imperative that is vague but recognizable through intuition, reason, and human experience.

The Islamic debate about how government might serve justice is remarkably similar to seventeenth-century Western discourse on the state of nature or the original condition of human beings. One view—advanced by Ibn Khaldun and al-Ghazali—argued that human beings are by nature fractious, contentious, and not inclined towards cooperation. So, government is necessary to force people to cooperate with each other, contrary to their natures, and to promote justice and the general interest.

Another school of thought, exemplified by al-Mawardi and Ibn Abi al-Rabi', argued that God created human beings weak and in need so that they would cooperate by necessity; cooperation would limit injustice by restraining the strong and safeguarding the rights of the weak. Furthermore, God created human beings different from one another so that they would need each other to achieve their aims. In this school of thought, human beings by nature desire justice and will tend to cooperate in order to achieve it. Even if human beings exploit the divine gift of intellect and the guidance of the law of God, through cooperation they are bound to reach a greater level of justice and moral fulfillment. And the ruler ascends to power through a contract with the people, pursuant to which he undertakes to further the cooperation of the people with the ultimate goal of achieving a just society.

In reflecting on the demands of justice the juristic argument about human diversity and cooperation is especially important. The Qur'an says that God created people different and grouped them into nations and tribes so that they would come to know one another. Muslim jurists reasoned that the expression "come to know one another" indicates the need for social cooperation and mutual assistance in order to achieve justice. The Qur'an also notes that people will remain different from one another until the end of human existence. It also states that the reality of human diversity is part of the divine wisdom and an intentional purpose of creation: "If thy Lord had so willed, He could have made mankind one people, but they will not cease to dispute. . ."

The Qur'anic celebration and sanctification of human diversity incorporates that diversity into the purposeful pursuit of justice and creates various possibilities for pluralistic commitment in modern Islam. That commitment could be developed into an ethic that respects dissent and honors the right of human beings to be different, including the right to adhere to different religious or nonreligious convictions. At the political level it could be appropriated into a normative stance that considers justice and diversity to be core values that a democratic constitutional order is bound to protect.

Furthermore, it could be developed into a notion of delegated powers, where the ruler is entrusted to serve the core value of justice by ensuring rights of assembly, cooperation, and dissent. Even more, a notion of limits could be developed that would restrain the government from derailing the quest for justice or from hampering the right of the people to cooperate, or dissent, in this quest. Importantly, if the government fails to discharge the obligations of its covenant, then it loses its legitimate claim to power.

Unfortunately, however, several factors militate against the fulfillment of these possibilities in modern Islam. At the theological and philosophical level the constituents of justice have not been subject to close examination in Islamic doctrine. And part of the explanation for that limitation lies in a basic tension in understanding the nature of justice. Does the divine law define justice or does justice define the divine law? If it is the former then whatever one concludes is the divine law therein is justice. If it is the latter, then whatever justice demands is, in fact, the demand of the divine.

If we can know what justice requires by first determining what the divine law is, then there is no point in investigating the demands of justice—whether justice means equality of opportunities or results, or fostering personal autonomy, or maximizing collective utility, or guarding basic human dignity. If the divine law is prior to justice, then the just society is no longer about rights of speech and assembly, or the right to explore the means to justice, but simply about the implementation of the divine law.

Suppose instead that we accept the primacy of justice in the Qur'anic discourse, the notion of human vicegerency, and the idea that the duty to foster justice has been assigned to humanity at large. A reasonable conclusion would be that the value of justice ought to control and guide all efforts at interpreting and understanding divine law. This requires a serious paradigm shift in Islamic thinking. In my view, justice is a divine imperative, and represents the sovereignty of the divine. God describes God's self as inherently just, and the Qur'an asserts that God has decreed mercy upon God's self. Furthermore, the very purpose of entrusting the divine message to the Prophet Muhammad was as a gift of mercy to human beings.

In the Qur'anic discourse mercy is not simply forgiveness, nor the willingness to ignore the faults and sins of people, but a state in which the individual is able to be just with him- or her and others, by giving each individual person his or her due. Fundamentally, mercy is tied to a state of genuine perception of others—that is why in the Qur'an mercy is coupled with the need for human beings to be patient and tolerant with each other. Most significantly, diversity and differences among human beings are claimed in the Qur'anic discourse as merciful divine gifts to humankind. Genuine perception that enables persons to understand, appreciate, and become enriched by the diversity of humanity is one of the constituent elements for founding a just society and achieving justice. The divine charge to human beings at large and Muslims in particular is, as the Qur'an puts it, "to know one another," and to utilize this genuine knowledge in an effort to pursue justice.

On this view, then, the divine mandate for a Muslim polity is to pursue justice by adhering to the need for mercy. Although coexistence is a basic necessity for mercy, in order to pursue genuine knowledge of the other and aspire to a state of justice, human beings need to cooperate in seeking the good and beautiful, and do so by engaging in a purposeful moral discourse. Implementing legalistic rules, even if such rules are the product of the interpretation of divine texts, is not sufficient for mercy—genuine perception of the other—or, ultimately, for justice.

So principles of mercy and justice are the primary divine charge, and God's sovereignty lies in the fact that God is the authority that delegated to human beings the charge to achieve justice on earth by fulfilling the virtues that approximate divinity.

This conception of divine sovereignty does not negate human agency by requiring a mechanical enforcement of rules; instead, it accommodates our agency and even promotes it insofar as it contributes to the fulfillment of justice. Significantly, according to the juristic discourses it is not possible to achieve justice unless every possessor of a right (haqq) is granted his or her right. The challenge for human vicegerents is to recognize that a right exists, to understand who is the possessor of such a right, and ultimately to ensure that the possessor enjoys the right. A society that fails in this task—no matter how many rules it applies—is neither merciful nor just. This puts us in a position to explore the possibility of individual rights in Islam.

Individual Rights

All constitutional democracies afford strong protections to certain individual interests through rights of free speech and assembly, equality before the law, rights to property, and guarantees of due process. But which rights ought to be protected, and to what extent, is subject to a large measure of variation in theory and practice. Here I will suppose that whatever the precise nature of rights, some individual interests ought to be treated as unassailable. These unassailable interests are that whose violation communicate to the individual in question a sense of worthlessness and tends to destroy the faculty of a human being to comprehend the necessary elements for a dignified existence. So, use of torture and denial of food, shelter, or means of sustenance, such as employment, are always unacceptable.

To understand the traditional place of protected interests in Islamic law it is important to note that the purpose of Shari'ah in jurisprudential theory is to assure the welfare of the people (tahqiq masalih al-'ibad). Typically, Muslim jurists divided the welfare of the people into three categories: necessities (daruriyyat), needs (hajiyyat), and luxuries (kamaliyyat or tahsiniyyat).

According to Muslim jurists the law and policies of the government must fulfill these interests, in descending order of importance—first necessities, then needs, then luxuries. The necessities are further divided into five basic values—al-daruriyyat al-khamsah: religion, life, intellect, lineage or honor, and property. But Muslim jurists did not develop the five basic values as broad categories and then explore the theoretical implications of each value. Rather, in a positivistic spirit, they examined existing legal injunctions that could be said to serve each value and concluded that by their codification of these specific injunctions, the five values would be sufficiently served.

So, for example, Muslim jurists contended that the prohibition of murder in Islamic law served the basic value of life, the law of apostasy protected religion, the prohibition of intoxicants protected the intellect, the prohibition of fornication and adultery protected lineage, and the right of compensation protected the right to property. But limiting the protection of the intellect to a prohibition of alcohol or the protection of life to the prohibition of murder is hardly thorough. Unfortunately, it appears that the juristic tradition reduced these five values to technical objectives. Still, the broad values asserted could serve as a foundation for a systematic theory of individual rights in the modern age.

To be sure, the juristic tradition articulated a wealth of positions that exhibit an orientation toward protections for individuals. For instance, Muslim jurists developed the idea of presumption of innocence in criminal and civil proceedings and argued that the accuser always carries the burden of proof (al-bayyina 'ala man idda'a). In matters related to heresy, Muslim jurists repeatedly argued that it is better to let a thousand heretics go free than to wrongfully punish a single sincere Muslim.

In criminal cases the jurists argued that it is always better to release a guilty person than to run the risk of punishing an innocent one. Moreover, many jurists condemned the practice of detaining or incarcerating heterodox groups even when such groups openly advocated and proselytized their heterodoxy (such as the Khawarij) and argued that such groups may not be harassed or molested until they carry arms and form a clear intent to rebel against the government.

Muslim jurists also condemned the use of torture, arguing that the Prophet forbade the use of muthla (the use of mutilations) in all situations, and opposed the use of coerced confessions in all legal and political matters. In fact, a large number of jurists articulated a doctrine similar to the American exculpatory doctrine—confessions or evidence obtained under coercion are inadmissible at trial. Interestingly, some jurists even asserted that judges who rely on a coerced confession in a criminal conviction are to be held liable for the wrongful conviction.

But perhaps the most intriguing discourse on the subject in the juristic tradition concerns the rights of God and the rights of people. The rights of God (huquq Allah) are rights retained by God in the sense that only God can say how the violation of these rights may be punished and only God has the right to forgive such violations. But all rights not explicitly retained by God are retained by people. And while violations of God's rights are only forgiven by God through adequate acts of repentance, the rights of people may be forgiven only by the people. Thus, a right to compensation is retained individually by a human being and may only be forgiven by the aggrieved individual. Neither the government nor even God have the right to forgive or compromise such a right of compensation if it is designated as part of the rights of human beings.

Muslim jurists did not imagine a set of unwavering and generalizable rights that are to be held by each individual at all times. Rather, they thought of individual rights as arising from a legal cause brought about by the suffering of a legal wrong. A person does not possess a right until he or she has been wronged and obtains a claim for retribution or compensation as a result.

To shift paradigms would require transformation of traditional conceptions of rights, so that rights become the property of individual holders, regardless of whether there is a legal cause of action. The set of rights recognized as immutable are those that are necessary to achieve a just society while promoting the element of mercy. In my view these must be the rights that guarantee the physical safety and moral dignity of a human being. It is quite possible that the relevant individual rights are the five values mentioned above, but this issue needs to be re-analyzed in light of the current diversity of human existence. In this context, the commitment to human rights does not signify a lack of commitment to God but is instead a necessary part of celebrating human diversity, honoring God's vicegerents, achieving mercy, and pursuing the ultimate goal of justice.

Interestingly enough, it is not the pre-modern juristic tradition that poses the greatest barrier to the development of individual rights in Islam. Rather, the most serious obstacle comes from modern Muslims themselves.

Especially in the second half of the last century, a considerable number of Muslims have made the unfounded assumption that Islamic law is concerned primarily with duties, not rights, and that the Islamic conception of rights is collectivist, not individualistic. Both assumptions, however, are based only on cultural assumptions about the non-Western "other." It is as if these interpreters fixed on a Judeo-Christian or perhaps Western conception of rights and assumed that Islam must be different.

In reality, claims about both individual and collectivist rights are largely anachronistic. Pre-modern Muslim jurists did not assert a collectivist vision of rights or an individualistic vision. They did speak of al-haqq al-'amm (public rights), and often asserted that public rights ought to be given preference over private entitlements. But this amounted to no more than an assertion that the many should not be made to suffer for the entitlements of the few. For example, as a legal maxim this was utilized to justify the notion of public takings or the right to public easements over private property.

This principle was also utilized in prohibiting unqualified doctors from practicing medicine. But as noted above, Muslim jurists did not, for instance, justify the killing or the torture of individuals in order to promote the welfare of the state or the public interest.

Perhaps the widespread assertion of a primacy of collectivist and duty-based perspectives in Islam points to the reactive nature of much contemporary discourse on Islamic law. But the notion of individual rights is actually easier to justify in Islam than a collectivist orientation. God created human beings as individuals, and their liability in the Hereafter is individually determined as well. To commit oneself to safeguarding and protecting the well-being of individuals is to take God's creation seriously. Each individual embodies a virtual universe of divine miracles. Why should a Muslim commit him- or herself to the rights and well-being of a fellow human being? The answer is that God already made such a commitment when God invested so much of the God-self in each and every person. This is why the Qur'an asserts that whomever kills a fellow human being unjustly has in effect murdered all of humanity; it is as if the killer has murdered the divine sanctity and defiled the very meaning of divinity.

Moreover, the Qur'an does not differentiate between the sanctity of a Muslim or non-Muslim. As the Qur'an repeatedly asserts, no human being can limit the divine mercy in any way, or even regulate who is entitled to it. This mean that non-Muslims as well as Muslims could be recipients and givers of divine mercy.

The measure of moral virtue on this earth is a person's proximity to divinity through justice, not a religious label. The measure in the Hereafter is a different matter, but that matter is God's exclusive jurisdiction. God will most certainly vindicate God's rights in the Hereafter in the fashion that God deems most fitting. But our primary moral responsibility on earth is the vindication of the rights of human beings. A commitment in favor of human rights is a commitment in favor of God's creation and ultimately a commitment in favor of God.

Shari'ah and the Democratic State

A case for democracy presented from within Islam must accept the idea of God's sovereignty: it cannot substitute popular sovereignty for divine sovereignty, but must instead show how popular sovereignty—with its idea that citizens have rights and a correlative responsibility to pursue justice with mercy—expresses God's authority, properly understood. Similarly, it cannot reject the idea that God's law is given prior to human action, but must show how democratic lawmaking respects that priority. I have reserved the issue of Shari'ah and the State for the end because it was necessary to first lay the foundation for addressing it. As part of this foundation, it is important to appreciate the centrality of Shari'ah to Muslim life. Shari'ah is God's Way; it is represented by a set of normative principles, methodologies for the production of legal injunctions, and a set of positive legal rules. As is well known, Shari'ah encompasses a variety of schools of thought and approaches, all of which are equally valid and equally orthodox.

The Shari'ah, for the most part, is not explicitly dictated by God. Rather, Shari'ah relies on the interpretive act of the human agent for its production and execution. Paradoxically, however, Shari'ah is the core value that society must serve. The paradox here is exemplified in the tension between the obligation to live by God's law and the fact that this law is manifested only through subjective interpretive determinations. Even if there is a unified realization that a particular positive command does express the divine law, there is still a vast array of possible subjective executions and applications. This dilemma was resolved somewhat in Islamic discourses by distinguishing between Shari'ah and fiqh. Shari'ah, it was argued, is the Divine Ideal, standing as if suspended in midair, unaffected and uncorrupted by life's vagaries. The fiqh is the human attempt to understand and apply the ideal. Therefore, Shari'ah is immutable, immaculate, and flawless—fiqh is not.

As part of the doctrinal foundations for this discourse, Sunni jurists focused on the tradition attributed to the Prophet, stating: "Every mujtahid (jurist who strives to find the correct answer) is correct" or "Every mujtahid will be [justly] rewarded." This implied that there could be more than a single correct answer to the same question. For Sunni jurists this raised the issue of the purpose or motivation behind the search for the Divine Will. What is the Divine

Purpose behind setting out indicators to the divine law and then requiring that human beings engage in a search? If the Divine wants human beings to reach the correct understanding, then how could every interpreter or jurist be correct? Put differently, is there a correct legal response to all legal problems, and are Muslims charged with the legal obligation of finding that response?

Mukhatti'ah

The overwhelming majority of Sunni jurists agreed that good faith diligence in searching for the Divine Will is sufficient to protect a researcher from liability before God. Beyond this, the jurists were divided into two main camps. The first school, known as the mukhatti'ah, argued that every legal problem ultimately has a correct answer; however, only God knows the correct response, and the truth will not be revealed until the Final Day.

Human beings for the most part cannot conclusively know whether they have found that correct response. In this sense every mujtahid is correct in trying to find the answer; however, one reader might reach the truth while the rest might mistake it. God, on the Final Day, will inform all readers of who was right and who was wrong. Correctness here means that the mujtahid is to be commended for putting in the effort, but it does not mean that all responses are equally valid.

Musawwibah

The second school, known as the musawwibah, argued that there is no specific and correct answer (hukm mu'ayyan) that God wants human beings to discover: after all, if there were a correct answer, God would have made the evidence indicating a divine rule conclusive and clear. God cannot charge human beings with the duty to find the correct answer when there is no objective means to discover the correctness of a textual or legal problem. If there were an objective truth to everything, God would have made such a truth ascertainable in this life.

Legal truth, or correctness, in most circumstances depends on belief and evidence, and the validity of a legal rule or act is often contingent on the rules of recognition that provide for its existence. Human beings are not charged with the obligation of finding some abstract or inaccessible, legally correct result. Rather, they are charged with the duty to diligently investigate a problem and then follow the results of their own ijtihad. According to al-Juwayni, for example, what God wants or intends is for human beings to search—to live a life fully and thoroughly engaged with the divine. Al-Juwayni explains: it is as if God has said to human beings, "My command to My servants is in accordance with the preponderance of their beliefs. So whoever preponderantly believes that they are obligated to do something, acting upon it becomes My command."

God's command to human beings is to diligently search and God's law is suspended until a human being forms a preponderance of belief about the law. At the point that a preponderance of belief is formed, God's law becomes in accordance with the preponderance of belief formed by that particular individual. In summary, if a person honestly and sincerely believes that such and such is the law of God, then as to that person it is in fact God's law.

The position of the second school in particular raises difficult questions about the application of the Shari'ah in society. This position implies that God's law is to search for God's law; otherwise the legal charge (taklif) is entirely dependent on the subjectivity and sincerity of belief. Under the first school of thought, whatever law the state applies, that law is only potentially the law of God, and we will not find out until the Final Day. Under the second school of thought, any law applied by the state is not the law of God unless the person to whom the law applies believes it to be

God's will and command. The first school suspends knowledge until we are done living and the second school hinges knowledge on the validity of the process and ultimate sincerity of belief.

Building upon this intellectual heritage, I would suggest Shari'ah ought to stand in an Islamic polity as a symbolic construct for the divine perfection that is unreachable by human effort. As Ibn Qayyim stated, it is the epitome of justice, goodness, and beauty as conceived and retained by God. Its perfection is preserved, so to speak, in the Mind of God, but anything that is channeled through human agency is necessarily marred by human imperfection. Put differently, Shari'ah as conceived by God is flawless, but as understood by human beings Shari'ah is imperfect and contingent. Jurists ought to continue to explore the ideal of Shari'ah and to expound their imperfect attempts at understanding God's perfection. As long as the argument constructed is normative it is unfulfilled potential to reach the Divine Will. Significantly, any law applied is necessarily a potential-unrealized. Shari'ah is not simply a collection of ahkam (a set of positive rules) but also a set of principles, a methodology, and a discoursive process that searches for the divine ideals. As such, Shari'ah is a work in progress that is never complete.

To put it more concretely: if a legal opinion is adopted and enforced by the state, it cannot be said to be God's law. By passing through the determinative and enforcement processes of the state, the legal opinion is no longer simply a potential—it has become an actual law, applied and enforced. But what has been applied and enforced is not God's law—it is the state's law. Effectively, a religious state law is a contradiction in terms. Either the law belongs to the state or it belongs to God, and as long as the law relies on the subjective agency of the state for its articulation and enforcement, any law enforced by the state is necessarily not God's law. Otherwise, we must be willing to admit that the failure of the law of the state is in fact the failure of God's law and, ultimately, of God Himself. In Islamic theology, this possibility cannot be entertained.

Of course, the most formidable challenge to this position is the argument that God and His Prophet have set out clear legal injunctions that cannot be ignored. Arguably, God provided unambiguous laws precisely because God wished to limit the role of human agency and foreclose the possibility of innovations.

But—to return one last time to a point I have emphasized throughout—regardless of how clear and precise the statements of the Qur'an and Sunna, the meaning derived from these sources is negotiated through human agency. For example, the Qur'an states: "As to the thief, male or female, cut off (faqta'u) their hands as a recompense for that which they committed, a punishment from God, and God is all-powerful and all-wise" (5:38).

Although the legal import of the verse seems to be clear, it requires at minimum that human agents struggle with the meaning of "thief," "cut off," "hands," and "recompense." The Qur'an uses the expression iqta'u, from the root word qata'a, which could mean to sever or cut off, but it could also mean to deal firmly, to bring to an end, to restrain, or to distance oneself from.

Whatever the meaning derived from the text, can the human interpreter claim with certainty that the determination reached is identical to God's? And even when the issue of meaning is resolved, can the law be enforced in such a fashion that one can claim that the result belongs to God? God's knowledge and justice are perfect, but it is impossible for human beings to determine or enforce the law in such a fashion that the possibility of a wrongful result is entirely excluded. This does not mean that the exploration of God's law is pointless; it only means that the interpretations of jurists are potential fulfillments of the Divine Will, but the laws as codified and implemented by the state cannot be considered as the actual fulfillment of these potentialities.

Institutionally, it is consistent with the Islamic experience that the 'ulama, the jurists, can and do act as the interpreters of the Divine Word, the custodians of the moral conscience of the community, and the curators reminding and pointing the nation towards the Ideal that is God. But the law of the state, regardless of its origins or basis, belongs to the state.

Under this conception, no religious laws can or may be enforced by the state. All laws articulated and applied in a state are thoroughly human and should be treated as such. These laws are a part of Shari'ah law only to the extent that any set of human legal opinions can be said to be a part of Shari'ah. A code, even if inspired by Shari'ah, is not Shari'ah. Put differently, creation, with all its textual and nontextual richness, can and should produce foundational rights and organizational laws that honor and promote those rights. But the rights and laws do not mirror the perfection of divine creation.

According to this paradigm, democracy is an appropriate system for Islam because it both expresses the special worth of human beings—the status of vicegerency—and at the same time deprives the state of any pretense of divinity by locating ultimate authority in the hands of the people rather than the 'ulama.

Moral educators have a serious role to play because they must be vigilant in urging society to approximate God. But not even the will of the majority—no matter how well educated morally—can embody the full majesty of God. And in the worst case—if the majority is not persuaded by the 'ulama, if the majority insists on turning away from God but still respects the fundamental rights of individuals, including the right to ponder creation and call to the way of God—those individuals who constituted the majority will still have to answer, in the Hereafter, to God.

Islamic Movements

The wide range of Islamic movements in social make-up, structure, and programme have left many observers baffled. Since the Iranian revolution there has been a sharpened distinction between two approaches which might be called, respectively, fundamentalism and Islamism. Islamism can embrace both "progressive" 'ulema and those urban intellectuals who believe Islamic tenets are compatible with such modern values as freedom and democracy. The Islamist view stands in sharp contrast to those held by fundamentalist, traditionalist 'ulema that have had a historical monopoly over the right to interpret Islam and its tenets.

There has been much confusion, especially, over the term "fundamentalist," which implies a return to the past in recapturing the roots of Islamic religion. There is also an implication here that other readings of Islam are illegitimate, since they supposedly neglect traditionally accepted concepts for innovations that are often imports from non-Islamic societies.

Robin Wright shows one side of this approach in pointing out those fundamentalist movements also incorporate a great deal of modernity and innovation. Thus, she denies that most Islamic movements today are: "fundamentalist": The various Islamic movements are often called "fundamentalist" in the West, but most are in fact not fundamentalist in their agendas. Fundamentalism generally urges passive adherence to literal reading of scriptures and does not advocate change of the social order, instead focusing on reforming the lives of the individual and family.

Most of today's Islamic movements resemble Catholic Liberation theologians who urge active use of original religious doctrine to better the temporal and political lives in a modern world. Islamist or Islamism more accurately describes their forward-looking, interpretive and often even innovative attempts to reconstruct the social order." The opposite standpoint is conveyed by Dr. Ibrahim Yazdi, who claims that all truly Islamic movements are "fundamentalist."

Trends in Islamic Movement

There is two major trends in Islamic movements. One, we call the traditionalist. (The term 'fundamentalism' does not reflect the true facts. All of us are fundamentalists according to the definition in Western culture, that whoever believes the Bible is the word of God is a fundamentalist.) There is the tradition-oriented Muslim intelligentsia, the so-called 'ulema. Then there are the reformist or modernist Muslim intellectuals." Both Islamic "fundamentalism" and "traditionalism" are used here interchangeably as referring to opposition to Islamic reformists, or "Islamists," who are less rigid in their views of Islamic law (Shari'a) and of non-Islamic cultures. In any case, the classification of Muslim movements into traditionalist/fundamentalist and Islamist/reformist can be confusing, since Islamic doctrine itself allows for different interpretations and therefore different opinions on Shari'a and its principles. It is quite possible for a traditionalist religious leader (alim) to share similar Islamic values with an Islamic reformer on the overall position of Islam in society, economy, and politics. The late Ayatollah Taleqani, who played an important role in Iran's revolution, had an activist vision of Islam and an Islamic state, for example, much closer to Islamist views than to those of Ayatollah Khomeini.

Thus it should be stressed that fundamental disagreements remain even among traditionalists over divine versus popular sovereignty. Some, like Abul A'la Mawdudi, founder of the Jamaat-i Islami in India, have argued that if democracy is conceived as a limited form of popular sovereignty, restricted and directed by God's law, there is no incompatibility with Islam, but Mawdudi concluded that Islam is the very antithesis of secular Western democracy based solely on the sovereignty of the people. On the other hand, Sayyid Qutb, a leading traditionalist theoretician of the Muslim Brotherhood, executed by the Egyptian government in 1966, objected to the idea of popular sovereignty altogether: Qutb believed that "the Islamic state must be based on the Quranic principle of consultation or shurah [on the interpretation of Shari'a], and that the Islamic law or Shari'a is so complete a legal and moral system that no further legislation is possible or necessary."

Yet the rapidly unfolding events of the 1980s and 1990s have helped popularize the message and broaden support for moderate Islamists, compared to the revolutionary fundamentalists who flourished following Iran's revolution. The more radical forces have been somewhat discredited by criticism of the Iranian model, their use of violence, and their failure to seize power. The current trend is for Muslim political leaders who favor participation in the electoral process as the way of taking control of the state, and intellectual reformists, who have been engaging in a lively debate on Islam and modernity (e.g., the outlook of Islam on democracy, equality and human, minority and women's rights). The 'ulema have historically preoccupied themselves with the literal interpretation of the Quran (Koran) and the development of Islamic Law (Shari'a) which relies basically on the Quran and Sunna ("path" or "tradition," referring to the traditions about the conduct of the Prophet).

In doing so, a great deal of analysis has been written on the contributions by such Muslim thinkers as al-Shafi'i (767-820), Ibn Hanbal (780-855), al-Ghazzali (1058-1111), Ibn-Taymiyya (1263-1328), and others. These thinkers paid less attention in their writings to the political dimension of Shari'a than to its theological aspects. Vital questions, such as the right of the individual versus the community (umma), the right to rule and the source of political legitimacy, and the right or duty to rebel against unjust government, have been left underdeveloped. Thus, the scholars have not examined the duties and functions of an Islamic government in detail. As a result, no concrete political philosophy based on Shari'a has ever developed, and Islamic political thought has remained purely speculative.

In short, while a detailed theological discussion of the relationship between Islam and democracy is outside the scope of this study, Islamists argue that shura (consultation) can be interpreted as a democratic principle, since it demands open debate among both the 'ulema and the community at large on issues that concern the public. But traditionalists' unilinear and rigid view of society and politics has also come increasingly under question among Muslims.

Their views on Islam and politics are too rigid and outmoded for modern problems, and are even, some would say, un-Islamic. The Taliban movement in Afghanistan in the 1990s under the religious guidance of some 'ulema, have imposed such restrictive "Islamic" laws in provinces under their military control that they have made both conservative and radical 'ulema in Iran look like liberal reformists. And Islamic militants, including Islamists in Egypt, Algeria, and elsewhere in the Islamic world, may be praised as martyrs by some clerics but are denounced as terrorists by others.

Not only are traditionalists everywhere under scrutiny in terms of what they say and what they do, but the foundation of their power as the only legitimate interpreters of the Shari'a has been shaken.

The Arab fundamentalists have even been accused of a false representation of Muslim history, the presentation of a biased and incoherent account of Islamic thought, to further their position and interest. And of course, their historically close association with the state further weakens the credibility of some fundamentalists.

The political and economic turmoil in the Middle East has sharpened the peoples' image and expectations of Muslim groups and their leadership. Increasingly, the capacity to deliver tangible economic goods and basic political rights has become more important than the politics of ideology and rhetoric, Islamic or not. The Islamic governments of Iran and the Sudan, for example, remain somewhat isolated in the international community and face tremendous domestic problems that have led to popular discontent and even uprisings. Saudi Arabia, a self-proclaimed Islamic state, faces increasing economic problems, and while the monarchy claims legitimacy through fundamentalist Wahhabi Islam, it denies the population fundamental political and civil rights that are respected in Islam. The latest phase of the Islamic movement that began in the 1980s varies distinctly from the Islamic experience in Iran in 1979, in Lebanon after 1982, and among a host of small groups in Egypt, Saudi Arabia, Kuwait, Syria, and elsewhere during the late 1970s and early 1980s. The most conspicuous difference is the tactics of the new Islamists.

If extremism characterized a first phase of fundamentalist movements, the new ones attempt to work within the state system rather than outside it. Islamists, in other word, have not failed to recognize that pluralism and interdependence are the catchwords of the 1990s. Historically, Islam as a religion had remained on the periphery of state politics, over-shadowed by authoritarian states that propagated secular ideologies and values. Furthermore, the overall structure of the post-World War II international political economy helped consolidate state power over most Muslim societies. The rent collected from oil and gas exports, and external support in the form of military, economic, and financial aid, for example, helped Middle Eastern states monopolize domestic power during the Cold War. The Arab-Israeli conflict also bolstered the Arab states' political hegemony by legitimizing their authoritarianism and providing an excuse for inadequacies in socio-economic performance.

It is clear to all Muslims that in the Quran and Shari'a, Allah are the ultimate sovereign, and everything on earth and heaven is under His command. Yet, there is nothing in either source to deny Muslims' freedom of action to improve their individual and communal lives; nor does Shari'a promote subservience to the state as a proof of proper Muslim behavior.

On the contrary, individuals are regarded as responsible for the salvation and well being of themselves, their families, and their communities so blind obedience to a self-proclaimed Islamic state can be as anti-Islamic as open defiance of such a state.

If a government rules in the name of Allah, then it must respect the fact that Allah regards individuals and not the state as responsible for their actions, for it is they who will be punished or rewarded accordingly on Judgment Day. On this basis, the Islamists dismiss the idea that further legislation beyond Shari'a is impossible, as confusing the boundary between the overall sovereignty of Allah and the particulars of popular sovereignty.

It is the extent of popular sovereignty and not its existence that is debated. Because of economic, technological, and environmental changes, further development of Shari'a seems inevitable to the Islamists. The development of Shari'a, they argue, need not be looked upon as a move away from Islamic principles, but, on the contrary, as a necessary stepping-stone towards reaching an ideal Islamic society — a materially and spiritually developed utopia. An indispensable element in building such a society is freedom of thought and expression, including freedom from government control and suppression. In short, accepting the sovereignty of Allah does not necessarily contradict popular sovereignty.

Thus, Islamic traditionalists' re-evaluation of their historical position on socioeconomic and political values is necessary to bring them more in line with the ongoing social and economic transformations in Muslim societies. Indeed, religious personalities such as the late Ayatollah Taleqani, among the most prominent leaders of the Iranian Revolution, cautioned Iranians on relations between Islam and politics and on the position of the 'ulema in society and polity. As Hasan Turabi puts it, Islam exists in society "as a matter of norms and laws. It is an integrated and total way of life. Therefore government must be limited, because Islamic government would be omnipotent.

Government has no business interfering in one's religion or religious practices." So, regarding dress codes in Muslim societies, for instance, society would definitely exercise a measure of censure and encouragement for one form of dress over another. But no organization like the Saudi amr bil-maarouf wal-nahi an al-munkar (the injunction "to command the good and forbid evil") has legal authority to stop women or harass them...Segregation of women is definitely not a part of Islam. This is just conventional, historical Islam. It was totally unknown in the model of Islam or the text of Islam. It is unjustified." As for the relation of civil society to the state, according to Turabi, "In general civil society should be left alone, but if a societal function fails, government should step in. Once society picks up the function, then it [the state] should withdraw once more to its limit of security, organizing those aspects of society which must be legally organized."

So, as one scholar of Islam has put it, "A major issue in democratization in Muslim societies is whether or not scholars and leaders have successfully made the transition from listing 'democratic doctrines of Islam' to creating coherent theories and structures of Islamic democracy that are not simply reformulations of Western perceptions in some Muslim idioms."

The absence of a constructive dialogue between the traditionalist 'ulema and the reformist Islamists has widened the gap among Islamic movements and their supporters.

4

Islam and Civil Society

Introduction

One recent premise about state-society relations in the Middle East is that states in the Middle East are weak and its societies are strong, while the opposite was long argued. The Iranian revolution, the rise of Islamist movements in the 1980s, and declining oil prices are cited as proof for this viewpoint. This is taken as grounds for optimism and has led to an increasing interest in state-society relations and in prospects for the emergence of civil society in the region in the 1980s and the 1990s.

Thus, "today most scholars confidently affirm that the bases of civil society-both intermediate powers and autonomous social groups — exist in the Middle East." Even traditional social formations based on blood and marriage, or tribal ties (as in the Gulf monarchies and Yemen), or bonyads — the semi-independent trusts (as in Iran) are thought to be a part of civil society in the Middle East. The mere presence of such groups, it is argued, deters the power of the state and leads to increased prospects for democratization.

But this position rests on shaky ground. Even the appearance of political parties and formal groups and associations in the Middle East by itself does not necessarily mean a fundamental move toward democracy by state or society. The augmentation of political parties in the region may be more a sign of the state's adjusting to pressure from Islamic groups and their allies than a genuine political opening on either side.

Political parties in the Middle East remain mainly ineffective and play a mostly ceremonial role that serves to legitimate the state and its policies. For example, in Iran the ruling religious elite affirmed the sovereignty of the people, but despite this, the new elite have been reluctant to share power with its political opposition. Although the formalities of a democratic state are in place (e.g., elections and debates), the people remain politically and economically without much functional power. What civil society there was in Iran is fading, although intellectual and associational life continues to resist the state which has come to dominate most aspects of life in Iran.

Moreover, embryonic associations, although they exist in Muslim countries, are poorly organized and remain dependent on patrons within the state. As Carrie Rosefsky Wickham puts it in discussing Egypt, "The emergence of independent sites of social and political expressions within an authoritarian setting is not the same as the emergence of civil society, at least not in its liberal conception." The emergence of state-controlled quasi-pluralism in countries like Egypt or Jordan should not be seen as a shift from one-party rule to pluralism (ta'addudiya) involving numerous political parties and associations.

The real basis of state power in Middle Eastern countries is largely informal and not institutional, for it is personal, family, and group ties that help sustain the executive power of the ruling elites. The pattern of patrimonial leadership is not confined to the Middle East, of course, as many developing countries display the same phenomenon. (Patrimonialism, though in milder and less rigid forms, have existed even in Portugal, Spain, and Greece, where they persisted longer than in most other European countries, except the Balkans; the modernization process has finally eradicated patrimonialism in Portugal, Spain, and Greece which have at last inaugurated or reestablished full formal democracy in the 1970s.)

The extent of ruling elites' autocratic power varies among the developing countries. Kuwait and the Persian Gulf sheikdoms, along with Saudi Arabia and Oman, are perhaps the primary examples of highly traditional autocratic rule. At the other extreme, South Korea, Taiwan, Malaysia, Turkey, Tunisia, and Brazil are examples that testify, to various degrees, to the changing balance of state-society relations in favor of society, as institutionalization of independent power relationships is gradually undermining informal and arbitrary state power associations.

The dominant position of the state in the Middle East has meant the domination of politics by powerful families, elites, and military and bureaucratic officers. The slow emergence and growth of independent groups and associations has been significant. For example, organized labor by itself, or through an alliance with the middle class, can be an effective force capable of checking the power of the state and promoting democracy, although most analysts ignore the role of organized labor in the civil society debate. But in any case, labor unions, a primary agent of civil society, in the Middle East remain either non-existent or are repressed by the state.

Rachid al-Ghannouchi, the founder of the Tunisian Islamic movement, al-Nahda, believes that, "Once the Islamists are given a chance to comprehend the values of Western modernity, such as democracy and human rights, they will search within Islam for a place for these values where they implant them, nurse them, and cherish them just as the Westerners did before, when they implanted such values in a much less fertile soil."

That is to say, Islam need not go through a process of secularization as did the West, but must face one of the foremost challenges it has encountered yet: "to outline a regime that is Islamic but also representative and accountable." Ghannouchi advocates "an Islamic system that features majority rule, free elections, a free press, protection of minorities, equality of all secular and religious parties, and full women's rights in everything from polling booths, dress codes, and divorce courts to the top job at the presidential palace. Islam's role is to provide the system with moral values."

Others, like the Iranian Islamic reformist, Abdul Karim Soroush, have argued that there is no contradiction between Islam and the freedoms inherent in democracy. "Islam and democracy are not only compatible, their association is inevitable. In a Muslim society, one without the other is not perfect." Soroush believes that the will and beliefs of the majority must shape the ideal Islamic state, and that Islam itself is evolving as a religion, which leaves it open to reinterpre-ztation: Sacred texts do not change, but interpretation of them is always in flux because the age and the changing conditions in which believers live influence understanding. Furthermore, everyone is entitled to his or her own understanding. No one group of people, including the clergy, has the exclusive right to interpret or reinterpret tenets of the faith. Some understanding may be more learned than others, but no version is automatically more authoritative than another.

The prospect for the emergence of civil society depends on the characteristics of the people who form that society in the first place. The better educated, healthier, wealthier, and more organized the people, and the more broadly these resources are spread, the stronger will the society be in protecting itself from domination by the state. Moreover, these resources allow for the formation of institutions that act as the focus of activity where differences in opinions and policies can be debated and resolved without resort to violence.

Thus, institutionalization is essential for political stability, for systematic, orderly channeling of contesting elites' demands for political leadership. To be democratic, political parties, whether religious or not, must function within an independent institutionalized organizational network where final decisions are made and executed without constant interference from various layers of their country's state bureaucracies. Associational groups and formal institutions that have played a critical role in Western political systems, however, have been considerably fewer in less developed countries. Chances for a crisis from their non-participation increase where the opposition lacks an institutional basis for exerting pressure for participation (e.g., religious opposition to the Shah prior to the Iranian revolution) or where the state and its participants fail to adapt to changing social and economic forces (e.g., Lebanon prior to 1975). On the other hand, institutionalized opposition, whether religious or not, can be successfully incorporated into the political process (e.g., Jewish religious parties in Israel and to some degree Islamic opposition in Jordan, Turkey, Pakistan and Egypt).

In fact, Samuel P. Huntington's pessimistic view of the incompatibility of Islam and democratic norms is undermined by his own argument for the destabilizing effects of modernization itself and for the stabilizing effects of institutionalization. He points to the revival of Islamic fundamentalism and the poverty of many Islamic states as the fundamental reasons for his pessimism. Yet the revival of Islam and the rise of fundamentalism in Iran and elsewhere in the Middle East has not been an anti-democratic movement aiming at the destruction of democratic values. Given the wide range of Islamic responses to the West and to each other, the appeal in Muslim countries to unconventional forms of political conduct, including mass uprisings and rioting, is not due to any inherent intolerance of Islam toward democracy and the peaceful settlements of disputes. Islam in its various denominations has always been, throughout its history, a source of both social protest against and social support for given regimes. The hostility toward the West by some - though not all -Islamic religious groups is aimed not at democratic values but at Western domination and interference in the domestic affairs of these countries.

Islamic States

The Islamic state is an institutional and constitutional one because the divine law, sharia, defines the rights and obligations of the ruled and the rulers. The Islamic rulership by the contract of the Caliphate or the imamate is a legal and historical fact. The Quran stresses that absolute sovereignty and authority belong only to God, and that anyone who is entrusted with authority from among the believers by them should be obeyed as long as such a person maintains divine justice and public consent. The Muslim people are not always expected to be obedient, as cases of variance and even clashes of views between rulers and ruled are possible. According to the Quran and sunnah, such differences should not be settled by suppression, but through a constitutional political and judicial process.

The rulers should not use their authority to conceal facts from public control or from judicial inquiry. Such a principle is reminiscent of the classical legal principle of habeas corpus, regarded as "the great writ of liberty" when it was formalized in the Habeas Corpus Act of 1679 in England.

Under this law, any authority who detains any person for any reason is forced to bring the detained person to a judge, to explain what has led to the detention, and to report procedures followed in affecting the detention. The judge, in addition to deciding what allegations are to be brought against the person being detained, must also ascertain that any harm which has befallen him/her - including death - has not been caused by the delivery authority.

No abuse of power on the side of the authorities should be tolerated, and all relevant evidence should be introduced. The responsibility of the authorities to provide relevant documents in general with certain specified and conditional exceptions has also been stated recently by certain legislations in the United States, Canada and a few other countries. Such a guarantee of freedom of information is required in principle by Islam and should be formulated in detail and sanctioned. Facts must be displayed by anyone who holds them, and Islamic authorities have greater responsibility than ordinary individuals in this respect, "to bear witness to the truth for the sake of God, even though it be against their own selves."

At the same time, Islam cannot ignore a reality accepted by contemporary legislation, namely, that in some cases freedom of expression and information may be restricted temporarily or partially to maintain other human rights or public interests. Privacy and justifiable security requirements, especially in time of war, have to be considered. According to Islamic legal principles, a line should be drawn, in practicing the right of expressing one's views, between criticizing an ordinary man and criticizing one who occupies a public office, especially a high office. Freedom of expression has a broader range, in the latter case than in the former, especially with regard to public activities and to behavior in personal life that may affect the practice of public authority. The ethical values and legal principles of Islam which secure privacy and forbid spying or any violation of personal rights should be observed. A groundless allegation cannot be tolerated:

"... if any iniquitous person comes to you with a tale, use your discernment lest you hurt people unwittingly, and afterward be filled with remorse for what you have done."

In sharî'ah, calumniation, libel and slander or any other offense of that kind are forbidden and punishable. However, the right of self-defense may justify some permissiveness in this respect:

"God does not like any evil to be mentioned openly, unless it be by him/her who has been wronged..."

"Yet indeed as for any who defend themselves after having been wronged - no blame whatever attaches to them; blame attaches but to those who oppress (other) people and behave outrageously on earth, offending against all right... but withal, if one is patient in adversity and forgives - this is indeed something to set one's heart upon."

In any expression of thoughts or feelings by words, drawings, music, performance or otherwise, one should observe the values of Islam and present them. A speech, writing, work of art or any other human expression cannot by any means persuade a deviation from Islamic values or a perpetration of what is prohibited. Any discussion which may arise about the beliefs and the laws of Islam should observe objectivity and avoid illegitimate offense, agitation and provocation. Arguing with non- believers, as the Quran cautions against, would necessarily draw them to defend their beliefs which are rejected by Islam or to give their opinions about what they are invited to follow.

Maintaining the human rights of expression and wisdom in presentation and argument are essential for such a dialogue which must be conducted on both sides within methodological and ethical guidelines in order to make it fruitful. Those who are born Muslims should not be deprived of the right to a similar discussion of their faith within the same lines.

Rights of expression and information should be protected by all authorities: legislative, executive and judiciary, internal and universal. A specific Islamic court for human rights should be established in every Muslim country and on a global level; the special court of the glorious historical precedent which was concerned specifically with cases of injustice committed by any of those who occupied public positions or were politically or socially influential should be revived.

Disputes with the rulers should be settled according to the superior legal sources: the Quran and sunnah. Any violation of human rights from rulers or from any group of the ruled (baghy) should be stopped. Islamic judicial protection of human rights must be more comprehensive and effective than what may be known in the contemporary world. It must show concern for any moral harm that is caused by the authorities to individuals, groups or the whole society, as well as for material transgression: "... and who can be a better lawgiver than God?"

Islamic Democracy

There seems to be no immediate resolution to the debate among traditionalists, Islamists, and intellectual reformers on Islam and democracy. However, the attempt to develop the political doctrine of Islam by Islamists, intellectual reformists, and some traditionalists need not necessarily be viewed by other traditionalists as an attempt to entirely undermine the legitimacy of the religious establishment in Muslim countries. (33) Traditional religious leaders in the Muslim world, whether in power (Iran, Saudi Arabia, and the Sudan) or in opposition, must face the fact that, in light of complex socioeconomic and political problems facing Muslim societies in the late twentieth and early twenty-first centuries, their position as legitimate religious/political leaders is bound to erode.

The greatest threat to the traditional 'ulema come from either their own meager performance as heads of state (e.g., in Iran, and the Sudan) or their failure in political opposition to formulate and propose comprehensive agendas for resolving socioeconomic and political problems (e.g., as in Egypt, Jordan, Kuwait) or their sectarian fighting that has resulted in violence and acts of terrorism. Further rifts among traditionalist 'ulema can be expected, as in Iran, as religious leadership in Muslim states finds itself under pressure to deal with modern problems. The progressive 'ulema will benefit from an open dialogue with the Islamists in streamlining the tenets of Islam to take into account modern values without abandoning the fundamentals of Islam itself. For example, "The experience of Iran and the Sudan has shown that fundamentalism in power cannot solve every problem, and actually complicates the challenge of implementing Islamic values in public life."

The potential for religious debate and political dialogue between traditionalists and Islamists, including the reformists, can be promising. The Islamists' pragmatic view of Islam and the popularity of the traditionalists in the late twentieth century can be mutually beneficial in their common struggle for political sovereignty and development.

This, however, can occur only when the religious establishment itself favors fundamental socioeconomic and political restructuring of the status quo. While it is not easy to predict the behavior of Islamist groups in their quest for power, it is possible to enhance cooperation between Islamists and secular groups in their common struggle against the state and in their future plans for their country. Thus, the question is whether the secular state can pursue a policy of political inclusiveness and allow Islamists to take part in the political process, given widespread concerns over the long-term fate of individual rights and liberties should the Islamists take control of the state. Some scholars have argued that where the popular will dictate it, Islamists must have the opportunity to rule, even if the future of such rights is not guaranteed. Some have advocated a slow and partial political inclusion of the Islamists. But, as Jerrold Green has argued, some sort of a "national pact must be devised as the best way to secure the democratization process, although devising a means to enforce the pact remain[s] unresolved."

Muslim countries, like other developing countries though in varying degrees, suffer from acute socioeconomic and political problems (e.g., strong and dominant states; weak associational opposition to the state, and an overall maldistribution of socioeconomic and power resources) that need to be addressed. Inauguration of democratic elections in Muslim countries without addressing the fundamental problem of uneven distribution of socioeconomic and political resources in these countries will not succeed. The religious debate on Islam and democracy must then deal with not only the question of justice and freedom, but also with developing mechanisms necessary to remedy the structural problem of maldistribution of resources.

An "Islamic" democracy will not embrace all the secular values adopted in the West. However, the initial steps taken toward such an end will need to include a process of institutionalization in Islam. The incorporation of an institutionalized Islam in the process of development will help the cause of democracy should Islamists successfully challenge the hegemony of the traditionalists in both the religious and political arenas. To play the democratic game, religious leaders will have to better organize themselves, to propose alternative plans for socio-economic and political issues facing the country. This in turn can help them maintain legitimacy and popular support, facilitating their struggle for political power. Organization is the key to the success of any group seeking to achieve its goals.

Freedom of Expression

The main goal of God's message to humankind is the attainment of justice in all of its fairness. This justice, the foundation of Islam, cannot be achieved unless human rights are secured for every individual and group in a

Muslim state. The member of such a state must be free to choose just rulers, to observe these rules as they practice their authority, and to stand firm against any injustice from them. Primary among human rights are the rights to believe, to express one's beliefs and to assemble to defend one's group's beliefs.

The rights of expression and information cannot be separated from rights to think and believe. Intellectual and linguistic capabilities characterize human beings, and thus, the right to form and express opinions represents an essential manifestation of human merits and of God's gifts. The right to express and to be informed should, therefore, be secured by all who are respectful of humanity or grateful to God.

Indeed, if one is allowed to think and believe, but not to communicate with others or exchange views, one's freedom of thought and belief is actually restricted. As the human being is a social creature, genuine intellectual activity in which a thinker considers more than one perspective on an idea and learns the strength and weakness of it debated, cannot be practiced individually or in isolation. Moreover, the basic condition for freedom of expression and information is that it extends to different viewpoints; otherwise, expression is merely an imposition of ideas and exercise in brain-washing.

Many national and international documents which declare human rights acknowledge the fact that freedom of thought and freedom of expression are intertwined. The Universal Declaration of Human Rights which was issued by the General Assembly of the United Nations in December 1948 has dealt with both in two successive articles (18, 19).

Freedom of thought and belief is repeatedly emphasized in the Quran:

"There shall be no coercion in matters of faith".

"And had your Lord so willed, all those who live on earth would have attained to faith - all of them, do you then think that you could compel people to believe?"

"Said (Noah): O my people - what do you think? If (it be true that) I am taking my stand on a clear evidence from my Lord... to which you have remained blind, can we force it on you even though it is hateful to you?"

"And so (O Prophet) exhort them; your task is only to exhort; you cannot compel".

As long as freedom of expression and information is maintained, different views should be expressed and respected:

"Call you (all humanity) unto your Lord's path with wisdom and goodly exhortation, and argue with them in the most kindly (and convincing) manner.

The Quran repeatedly reports the arguments of atheists and polytheists and replies to them objectively in order to teach Muslims how freedom of expression and information should be maintained to make such a dialogue fruitful. According to Islam, freedom of expression and information is a basic human right. Islam condemns spreading lies and false information as well as passiveness and reluctance when the truth should be spoken:

"And do not overlay the truth with falsehood, and do not knowingly suppress the truth".

A believer who is conscious of God should always maintain and defend truth and justice:

"O you who have attained to faith! Be ever steadfast in upholding equity, bearing witness to the truth, for the sake of God, even though it be against your own selves or your parents and kinsfolk.... "

"... Be ever steadfast in your devotion to God, bearing witness to the truth in all equity, and never let hatred lead you into the sins of deviation from justice....

Providing false information about an event which one has witnessed as well as refraining from providing the facts that one knows are both considered grave sins that should be avoided and prevented by every possible means.

The teachings of the divine message should be revealed to the public and not concealed, even when the message criticizes or condemns an influential party or authority. It is significant that the Arabic word kafir and its origin kafara mean originally "to conceal, or to hide."

The vice of hypocrisy (nifaq) is not less condemned in the Quran than kufr:

"They (the hypocrites) are the real enemies..., how perverted are their minds."

"Behold, together with those who deny the truth, God will gather in hell the hypocrites..."

"Verily the hypocrites shall be in the lowest depth of hell..."

Likewise, one who is reluctant to provide the facts is actually concealing the truth and such a person is described as "evil at heart" in the Quran, and as "a muted devil" in the tradition of the Prophet. Providing the known facts and cooperating constructively so that truth may prevail are fundamental parts of the Islamic obligation of enjoining the doing of what is right and forbidding the doing of what is wrong.

One who provides false information or is reluctant to provide the right information becomes a participant in the prevalence of falsehood and evil. Every believer is a witness and protector of the truth during his/her whole life:

"... So that you may bear witness to the truth before all humanity...."

God Himself is the "Ultimate Truth" according to the Quran and it is incumbent upon every believer to support the truth in all forms so that it will always prevail. Muslims are addressed as a community to work together in their efforts for progress. The right of assembly is thus essential to secure correctional efforts against any powerful supporter of deviation from truth and righteousness:

"And the believers, both men and women, are responsible for (or the supporters of) one another; they all enjoin the doing of what is right and forbid the doing of what is wrong"

"And that there should arise among you a band of people who invite unto all that is good and enjoin the doing of what is right and forbid the doing of what is wrong"

"But help one another in furthering virtue and God-consciousness, and not in furthering evil and enmity."

"And enjoin upon one another the keeping to truth... and enjoin upon one another patience (and firmness) in adversity"

Freedom of expression and information, constituting both a right and a duty for every believer, should be established and maintained by all Muslims - men and women, rulers and ruled. The Quran orders those who have been entrusted with authority:

"To deliver all that you have been entrusted with unto those who are entitled thereto, and whenever you rule between people to rule with justice".

The rulers are responsible for securing the doing of what is good and preventing the doing of what is evil. Their responsibility is not limited only to allowing the people to express themselves as individuals or groups, but they must develop a sound public opinion by also providing correct information to the people. The authorities cannot maintain their credibility among the people, if they expose only what supports their position while concealing what may arouse criticism of their rule. If individuals can be blamed for not revealing the truth, then rulers must receive greater blame for such an evil: they have been entrusted with authority by the people for the public benefit; moreover, they have the sources of information and the authority and capability to obtain information. How can Muslim rulers discharge their responsibility of forbidding what is wrong unless they themselves provide a model by courageously airing their faults?

"Do you bid other people to be pious, while you forget your own selves, and yet you recited the divine writ; will you not then use your reason?"

Rulers may not, by concealing or manipulating information whose sources they may monopolize, use their authority to conceal facts that may hurt them personally or hurt their authority. Their responsibility is to maintain freedom of information, allow its flow and tolerate any individual effort to obtain essential information from governmental sources within reasonable limits of state security, which themselves ought to be delineated by the people. Rulers have the obligation to display all facts and release required evidence about an issue, either at their own initiative or in response to a request even if their interests suffer:

"... if they but refer - any matter pertaining to peace or war - unto the Conveyer of the (divine) Message and unto those from among them who have been entrusted with authority, such of those who are engaged in investigating the matter would indeed know it (directly and properly)."

According to Islamic teachings, the Muslim people may not be passive subjects, and the Muslim rulers do not enjoy absolute powers. To use political terminology, Islam establishes an institutional and constitutional authority, not a personalized one.

This set of restrictions on Muslim rulers is similar to which Rousseau has elaborated on: In any society past the primitive level, the ruler's authority and the citizen's rights and liberties may not conflict with each other. The citizens' rights are opposed by the ruler's authority only in a society which is deprived as a whole of participation in the practice of political power; in such a society only the rulers enjoy absolute authority.

The Place of Tolerance in Islam

The terrorist attacks on New York City and the Pentagon have focused public attention on the state of Muslim theology. For most Americans, the utter indifference to the value of human life and the unmitigated hostility to the United States shown by some Muslims came as a great shock. Others were confirmed in their belief that we face a great struggle between civilizations. Islamic values, they say, are fundamentally at odds with Western liberal values.

The terrorist attacks are symptomatic of a clash between Judeo-Christian civilization, with its values of individual freedom, pluralism, and secularism, and an amoral, un-Westernized, so-called "authentic Islam." Indeed, Islamic civilization is associated with the ideas of collective rights, individual duties, legalism, despotism, and intolerance that we associated with our former civilizational rival, the Soviet bloc. We seem to project onto the other everything we like to think that we are not.

This intellectual trap is easy to fall into when we deal with the theology of Osama Bin Laden, the Taliban, the Wahhabis of Saudi Arabia, and the Jihad organizations. The theologically-based attitudes of these Muslim puritans are fundamentally at odds not only with a Western way of life, but also with the very idea of an international society or the notion of universal human values. They display an intolerant exclusiveness, and a belligerent sense of supremacy vis-à-vis the other. According to their theologies, Islam is the only way of life, and must be pursued regardless of its impact on the rights and well-being of others. The straight path (al-sirat al-mustaqim) is fixed, they say, by a system of Divine laws (shari-ah) that trump any moral considerations or ethical values that are not fully codified in the law. God is manifested through a set of determinate legal commands that specify the right way to act in virtually all circumstances. The sole purpose of human life on earth is to realize the Divine manifestation by dutifully and faithfully implementing God's law. Morality itself begins and ends in the mechanics and technicalities of Islamic law (though different schools of Islamic law understand the content of those laws differently).

A life devoted to compliance with this legal code is considered inherently superior to all others, and the followers of any other way are considered either infidels (kuffar), hypocrites (munafiqun), or iniquitous (fasiqun). Anchored in the security and assuredness of a determinable law, it becomes fairly easy to differentiate between the rightly-guided and the misguided. The rightly-guided obey the law; the misguided either deny, attempt to dilute, or argue about the law. Naturally, the rightly-guided are superior because they have God on their side. The Muslim puritans imagine that God's perfection and immutability are fully attainable on earth—as if God's perfection had been deposited in the Divine law, and, by giving effect to this law, we could create a social order that mirrors Divine Truth. By attaching themselves to the Supreme Being, puritan groups are able to claim a self-righteous perfectionism that easily slips into a pretense of supremacy.

Extremism in Islamic History

Perhaps all firmly held systems of belief, especially those founded on religious conviction, are in some way supremacist: believers are understood to have some special virtue that distinguishes them from adherents of other faiths. But the supremacist creed of the puritan groups is distinctive and uniquely dangerous. The supremacist thinking of Muslim puritans has a powerful nationalist component, which is strongly oriented towards cultural and political dominance. These groups are not satisfied with living according to their own dictates, but are actively dissatisfied with all alternative ways of life. They do not merely seek self-empowerment, but aggressively seek to disempower, dominate, or destroy others. The crux of the matter is that all lives lived outside the law are considered an offense against God that must be actively resisted and fought.

The existence of Muslim Puritanism is hardly surprising. Most religious systems have suffered at one time or another from absolutist extremism and Islam is no exception. Within the first century of Islam, religious extremists known as the Khawarij (literally, the secessionists) slaughtered a large number of Muslims and non-Muslims, and were even responsible for the assassination of the Prophet's cousin and companion, the Caliph Ali b. Abi Talib. The descendants of the Khawarij exist today in Oman and Algeria, but after centuries of bloodshed, they became moderates if not pacifists. Similarly, the Qaramites and Assassins, for whom terror became a raison d'etre, earned unmitigated infamy in the writings of Muslim historians, theologians, and jurists. Again, after centuries of bloodshed, these two groups learned moderation, and they continue to exist in small numbers in North Africa and Iraq. The essential lesson taught by Islamic history is that extremist groups are ejected from the mainstream of Islam; they are marginalized, and eventually treated as heretical aberrations to the Islamic message.

But Islam is now living through a major shift, unlike any it has experienced in the past. The Islamic civilization has crumbled, and the traditional institutions that once sustained and propagated Islamic orthodoxy—and marginalized Islamic extremism—have been dismantled. Traditionally, Islamic epistemology tolerated and even celebrated divergent opinions and schools of thought. The guardians of the Islamic tradition were the jurists (fuqaha), whose legitimacy rested largely on their semi-independence from a decentralized political system, and their dual function of representing the interests of the state to the laity and the interests of the laity to the state.

But in Muslim countries today, the state has grown extremely powerful and meddlesome, and is centralized in ways that were inconceivable two centuries ago. In the vast majority of Muslim countries, the state now controls the private religious endowments (awqaf) that once sustained the juristic class. Moreover, the state has co-opted the clergy, and transformed them into its salaried employees. This transformation has reduced the clergy's legitimacy, and produced a profound vacuum in religious authority. Hence, there is a state of virtual anarchy in modern Islam: it is not clear who speaks with authority on religious issues. Such a state of virtual religious anarchy is perhaps not problematic in secular societies where religion is essentially reduced to a private matter. But where religion remains central to the dynamics of public legitimacy and cultural meaning, the question of who represents the voice of God is of central significance.

Puritanism and Modern Islam

It would be wrong to say that fanatic supremacist groups such as the al-Qa'ida or al-Jihad organizations now fill the vacuum of authority in contemporary Islam. Though they are obviously able to commit highly visible acts of violence that command the public stage, fanatic groups remains sociologically and intellectually marginalized in Islam. Still, they are extreme manifestations of more prevalent intellectual and theological currents in modern Islam.

Fanatic groups derive their theological premises from the intolerant Puritanism of the Wahhabi and Salafi creeds.

Wahhabism was founded by the eighteenth-century evangelist Muhammad ibn 'Abd al-Wahhab in the Arabian Peninsula. 'Abd al-Wahhab sought to rid Islam of the corruptions that he believed had crept into the religion. He advocated a strict literalism in which the text became the sole source of legitimate authority, and displayed an extreme hostility to intellectualism, mysticism, and any sectarian divisions within Islam.

According to the Wahhabi creed, it was imperative to return to a presumed pristine, simple, straightforward Islam, which could be entirely reclaimed by literal implementation of the commands of the Prophet, and by strict adherence to correct ritual practice. Importantly, Wahhabism rejected any attempt to interpret the divine law historically or contextually, with attendant possibilities of reinterpretation under changed circumstances. It treated the vast majority of Islamic history as a corruption of the true and authentic Islam. Furthermore, Wahhabism narrowly defined orthodoxy, and was extremely intolerant of any creed that contradicted its own.

In the late eighteenth century, the Al Sa'ud family united with the Wahhabi movement and rebelled against Ottoman rule in Arabia. The rebellions were very bloody because the Wahhabis indiscriminately slaughtered and terrorized Muslims and non-Muslims alike. Interestingly, mainstream jurists writing at the time, such as the Hanafi Ibn 'Abidin and the Maliki al-Sawi, branded the Wahhabis the modern day Khawarij of Islam, and condemned their fanaticism and intolerance. In 1818, Egyptian forces under the leadership of Muhammad Ali defeated this rebellion, and Wahhabism seemed destined to become another fringe historical experience with no lasting impact on Islamic theology. But the Wahhabi creed was resuscitated in the early twentieth century under the leadership of 'Abd al-'Aziz ibn Sa'ud, who allied himself with Wahhabi militant rebels known as the Ikhwan, in the beginnings of what would become Saudi Arabia. Even with the formation of the Saudi state, Wahhabism remained a creed of limited influence until the mid-1970s when the sharp rise in oil prices, together with aggressive Saudi proselytizing, dramatically contributed to its wide dissemination in the Muslim world.

Wahhabism did not propagate itself as one school of thought or a particular orientation within Islam. Rather, it asserted itself as the orthodox "straight path" of Islam. By claiming literal fidelity to the Islamic text, it was able to make a credible claim to authenticity at a time when Islamic identity was contested. Moreover, the proponents of Wahhabism refused to be labeled or categorized as the followers of any particular figure including 'Abd al-Wahhab himself. Its proponents insisted that they were simply abiding by the dictates of al-salaf al-salih (the rightly-guided predecessors, namely the Prophet and his companions), and in doing so, Wahhabis were able to appropriate the symbolisms and categories of Salafism.

Ironically, Salafism was founded in the early twentieth century by al-Afghani, Muhammad Abduh, and Rashid Rida as a liberal theological orientation. To respond to the demands of modernity, they argued, Muslims needed to return to the original sources of the Qur'an and Sunnah (tradition of the Prophet), and engage in de novo interpretations of the text.

By the 1970s, however, Wahhabism had succeeded in transforming Salafism from a liberal modernist orientation to a literalist, puritan, and conservative theology. The sharp rise in oil prices in 1975 enabled Saudi Arabia, the main proponent of Wahhabism, to disseminate the Wahhabi creed under a Salafi guise, which purported to revert back to the authentic fundamentals of religion uncorrupted by the accretions of historical practice. In reality, however, Saudi Arabia projected its own fairly conservative cultural practices onto the textual sources of Islam and went on to proselytize these projections as the embodiment of Islamic orthodoxy.

Despite its intolerance and rigidity, however, Wahhabism itself does not bear primary responsibility for the existence of terrorist groups in Islam today. To be sure, Wahhabism and its militant offshoots share both attitudinal and ideological orientations. Both insist on a normative particularism that is fundamentally text-centered; both reject the notion of universal human values; and both deal with the other, however defined, in a functionalist and even opportunistic fashion. But Wahhabism is distinctively inward-looking—although focused on power, it primarily asserts power over other Muslims.

This is consistent with its obsession with orthodoxy and correct ritualistic practice. Militant puritan groups, however, are both introverted and extroverted—they attempt to assert power against both Muslims and non-Muslims. As populist movements, they are a reaction to the disempowerment most Muslims have suffered in the modern age at the hands of harshly despotic governments, and at the hands of interventionist foreign powers.

These groups compensate for extreme feelings of disempowerment by extreme and vulgar claims to power. Fueled by supremacist and puritan theological creeds, their symbolic acts of power become uncompromisingly fanatic and violent.

The Theology of Intolerance

Islamic puritans, whether of the Wahhabi or more militant varieties, offer a set of textual references in support of their exclusionary and intolerant theological orientation. For instance, they frequently cite the Qur'anic verse that states: "O' you who believe, do not take the Jews and Christians as allies. They are allies of each other, and he amongst you who becomes their ally is one of them. Verily, God does not guide the unjust." Wahhabi and militant Puritanism read this and similar Qur'anic verses literally and ahistorically, and therefore reach highly exclusionary conclusions. For example, while Muslims may elicit the support or aid of non-Muslims over particular issues when the self-interests of Muslims so require, they may not befriend or share the normative values of non-Muslims. This orientation often demands the performance of symbolic acts, which aim to distinguish Muslims from non-Muslims—for instance, dressing in a particular way or marking non-Muslims with distinctive symbols.

Islamic puritanism also often invokes the Qur'anic verse asserting that, "whosoever follows a religion other than Islam this will not be accepted from him, and in the Hereafter he will be among the losers." This verse is invoked in arguing that the theology and rituals of Islam is the exclusive path to salvation. Moreover, a mere testament of faith or a general act of submission to God is insufficient to attain salvation in the Hereafter; rather, a person must comply with the particulars of the Divine law in order to qualify as a "true" believer. The puritan trend is thus uncompromising in its rejection of all forms of belief and ritual that do not qualify as the "true" religion of God.

As to the principles that should guide the interaction between Muslims and non-Muslims, the puritan trend cites the Qur'anic verse commanding Muslims to fight the unbelievers, "until there is no more tumult or oppression, and until faith and all judgment belong to God." Moreover, justifying an essentially supremacist view towards non-Muslims, proponents of Puritanism often quote the following Qur'anic injunction: "Fight those among the People of the Book (Jews and Christians) who do not believe in God or the Hereafter, who do not forbid what God and His Prophet have forbidden, and who do not acknowledge the religion of truth—fight them until they pay the poll tax (jizyah) with willing submission and feel themselves subdued."

Relying on such textual evidence, Muslim puritans assert that Muslims are the inheritors of an objectively ascertainable and realizable Divine Truth; while Jews and Christians may be tolerated, they cannot be befriended. Ultimately, however, they must be subdued and forced to acknowledge Muslim supremacy by paying a poll tax. The puritan doctrine is not necessarily or entirely dismissive of the rights of non-Muslims, and it does not necessarily lead to the persecution of Jews and Christians. But it does assert a hierarchy of importance, and the commitment to toleration is correspondingly fragile and contingent. So it is conducive to an arrogance that can easily descend into a lack of respect or concern for the well-being or dignity of non-Muslims. When this arrogant orientation is coupled with textual sources that exhort Muslims to fight against unbelievers (kuffar), it can produce a radical belligerency.

Religious Beliefs and Laws

The puritans construct their exclusionary and intolerant theology by reading Qur'anic verses in isolation, as if the meaning of the verses were transparent—as if moral ideas and historical context were irrelevant to their interpretation. In fact, however, it is impossible to analyze these and other verses except in light of the overall moral thrust of the Qur'anic message.

The Qur'an itself refers to general moral imperatives such as mercy, justice, kindness, or goodness. The Qur'an does not clearly define any of these categories, but presumes a certain amount of moral probity on part of the reader. For instance, the Qur'an persistently commands Muslims to enjoin the good. The word used for "the good" is ma'ruf, which means that which is commonly known to be good. Goodness, in the Qur'anic discourse, is part of what one may call a lived reality—it is the product of human experience and constructed normative understandings. Similarly, the Qur'anic term for kindness is ihsan, which literally means to beautify and improve upon. But beautification or improving upon can have meaning only in the context of a certain sociological understanding and practice.

In a further example, as to justice, the Qur'an states: "O you who believe, stand firmly for justice, as witnesses for God, even if it means testifying against yourselves, or your parents, or you kin, and whether it is against the rich or poor, for God prevails upon all.

Follow not the lusts of your hearts, lest you swerve, and if you distort justice or decline to do justice, verily God knows what you do." The idea that Muslims must stand up for justice even against their own self-interests is predicated on the notion that human beings are capable of achieving a high level of moral agency.

As agents, Muslims are expected to achieve a level of moral conscientiousness, which they will bring to their relationship with God. In regards to every ethical obligation, the Qur'anic text assumes that readers will bring a pre-existing, innate moral sense to the text. Hence, the text will morally enrich the reader, but only if the reader will morally enrich the text. The meaning of the religious text is not fixed simply by the literal meaning of its words, but depends, too, on the moral construction given to it by the reader. So if the reader approaches the text without moral commitments, it will almost inevitably yield nothing but discrete, legalistic, technical insights.

Similarly, it is imperative to analyze the historical circumstances in which specific Qur'anic ethical norms were negotiated. Many of the institutions referenced in the Qur'an—such as the poll tax or the formation of alliances with non-Muslims—can be understood only if the reader is aware of the historical practices surrounding the revelation of the text. By emptying the Qur'an both of its historical and moral contexts, the puritan trend ends up transforming the text into a long list of morally non-committal legal commands.

The Qur'anic discourse, for instance, can readily support an ethic of diversity and tolerance. The Qur'an not only expects, but even accepts the reality of difference and diversity within human society: "O humankind, God has created you from male and female and made you into diverse nations and tribes so that you may come to know each other.

Verily, the most honored of you in the sight of God is he who is the most righteous." Elsewhere, the Qur'an asserts that diversity is part of the Divine intent and purpose in creation: "If thy Lord had willed, He would have made humankind into a single nation, but they will not cease to be diverse... and, for this God created them [humankind]."

The classical commentators on the Qur'an did not fully explore the implications of this sanctioning of diversity, or the role of peaceful conflict resolution in perpetuating the type of social interaction that would result in people "knowing each other." Nor does the Qur'an provide specific rules or instructions about how "diverse nations and tribes" are to acquire such knowledge. In fact, the existence of diversity as a primary purpose of creation, as suggested by the verse above, remained underdeveloped in Islamic theology. Pre-modern Muslim scholars did not have a strong incentive to explore the meaning and implications of the Qur'anic endorsement of diversity and cross-cultural intercourse.

This is partly because of the political dominance and superiority of the Islamic Civilization, which left Muslim scholars with a sense of self-sufficient confidence. Nevertheless, it is fair to say that the Islamic civilization was pluralistic and unusually tolerant of various social and religious denominations. Working out the implications of a commitment to human diversity and mutual knowledge under contemporary conditions requires moral reflection and attention to historical circumstance precisely what is missing from puritan theology and doctrine.

Other than a general endorsement of human diversity, the Qur'an also accepted the more specific notion of a plurality of religious beliefs and laws. Although the Qur'an clearly claims that Islam is the Divine Truth, and demands belief in Muhammad as the final messenger in a long line of Abrahamic prophets, it does not completely exclude the possibility that there might be other paths to salvation. The Qur'an insists on God's unfettered discretion to accept in His mercy whomever He wishes.

In a rather remarkable set of passages that, again, have not been adequately theorized by Muslim theologians, the Qur'an recognizes the legitimate multiplicity of religious convictions and laws. In one such passage, for example, the Qur'an asserts: "To each of you God has prescribed a Law and a Way. If God would have willed, He would have made you a single people.

But God's purpose is to test you in what he has given each of you, so strive in the pursuit of virtue, and know that you will all return to God [in the Hereafter], and He will resolve all the matters in which you disagree." On this and other occasions the Qur'an goes on to state that it is possible for non-Muslims to attain the blessing of salvation: "Those who believe, those who follow Jewish scriptures, the Christians, the Sabians, and any who believe in God and the Final Day, and do good, all shall have their reward with their Lord and they will not come to fear or grief." Significantly, this passage occurs in the same chapter that instructs Muslims not to take the Jews and Christians as allies. How can these different verses be reconciled?

If we read the text with moral and historical guidance, we can see the different passages as part of a complex and layered discourse about reciprocity and its implications in the historical situation in Mohammed's Medina. In part, the chapter exhorts Muslims to support the newly established Muslim community in Medina.

But its point is not to issue a blanket condemnation against Jews and Christians (who "shall have their reward with their Lord"). Instead, it accepts the distinctiveness of the Jewish and Christian communities and their laws, while also insisting that Muslims are entitled to the same treatment as those other communities. Thus it sets out an expectation of reciprocity for Muslims: while calling upon Muslims to support the Prophet of Islam against his Jewish and Christian detractors, it also recognizes the moral worth and rights of the non-Muslim "other."

The challenge most often invoked against an argument for tolerance in Islam is the issue of jihad. Jihad, especially as portrayed in the Western media, is often associated with the idea of a holy war that is propagated in the name of God against the unbelievers. Therefore, jihad is often equated with the most vulgar images of religious intolerance.

At the most rudimentary level, the Qur'an itself is explicit in prohibiting any form of coerced conversions to Islam. It contends that truth and falsity are clear and distinct, and so whomever wishes to believe may do so, but no duress is permitted in religion: "There is no compulsion in matter of faith." Of course, this response is incomplete—even if forced conversions to Islam are prohibited, aggressive warfare to spread Islamic power over non-believers might still be allowed. Does the Qur'an condone such expansionist wars?

Interestingly, Islamic tradition does not have a notion of holy war. "Jihad" simply means to strive hard or struggle in pursuit of a just cause, and according to the Prophet of Islam, the highest form of jihad is the struggle waged to cleanse oneself from the vices of the heart. Holy war (in Arabic al-harb al-muqaddasah) is not an expression used by the Qur'anic text or Muslim theologians.

In Islamic theology, war is never holy; it is either justified or not, and if it is justified, those killed in battle are considered martyrs. The Qur'anic text does not recognize the idea of unlimited warfare, and does not consider the simple fact of the belligerent's Muslim identity to be sufficient to establish the justness of his cause. In other words, the Qur'an entertains the possibility that the Muslim combatant might be the unjust party in a conflict.

Moreover, while the Qur'an emphasizes that Muslims may fight those who fight them, it also insists that Muslims may not transgress. Transgression is an ambiguous term, but on several occasions the Qur'an intimates that in order not to transgress, Muslims must be constrained by a requirement of proportionality, even when the cause is just. For instance, it states, "Mandated is the law of equality, so that who transgresses against you, respond in kind, and fear God, and know that God is with those who exercise restraint."

Despite the prohibition against transgression and the condemnation of unlimited warfare, many classical jurists adopted an imperialist orientation, which divided the world into the abode of Islam and the abode of war, and supported expansionist wars against unbelievers. But this view was not unanimous. Classical Muslim jurists debated whether unbelief is a sufficient justification for warfare, with a sizeable number of classical jurists arguing that non-Muslims may not be fought unless they pose a physical threat to Muslims. If non-Muslims seek peace, Muslims should make an effort to achieve such a peace.

This discourse was partly inspired by the Qur'anic injunctions concerning peace. The Qur'an asserts that God does not prohibit Muslims from making peace with those who do not fight Muslims, but God does prohibit Muslims from making peace with those who have expelled Muslims from their homes and continue to persecute them. Elsewhere, the Qur'an pronounces a stronger mandate in favor of peace in stating: "If your enemy inclines towards peace, then you should seek peace and trust in God."

Moreover, the Qur'an instructs Muslims not to haughtily turn away unbelievers who seek to make peace with Muslims, and reminds Muslims that, "If God would have willed, He would have given the unbelievers power over you [Muslims], and they would have fought you [Muslims]. Therefore, if they [the unbelievers] withdraw from you and refuse to fight you, and instead send you guarantees of peace, know that God has not given you a license [to fight them]." These discussions of peace would not make sense if Muslims were in a permanent state of war with non-believers, and if non-believers were a permanent enemy and always a legitimate target.

The other major issue on the point of tolerance in Islam is that of the poll tax (jizyah) imposed on the People of Book (Christians and Jews) who live in Muslim territory. When the Qur'an was revealed, it was common inside and outside of Arabia to levy poll taxes against alien groups. Building upon the historical practice, classical Muslim jurists argued that the poll tax is money collected by the Islamic polity from non-Muslims in return for the protection of the Muslim state.

If the Muslim state was incapable of extending such protection to non-Muslims, it was not supposed to levy a poll tax. In fact, 'Umar (r. 13-23/634-644), the second Rightly-Guided Caliph and close companion of the Prophet, returned the poll tax to an Arab Christian tribe that he was incapable of protecting from Byzantine aggression.

Aside from the juristic theory justifying the poll tax, the Qur'an does not, however, pronounce an absolute and unwavering rule in favor of such an institution. Once more, attention to historical circumstance is essential. The Qur'an endorsed a poll tax as a response to particular groups in Arabia who were persistently hostile to the early Muslims. Importantly, the Prophet did not collect a poll tax from every non-Muslim tribe that submitted to Muslim sovereignty, and in fact, in the case of a large number of non-Muslim but non-hostile tribes, he paid them a periodic sum of money or goods.

These tribes were known as "those whose hearts have been reconciled." Furthermore, 'Umar entered into a peace settlement with Arab Christian tribes pursuant to which these tribes were obligated to pay the Islamic annual tax known as the zakah (almsgiving), and not the poll tax. Reportedly, although they refused to convert to Islam, the Christian tribes contended that paying the jizyah (poll tax) was degrading, and instead, asked to pay the zakah, and 'Umar accommodated their request.

In short, there are various indicators that the poll tax is not a theologically mandated practice, but a functional solution that was adopted in response to a specific set of historical circumstances. Only an entirely ahistorical reading of the text could conclude that it is an essential element in a Divinely-sanctioned program of subordinating the non-believer.

Final Thoughts

Ultimately, the Qur'an, or any text, speaks through its reader. This ability of human beings to interpret texts is both a blessing and a burden. It is a blessing because it provides us with the flexibility to adapt texts to changing circumstances. It is a burden because the reader must take responsibility for the normative values he or she brings to the text. Any text, including those that are Islamic, provides possibilities for meaning, not inevitabilities. And those possibilities are exploited, developed and ultimately determined by the reader's efforts—good faith efforts, we hope—at making sense of the text's complexities. Consequently, the meaning of the text is often only as moral as its reader. If the reader is intolerant, hateful, or oppressive, so will be the interpretation of the text.

It would be disingenuous to deny that the Qur'an and other Islamic sources offer possibilities of intolerant interpretation. Clearly these possibilities are exploited by the contemporary puritans and supremacists. But the text does not command such intolerant readings. Historically, Islamic civilization has displayed a remarkable ability to recognize possibilities of tolerance, and to act upon these possibilities.

Islamic civilization produced a moral and humanistic tradition that preserved Greek philosophy, and generated much science, art, and socially benevolent thought. Unfortunately, however, the modern puritans are dissipating and wasting this inspiring moral tradition. They are increasingly shutting off the possibilities for a tolerant interpretation of the Islamic tradition.

If we assess the moral trajectory of a civilization in light of its past record, then we have ample reason to be optimistic about the future. But the burden and blessing of sustaining that moral trajectory—of accentuating the Qur'anic message of tolerance and openness to the other—falls squarely on the shoulders of contemporary Muslim interpreters of the tradition.

5

The Issue of Riba in Islamic Faith and Law

Introduction

Perhaps one of the most difficult issues in Islamic concern for fairness in business dealings is its prohibition of business transactions that call for charging riba (usury and interest). Riba, in its Qur'anic meaning, means paying money for the use of money. Muslims have struggled with the problem ever since the Qur'an categorically denounced riba. From the Islamic perspective, with its bias towards fair distribution of wealth and social justice, the Qur'an's strictures against riba have implications for international political economy. The issue also confronts devout Muslim business people as they struggle to make their investments religiously and morally legitimate.

This essay will analyze the controversy around riba as a prime example of how Muslims engage in ethical reasoning about business practice. It will show that ethical judgements in Islam amalgamate cultural elements derived from the particular experience of Muslims living in a specific place and time, as verified by the timeless universal norms derived from the scriptural sources like the Qur'an and the Tradition (Sunna), which themselves possess common elements applicable to all humans as humans.

Although the business world today is moving towards globalization in which small businesses are going to be further marginalized, the paragon of business ethics in the Muslim world as well as the West remains a devout individual who exhibits unusual sense of ethical-religious responsibility towards the higher goals set by his/her religious teachings.

To dismiss this dimension from discussions about the business world today is equivalent to saying that the highly technicalized business world is moving at a pace uncontrollable by human beings and that no human conscience is able to direct the moral consequences of wealth-generating enterprises, however exploitative or corruptive they might appear to morally conscious individual or group of individuals. The following case illustrates the ethical dilemma presented by the Qur'anic stricture against paying and charging interest in business dealings.

Religious Ethical Dilemma for a Muslim Businessman

A highly successful businessman was faced with an ethical dilemma of a religious kind when he bought his company some twenty-three years ago. At first he did not let the owner of the property know that he had an ethical and religious problem with a transaction that involved him paying interest, because he was concerned that the seller would have factored that interest into his selling price. So after he had negotiated the price, he told the owner that he make a down payment, and then covers the rest in installments over a period of time.

However, he could not pay interest on the unpaid balance because that was not allowed by his religion. The owner suggested that the selling price be increased to cover the interest. He argued that it would amount to the same thing as paying interest and in good conscience he could not justify that. He also made it clear that if this were not acceptable then he would simply not proceed with the transaction. At this point, the owner agreed not to charge the interest and the businessman finalized the deal and bought the business.

In this case the amount of the interest was not significant and the owner was not going to lose much money. Nevertheless, it is hard to predict what the owner would have done had the amount of the interest been significant. And because the stakes are often much higher, the prohibition on interest-taking presents serious problems to Muslim business people.

While the businessman had enough resources to make the down payment, those Muslims who don't, face a quandary. Either they would have to apply for a loan to an interest-charging bank or they would simply have to give up an opportunity to start a new business.

Conscience and Social Responsibility in Islam

Religious rulings related to the charging, paying and taking of interest in Islamic legal tradition have been at the center of ethical deliberations among Muslims for many centuries. Around the world, mainstream Islamic opinion continues to regard interest as an impediment to social justice. As a result the question of whether interest is a legitimate financial instrument or not remains an important issue of conscience.

In the Islamic tradition, human acts have a direct impact upon the development of conscience, the source of determining the rightness or wrongness of human undertakings. The conscience must be constantly guarded against being corrupted.

For when the conscience of individuals becomes corrupted as a result of neglecting ethical matters related to the production of daily sustenance, there remains no moral safeguard to prevent these individuals from engaging into more serious acts that would lead to the destruction of the very fabric of social relations founded upon divinely ingrained sense of justice and fairness.

Islam, as it developed in the regions inhabited by other monotheistic faiths like Judaism, Christianity and Zoroastrianism, shared an ethos of public order founded upon justice. It required the practice of a minimum of moral virtues intended to be a kind of "rule of life," to foster a sense of social responsibility.

In the Islamic view, both reflection and intention must precede all human acts which infringe upon the spiritual and temporal well being of others. To guide such reflection and inform such intention, Islam has developed a cohesive body of ethical reflection. Islam, the third and last of the Abrahamic religions to emerge, literally means "submission to God's will". It was proclaimed by Muhammad (born 570 C.E.), the Prophet of Islam and the founder of Islamic public order during the 600s in Mecca, Arabia.

Along with certain rules, which were practical and material, temporary and external, Muslim jurists explicitly decreed various permanent restrictions designed to discipline both the body (rules about lawful foods and earning, about dress and public behavior) and the mind (prohibited subjects of thought and conversation that led to the corruption of conscience). In addition, Islam required certain expiatory works of charity to compensate for the sins of omission and commission.

These works were intended primarily to inculcate a sense of social responsibility. Whereas the ritual acts, whether performed publicly in a group or privately, were the homage humankind paid to God and were intended to affect the conscience of the practicing believer, commercial engagements were closely tied to the notions of interpersonal justice and were intended to affect public behavior. In this latter sense, the rites are instruments provided by God for developing the conscience in the direction of greater social responsibility.

Islamic Juridical Discourse on the Market

Islam required a good public order in which spiritual interests were organically related to individual material well-being. Hence the law of the marketplace was given almost equal weight with the regulations connected with acts of worship in the mosque. This emphasis on economic relations in the context of commercial markets was not suprising, given that Mecca was the most important trading center of western and central Arabia. Meccans played a dominant role in the creation of a culture that nurtured the cultivation and development of socioeconomic system based on Islamic justice.

The market mechanism is an integral part of the Islamic economic system because the institution of private property depends on it for its operation. It also provides the consumers to express their desires for the production of goods of their liking by their willingness to pay the price. But the profit motive that is essential for the operation of free enterprise, if not controlled, can also become a tool of greed and violate the Islamic goals of social and economic justice and equitable distribution of income and wealth. The strictures against usury in the Qur'an can be seen in the clear distinction Islam makes between legitimate trade with profit motive and unchecked individual greed to increase one's possessions manifold without engaging in precarious trade in a market economy. According to Muslim jurists:

The law in order for benefit mutually permits the people of buying and selling. There is no doubt that this can also be a cause of injustice, because both buyer and seller desire more profit and the Lawgiver has neither prohibited profit nor has He set limits to it. He has, however, prohibited fraud and cheating and ascribing to a commodity attributes that it does not possess.

The main concern of the Islamic public order was not so much collective interest as individual justice in transactions that had to be protected outside of close friendship and family ties. It was expected that, contrary to the claims of tribal kinship and noble family lineage that determined social relations in pre-Islamic Arabia, most human relations under Islam would take the form of contractual relations rather than be determined in advance by social status. Many provisions in the law attempted to back those who were weak in one way or another against the strong who might take advantage of them. While on the whole, faith in Islam constituted ten parts, only one part was related to the God-human relationship and claimed the status of a common universal obligation. The remaining nine parts were related to human relationships, and determined by contractual responsibilities and specific social and cultural experience.

Muslim juridical writings give detailed rulings related to the acquisition and disposal of private and business property and purchase and sale of merchandise. The underlying principle operative in market law is twofold: the autonomy of individual to own productive resources to further her or his economic interest, and the protection of the consumer from harm. The pursuit of individual economic interest was to be regulated within a communitarian ethic requiring the individual to take the competing interests of the community at large as morally binding. Therefore, any individual business undertaking seen to cause harm to the moral and spiritual fabric of the society was to be condemned and prohibited.

The protection of the consumer was regulated through the principle of non-maleficence (al-darar al-muhtamal). This principle required that resource-owners could not seek to cause harm to the buyers by using false information and other means to raise sales. Hence, deceptive advertising was regarded as morally wrong and legally punishable. The principle of public interest (maslahah) required that free mutual consent of the buyer and the seller be regarded as a necessary condition for any business transaction. The Qur'an provides the grounds for the ruling: "O believers, consume not your goods between you in vanity, except there be trading, by your agreeing together". Individual freedom in negotiating business transactions was recognized in the directive given by the Prophet: "Leave people alone for God provides them sustenance through each other". Thus freedom of enterprise leaves much of the production and distribution of goods and services to individuals or voluntarily constituted groups. However, even this otherwise absolute freedom was regulated by the legal principle of public interest that requires that faithful Muslims produce more good than harm.

The integration of ethics and law was most clearly worked out in Islamic economics. The need to regulate an economic system that would be compatible with Islamic concern for redistribution of wealth and social justice required Muslim jurists to resort to legal doctrines and practical rules where the validity of their rulings against certain forms of usury received judicious legal elaboration. The apparent meaning of those verses of the Qur'an that spoke about the prohibition of usury in a straightforward manner were developed through the legal principles and rules, case by case, to create the framework for a morally accountable financial exchange. The nature of this process of legal and ethical construction is taken up next.

Shari'ah and the Emergence of Principles from Cases

Islamic ethics, mediated through God's will, is an integral part of Islamic law: the Shari'ah. The Shari'ah is the divinely ordained blueprint for human conduct, which was inherently and essentially religious. It enjoys comprehensive scope, for it encompasses judgments of public interest and equity which link the overall prosperity of the community in this life and the next. The end of humanity is happiness, and this is attained fully through the rewards of God on the Day of Judgment for everything that humans do to improve the quality of spiritual and moral and material life of humanity.

Islamic jurisprudence (fiqh) was developed to determine normative Islamic conduct as detailed in the Shari'ah. The legal precedents and principles provided by the Qur'an and Sunna were used to develop an elaborate system of rules of jurisprudence. By the middle of the eighth century, Islamic jurists had developed and laid down a legal theory to allow a judge or a mufti to find out in all circumstances what was the legal and moral action.

The two sources for deriving authoritative guidance were the Qur'an, the basic scripture of Islam, and the Sunna, the normative directives deduced from the Prophet Muhammad's own actions. Two further resources in Sunni law were provided by the consensus (ijma') of the scholars of legal tradition, and by a method of analogical deduction (qiyas). Sunni jurists used qiyas to project a new ruling from a known ruling by using data furnished by the Qur'an and the Sunna.

Al-Shafi'i (d. 820), a rigorous legal thinker, systematically and comprehensively linked these four sources to extend Shari'ah to cover all possible contingencies. In the Shi'ite jurisrudence, the methodology of their founding scholar and Imam Ja'far al-Sadiq (d. 748) allowed greater use of human reason in deriving the entire system of the Shari'ah. Shi'ite jurists perfected the principle of the correlation between a judgment derived from reason and the one promulgated by the Qur'an and the Sunna, thereby giving human intuitive reason a substantial role in deriving legal decisions at all times. The 'rule of correlation' (qa'idat al-mulazama) in Shi'ite law allows the jurists to infer the rulings in the Shari'ah from the sole verdict of reason.

Legal scholars and other administrative officials exercising judicial powers usually issued judgments of public interest, convenience or similar considerations. Duties and right actions that were not mentioned in the Qur'an and Sunna were to be determined by the exercise of independent personal judgment of lawyers.

As developed in the classical Islamic legal theory (usul al-fiqh), justifications in religious-moral action consists of a dialectic between judgments (fatawa) in specific cases and the generalizations derived from effective causes ('ilal) in cases in the light of which generalizations themselves are modified. Hence, to derive a specific ethical judgment - for example, that an act of distribution of surplus wealth among the needy is obligatory - is to confirm that it satisfies a certain description of the religious-moral concept of justice according to one's belief in social responsibility. Social responsibility as part of the generalizable command to be just could then be applied to other acts.

The criterion of social responsibility has made it necessary for Islamic jurists to nuance the stringency of moral rules. In contemporary Islamic thinking, human conduct is to be determined in terms of how much legal weight is borne by a particular rule, and whether a rule renders a given practice obligatory or merely recommended. For instance, bribery is ethically and legally forbidden. But if it becomes necessary under an unjust system in order to influence a decision leading to the betterment of the community, then Islamic law excuses it after a careful risk-benefit analysis.

The underlying principle in deciding such cases was the proportion of benefit as compared to harm to the well being of the community. Some rules are categorical. For example, cases involving blatant moral-spiritual corruption are excluded from risk-benefit analysis. Another factor in determining the weight of a rule is whether it is to be enforced by penalties in the courts because it occurs in Muslim territory, or whether it is to be left to God's judgment in the hereafter because it occurs outside. Thus, for instance, transactions involving selling or buying of alcohol are regarded as illicit and punishable by the Shari'ah courts when they occur within Muslim communities. However, when a Muslim businessman living in the West sometimes has to entertain his non-Muslim clients with alcohol while abstaining himself, his action, although sinful in itself, is regarded as being beyond the jurisdiction of the Shari'ah court.

Reason and Revelation in Islamic Moral Reasoning

In recent years, attempts have been made to engage Muslim scholars in the ongoing debate in the area of business ethics in the West. At the center of this debate is the role of ethical principles and rules in the moral assessment of an action in Western thinking. Such assessment can be developed from at least four different perspectives: those of the agent, the act itself, the end, and the consequences. They offer different viewpoints about the meaning and nature of moral principles and rules as they are applied to different types of moral dilemmas. In fact, many disputes in applied ethics in the West stem from disputes about the generalizability and applicability of more than one of these normative principles that function as action-guides, categorizing actions as morally required, prohibited, or permitted. Moreover, there exists the great variety of principle-based approaches that focus on general principles as sources of rules, and rules that specify type of prohibited, required, or permitted actions before any particular judgments can be derived in cases dealing with questionable business practices.

While this conceptual apparatus is helpful, it does not enable Westerners to delineate the pattern of Islamic moral reasoning. Without adequate training in the Islamic legal sciences, especially legal theory, one cannot pinpoint the principles and the rules that Muslim jurists utilize to justify and assess moral-legal decisions within their own cultural environment. The process has combined revelation and reason. The convergence between the divine command that human beings must treat each other justly and the rational cognition of justice being good encouraged Islamic jurists to formulate specific moral-legal judgments first and then to search for principles that can be generalized and then applied to new cases. The method, refined over centuries, yields certitude in moral judgment. By working back and forth between legal doctrines and rules, on the one hand, and analogical reasoning based on paradigm cases, on the other, Muslim jurists are able to resolve ethical dilemmas that face the community in dealing with immediate questions about economic issues: banking, taking interest, advertising, and so on. The practical judgments or legal opinions, known as fatawa, reflect the insights of a jurist who has been able to connect cases to an appropriate set of linguistic and rational principles and rules that provide keys to a valid conclusion of a case under consideration.

This pattern of moral reasoning should not be seen as a lock-step deductive model. The Qur'an uses the word al-ma'ruf (the "commonly known" paradigms) for the generalized principles which must be inferred from concrete ethical practice of everyday life. It made no attempt to lay down a comprehensive moral system because it treated morality as "the known," al-ma'ruf. Al-ma'ruf, in the meaning of moral behavior in the Qur'an, signifies "goodness," a "good quality or action," gentleness in any action, or deed, of which goodness is known by reason and by the revelation." Muslim jurists have been working out practical ways of carrying out more efficient proceedings in view of the changed circumstances of commercial life, without setting aside the more idealistic provisions of the law as basic norms. The justification provided by these jurists was to argue that there is a correlation between "known" moral convictions and God's purposes as mentioned in revelation.

Market Ethics and the Charging of Interest

In general, it can be said that in every ethical situation Islamic juridical tradition seeks to address and accommodate the demands of justice and public good. Perhaps one of the most difficult issues to test the Islamic concern for fairness in business dealings was its early prohibition of business transactions that called for charging interest (riba). Often translated by "usury", this term in its Qur`anic meaning, refers to using money to buy the use of money. Muslims have struggled with the problem of interest ever since the Qur`an categorically denounced it, and have not achieved agreement among themselves. Some jurists have interpreted the Qur`anic prohibition to permit exceptions as cases required in different contexts. There have been a number of rulings issued at different times in the history of Islamic jurisprudence making a distinction between `usury' (riba) and `interest' to circumvent the categorical prohibition. Other scholars believe that there is a difference between Muslim and non-Muslim financial institutions, allowing Muslims to receive interest from the latter institutions while prohibiting it from the former.

This lack of unanimity reflects a common but misleading practice among Muslims: sweeping larger questions about the nature of divine revelation under the rug when it comes to addressing interest and usury and other major ethical problems exacerbated by the introdu-ction of laissez faire economics. This uncritical approach to the normative sources has deep roots in the theology of revelation in Islam. Briefly stated, there are two major trends about the meaning and relevance of revelation for Muslims. According to one, Islamic revelation in its present form was 'created' in time and space. As such, it reflects historical circumstances of that original divine command. According to the other view, revelation was 'uncreated' and hence its current form is not conditioned by place and time. Most devout Muslims reject any hints that the interpretation of revelation reflects cultural or historical variables.

In the wake of both quantitative and qualitative change in the modern Muslim economies, the question arises as to how far traditional readings of the revelation are relevant in assessing the negative and positive limits governing the present economic system? It is this critical theological question with drastic ramifications for the overall status of normative tradition that is usually swept under the rug.

Rather than peek further under this rug, I will consider some of this historical and theological issues connected with the institution of riba. At the time that the Prophet emerged in Mecca, transactions with a fixed time limit and payment of interest (riba), as well as speculations of all kinds, formed an essential element in the highly developed regional system of trade in Arabia.

A debtor who could not repay the capital (money or goods) with the accumulated interest at the time it became due was given an extension of time in which to pay, but at the same time the sum due was doubled. The practice was prevalent during the early part of the Prophet's mission in Mecca before he migrated to Medina in 622 CE, where he denounced it. Like other social reforms the Prophet introduced into his growing community, the prohibition against interest was introduced in stages in the Qur'an. It began with a caution: "O believers, devour not usury (riba) doubled and redoubled, and fear you God." Later the prohibition was proclaimed in no uncertain terms.

It is important to note that instructions about usury are connected to the message about "freewill offerings" (sadaqat), encouraging people to "spend in the path of God." The Qur`an compares and contrasts two practices:

usury earned without giving anything in return, and charity given without taking anything in return. Measured in risk-benefit terms, the evil effects of usury surpass by far the good effects of charity. The Qur`an indicates that the practice of usury leads to the concentration of wealth in few hands, giving these people power over the less fortunate in society: "And they accepted usury even though they had been forbidden to do so; and they devoured and misappropriated the goods and monies of others in their greed." The practice is seen to lead to social unrest and corruption because the rich become richer as a result of reckless profiteering, whereas the poor remain poor: "That which you entrust to commercial organizations with a view to making profit will not be increased by God; nor will it increase your sustenance...Corruption appears on land and sea because of the evil that human hands have done..." Clearly, the Qur`an regards usury a practice of unbelievers. It requires, as a test of belief, that it be abandoned. The Prophetic traditions which elaborate the Qur`anic passages declare that taking interest on loans is one of the gravest of sins. All who take part in transactions involving interest is cursed, and the guilty are threatened with hell. Various kinds of punishment are described.

The Qur'anic denunciations of usury were occasioned by the needs of a developing community faced with socio-economic imbalances. But such denunciations were not consistently absolute. The Qur'an sometimes softens its position on a matter of interpersonal justice it has fulminated against just before, recognizing the human conditions that prompt such behavior. At other times, the Prophet, as its interpreter, moderated the Qur'anic stance by providing exceptions to the overall prohibition. The case of usury points to this confrontation between revelation and social inertia in the early community.

In spite of all the deterrent threats voiced in the Qur'an, some jurists foresaw that transactions involving interest would prevail. In pre-modern judicial decisions, gold and silver were generally regarded as items capable of riba. A number of traditions show that the severe prohibition of usury was moderated by reference to the changed circumstances of a transaction involving specific items and the way they exchanged hands in active trade. In general, Muslim jurists developed cases to permit exceptions to the categorical prohibition in the Qur'an.

The cases were reported in the traditions that were open to various interpretations. There were monetary transactions that led to principles that now govern when and where interest may be accepted. For instance, some Muslims practiced money exchange during the Prophet's life time. They asked the Prophet if this was alright. The Prophet said: "If it is from hand to hand (yadan bi-yadin, that is, immediately), there is no harm in it; but if it is delayed (nasa'an) it is not right." Some jurists extrapolated these traditions to maintain the view that riba consists only in the increase of original amount of a loan in a business agreement with a fixed period (dayn); others opined that there is no riba if the transfer of ownership takes place immediately. In other words, interest was to be permitted if transfer of ownership took place at once.

Contemporary Attitudes towards Interest

Because the rulings inferred by earlier jurists were not strictly uniform, there exists a variety of views regarding the permissibility of charging interest in the buying and selling of goods. Outside of precious metals there remain differences of opinion about the items that are liable to usury ordinances. Thus, for instance, should all business dealings in things of the same kind be considered capable of riba? The opinions vary according to the documentation used to deduce juridical decision. Some argue that interest is permitted if the transfer of ownership of goods capable of riba takes place immediately. This is also known as riba al-fadl ('immediate' credit), which occurs in a contract of sales when there is an increase in the terms of exchange themselves. The more strict Muslims limit riba to the exchange of goods of same kind in equal quantities in accordance with a tradition that says: 'Gold for gold, silver for silver, wheat for wheat, barley for barley, dates for dates, salt for salt, each kind for each kind, in hand. He who increases or asks for an increase commits riba, alike whether he gives or takes.' In the case of loans, which occasioned the Qur'anic prohibition of interest in the first place, it is forbidden to make a condition that a larger quantity shall be returned without regard to the kind of article. This is known as riba al-nasi'a ('delayed' credit) which entails a fixed increase in the amount of money over a time period. This kind of riba is the main source of contention.

The law regarding interest in lending is formally stricter. Muslims are prohibited either from taking or paying interest. Much of the Islamic law of contract is aimed at enforcing this prohibition of usury and risk (maysir). Riba in a loan exists not only when one insists upon the repayment of larger quantity, but also if any advantage at all is demanded. Therefore, it can even be forbidden to draw up a bill of exchange (suftaja) because the vendor, who is regarded as the creditor, reaps the advantage of avoiding the cost of transport. To be sure, many merchants used bills of exchange in the Muslim Middle Ages. But they were always conscious that a direct breach of the prohibition of usury was a grave sin.

Remembering such strict interpretations, conscientious Muslims to this day therefore not infrequently refuse to take bank interest. It is accurate to say that riba has operated in a negative manner. The thrust of the debate over riba has centered on the definition of the term, and has included little by way of a positive construction of a viable alternative in the contemporary financial world. The oil boom changed the picture of money flow radically, and one urgent problem facing the Arab and Islamic world was how to utilize effectively the petrodollars without openly flouting the Shari'ah. The question of riba emerged again, but in a different context. For many concerned with its prohibition, the premise was that riba simply meant interest, and loans for interest could consequently not be accepted. Still, the importance of riba-based commerce and its requirement to charge interest have given rise to a number of methods to evade the prohibition. Some Sunni schools and the Shi'ites have recognized such methods of evasion in their discussion about the purpose of divinely ordained restrictions. In applied jurisprudence, these methods are not seen as contrary to the strict enforcement of the prohibition. Legal interpreters argue that two firm principles-"Necessity overrides prohibition" and "No harm and harrassment in Islam"-provide a reason to take into consideration the situational aspects (mawdu'at) of the original prohibition, to the extent that these two principles reflect the effective causes ('ilal) and inner significance (maqasid) of the Qur'anic ordinance.

Still, more strict jurists continue to regard any loan contract specifying a fixed return to the lender as immoral and illegal, regardless of the purpose for which a loan is sought, its amount and, or the prevailing institutional framework. The reason is that a distinction made in the loan operation by those who justify this operation, between the money on which the contract is made and the operation of lending itself is actually money rewarding money,which is unacceptable under the Shari'ah. This vocal minority in juridical opinion takes the Qur'anic prohibition as categorical, and hence, not open to any further debate or discussion. There is little doubt that in the case cited for this study, Mr. Kamaluddin's religious tenets were governed by the directives received from the latter group of scholars.

In general, it is safe to assume that majority of the Muslim businesses have come to recognize a fait accompli in dealing with interest-based transactions. Devout Muslims may remain hesitant to invest their money in the international stock market, but continue to avail themselves of modern banking with its religiously questionable practice of charging or paying interest.

Most businesspeople simply consent to the western model as long as the financial institution happens to be non-Muslim. And some jurists regard banking with interest permissible, as long as, a person does not negotiate the interest and the bank is non-Muslim. Others seek to justify such excusatory thinking. Some leading Sunni jurists in Egypt defend their positive rulings on bank interest by regarding the modern bank interest as something different than the riba (usury) forbidden in the Qur'an. Their judgment rests on the ordinary lexical meaning of the term riba, which literally and simply means "increase" (ziyadah).

They argue that since not every increase or profit is unlawful in the Shari'ah, the Qur'anic text remains open to further extrapolation as to what type of increase God intends to forbid. Another tactic is used by Islamic banking institutions in many countries, including traditionally Muslim countries like Algeria and United Arab Emirates. They maintain their economic viability by describing themselves using the Islamic legal concept of "partnership for profit and loss" (mudaraba).

There are basically three parties to the "partnership": the depositor (mudarib), the entrepreneur-investor (mudarab) or agent ('amil) and the bank which is intermediary between the depositer and the entrepreneur, as well as the agent of the owner of capital deposited in its safes. In this form of organization, all the parites to the mudaraba share in the profit and losses of the enterprises.

Despite efforts to evade it, the prohibition of interest remains a key element in the Islamic vision of a socially responsible economy, and an important element in Islamic business practice. In the last few decades of the twentieth century, according to a report by the Institute of Islamic Banking and Insurance, as many as 150 Islamic banking institutions manage $100 billion in the Muslim countries and abroad. There is a huge market demand for religiously guided investing among Muslims.

Committees of Muslim jurists are consulted to decide what companies are Qur'an-safe (i.e., for example, do not sell alcohol, pork products, tobacco or charge interest on loans) for investment. Interest in Islamic investment is growing, with international stock markets launching their own Islamic market index to track Qur'an-safe stocks.

The influence of Islamic ethics extends further. Besides ruling out certain items as forbidden, the Shari'ah (Muslim religious law) also governs how much debt a company can carry and how much it can earn from interest. From the Islamic perspective, with its bias towards fair distribution of wealth and social justice, the Qur'an's strictures against riba remains at the heart of the Muslim individual as well as national financial institutions in international economic activity.

The prohibition of interest may become an important benchmark of justice in international political economy. As the world economies move closer to integration there is a growing consensus in the international community to move towards a more or less transcultural framework of ethical principles and rules. What is needed is a meta-ethics, a way for the different cultures and religions of the world to interpret their norms and practices to each other.

From a normative Islamic point of view, the aim of this dialogical mode should be to engage theologians, scholars and policy makers in the world economic system to search for better ways of redistributing wealth and preserving social justice across nations. This normative focus clearly is evident in Islamic jurisprudence regarding the charging or paying of interest. When the Qur'an banned transactions involving interest, the purpose was to protect financially weak in one way or another against the wealthy who might take advantage of them.

The attitude which dominated Islamic jurists was fear of arbitrariness in the decisions of those who held financial and political power. It is an appropriate attitude today.

The Islamic position is an important contribution to international business ethics, for it is supported by a general cross-cultural moral belief that the poor ought to be protected as well as a specific revelation within Islam that regards interest as a form of disregard for the downtrodden in society.

All cultures share certain moral principles like beneficence or nonmaleficence. All require rules like truthfulness in advertising as an essential element in regulating morally responsible merchant-consumer relationship. The Islamic prohibition of interest therefore seems to be an extension of the ethical requirement that human beings must treat each other fairly, rather than an obstruction to commerce.

6

Islam and Ecology

The Qur'an' and the Hadith are rich in proverbs and precepts that speak of the Almighty's design for creation and humanity's responsibility for preserving it. For many Muslims, citing these is enough to prove that Islam has always embraced a complete environmental ethic. Others are more critical. They readily acknowledge that the guidelines are all there in Islamic doctrine. Tawhid (unity), khilafa (trusteeship), and akhirah (accountability, or literally, the hereafter), three central concepts of Islam, are also the pillars of Islam's environmental ethic. But they add that Muslims have strayed from this nexus of values and need to return to it.

Although many Muslims with whom we have talked are familiar with these broad Qur'anic principles, few see any need to move an ecological ethic to the center of their awareness. True, some Muslims have become heads of national and international environmental organizations, but the average citizen is only vaguely aware of the extent of the crisis; most political and educational leaders perceive only a few of the problems, and those in isolation.

Moreover, many advance the common argument that "when we catch up with the technological superiority of the West, then we can begin to focus on this issue." Not a few Muslims see environmentalism as still another form of

Western control, intended to keep Islam from developing and Muslims from realizing their economic potential. Hence it is hardly surprising that, generally speaking, there is little discussion about actually applying Islamic principles to environmental practice. A few scholars and grassroots leaders, however, have begun to grapple with the question.

While Islamic writing in general lacks the self-criticism that Westerners value, and the study of comparative religion is seldom considered important, the view of the distinguished philosopher Seyyed Hossein Nasr is wider in scope. Born in Iran, he studied physics and math at the Massachusetts Institute of Technology, obtained a doctorate in science and philosophy at Harvard, and then returned to Iran, where he eventually became chancellor of Aryamehr University. After the Khomeini revolution in 1979, he began teaching Islamic studies in the United States. Although most of his twenty-odd books focus on Islamic civilization, some deal with the spiritual crisis facing humanity today, and all evidence his knowledge of Western and Eastern scientific and religious traditions.

Ecology in Muslim Countries

In Islamic countries religion is a stronger force. In a true Islamic society, political leadership could act in accordance with the shari'ah as set out by doctors of the law. If they pronounced polluting industries and certain kinds of development in violation of Islamic principles, political leaders would have to take strong measures against transgressors. Unfortunately, today the West dominates the world economy, so Islam reacts to the West both economically and politically. The West sets the agenda.

In the 1960s, Iran was the most advanced Muslim country in the Middle East. While industrializing rapidly, we created nature parks, and in the 1970s we held environmental conferences attended by Ivan Illich and other notables. Yet when the Shah asked for advice about shifting to nuclear power, and I suggested he should rely instead on resources like wind and solar energy, my advice was not followed by the government.

Today there are basically three types of Islam: traditionalism, modernism, and a variety of forms of revivalism usually brought together as fundamentalism. Until two hundred years ago, in spite of the many schools and interpretations, all Muslims lived within the tradition, with its roots in the Qur'an, Hadith, and the shari'ah. It was a living tradition, emphasizing the harmony of law, art, and all forms of knowledge. In the eighteenth century modernism, with its roots in secular humanism, entered this world, in all fields from science and philosophy to art, and traditional Islam began to weaken. Today we also see it struggling against many of the forms of violent revivalism usually called Islamic fundamentalism, which speaks of reviving Islam in opposition to modernism. But most so-called fundamentalists are pseudo-traditional, as can be seen in their attitude toward modern technologies and the destruction of the environment.

Many of the so-called fundamentalists, like Christian fundamentalists, pull out a verse from the scriptures and give it a meaning quite contrary to its traditional commentary. Also, even while denouncing modernism as the 'Great Satan,' many fundamentalists accept its foundations, especially science and technology. For traditionalists, there is beauty in nature which must be preserved and beauty in every aspect of traditional life, from chanting the Qur'an to the artisan's fashioning a bowl or everyday pot. Both fundamentalists and modernists, however, could just as easily produce mosques that look like factories. Many fundamentalists even seek a Qur'anic basis for modern man's domination and destruction of nature by referring to the injunction to 'dominate the earth' - misconstruing entirely the basic idea of vicegerency: that man is expected to be the perfect servant of God.

"To turn to a very tangible environmental problem like overpopulation — what would traditionalists say about that?"

Overpopulation is a major problem but it is not soluble as an entity unto itself; it is connected with other issues. Because of the imbalances in the political situation, many in Muslim countries have felt that power lies in numbers. But in the end, overpopulation is simply too great a burden, and there are now new interpretations among religious scholars who try to interpret the teachings of the Prophet to enable planning for one's family in accordance with one's possibility of supporting them. But isn't the real question how many can the earth support? And doesn't a just and workable solution involve allowing more women to become Islamic scholars and jurists?

Seyyed Hossein Nasr's writings spell out many of these ideas in greater detail. Running through them is the theme of "man's total disharmony with his environment." He sees the crisis as the externalization of an inner malaise that cannot be solved without "the spiritual rebirth of Western man." The human destiny, says Nasr, entails fulfilling the role of God's vicegerent on earth and protecting the natural order, thus bearing witness to the truth that the whole of nature speaks of God.

The Renaissance led to the separation of philosophy from theology, reason from faith, and mysticism from gnosis. In medieval times Christianity, like Islam, was steeped in tradition. But as the West emphasized the rigid logic of Aristotelian thinking, the sense of the sacred diminished. By the seventeenth century the science of the cosmos was secularized. The scientific revolution mechanized the Western worldview, and, with the appearance of the nineteenth-century sociologist Auguste Comte, led to examining the person and society as elements that could be measured with the aim of manipulation and predictability.

Nasr attacks what he calls the "hypothesis" of evolution. He uses the term not to mean modifications within a particular species (which do occur, he says, as a species adapts itself to changed natural conditions) but the belief that through natural processes one species is actually transformed into another. Nasr passionately criticizes this on a wide variety of grounds – metaphysical, cosmological, religious, logical, mathematical, physical, biological, and paleontological - building arguments too complex to recapitulate here. His central concern is that what he calls "the deification of historical process" has become so powerful that in many souls it has replaced religion and veils the archetypal realities.

Among his arguments is the contention that there is a remarkable unanimity that humankind descends from a celestial archetype but does not ascend from the ape or any other creature. Hinduism, Jainism, Buddhism, Islam, and many other traditions do demonstrate awareness that other creatures have preceded humankind on earth and that the earth's geological configuration has changed. For example, over a thousand years ago Muslim scientists knew that sea shells on top of mountains meant that mountains had turned into seas and seas into mountains, and that land animals had preceded humans on earth. But no sacred scriptures, whether they speak of creation in six days or of cosmic cycles enduring over vast expanses of time, speak of higher life forms as evolving from lower ones.

A number of scientists have found difficulties with the theory of evolution, Nasr says. For example, the lack of fossils intermediate between the great groups requires explanation. Contrary to Darwinian Theory, each new species enters life quite suddenly, over an extended region, and with all its essential characteristics. A truly scientific statement would be that nature produces species that are constant and unchanging, but occasionally disappear. Nasr comes to the rather startling conclusion that as long as humans have lived on earth, they have not evolved at all. Moreover, Nasr says in Man and Nature the same species still live, die, and regenerate themselves - except for the unfortunate species that modern humanity has made extinct.

Underlying these developments, Nasr says, was the absence of a higher form of knowledge which encompasses all learning and all phenomena: metaphysics. In the East, this "sacred science" endures to this day. Some early Christian thinkers were metaphysicians - Origen and Gregory of Nyssa, for example - and so were such later mystics and theologians as Eckhart, Erigena, and Nicolas of Cusa.

For Nasr, Muslims are a kind of "middle people," geographically and metaphysically located between other Oriental traditions and Western Christianity. Islam's elaborate hierarchy of knowledge is integrated by the principle of unity (tawhid), running as an axis through every mode of knowledge and being.

There are juridical, social, theological, gnostic, and metaphysical sciences, their principles all derived from the Qur'an. Within Islamic civilization, too, there have developed philosophical, natural, and mathematical sciences that became integrated with the worldview of Islam. On each level of knowledge, nature is seen in a particular way. For jurists it is the background for human action, for scientists a domain to be analyzed, and for metaphysicians the object of contemplation. Ultimately, all Islamic sciences affirm the Divine Unity.

Nasr finds throughout Islamic history an intimate connection between the metaphysical dimension of the tradition and the study of nature. Muslim scientists were Sufis. In Islamic as in Chinese civilization, observation of nature and even experimentation generally stood on the gnostic and mystic side of the tradition. In Islam the indivisible link between humans and nature and between religion and the sciences lies in the Qur'an itself, the Logos or Word of God. "By refusing to separate man and nature completely, Islam has preserved an integral view of the Universe and sees in the arteries of the cosmic and natural world order the flow of divine grace, or barakah... Man can learn to contemplate it, not as an independent domain of reality but as a mirror reflecting a higher reality".

In Islam, then, nature has never been considered profane. Someone like Avicenna could be both a physician and a philosopher who sought knowledge through illumination. That modern science did not develop in the bosom of Islam is a sign not of decadence, but of the Islamic refusal to consider any form of knowledge as purely secular and divorced from the ultimate goal of human existence.

Across the centuries, the same principles of the Divine Unity have guided Islamic science, art, and law. Islamic cosmology and cosmography have served as matrix for the Islamic sciences, from geography to alchemy. Maps were based on observation, and remain amazingly accurate. Yet they were also works of art. Islamic medicine produced detailed, accurate anatomical studies, even while following the ancient injunction against dissection.

Founded on the doctrines of unity and balance, Islamic medicine is to this day practiced with success in places like the Hamdard Institutes. The plant world was studied with minute care, but with the goal of drawing spiritual lessons from it. Muslim scientists have always recognized that nature is, above all, a reflection of the Paradise whose memories we still bear in the depths of our souls.

This symbolic approach to creation can be likened to the Orthodox Christian view that icons are an image of the divine world. Indeed, at one point Nasr observes that Islamic science is in the most profound sense an art, one that enables the human to contemplate the visible cosmos as an icon revealing the spiritual world beyond it. Thus, we humans have studied animals not only for their own sake, but also to know better our own inner reality. This reality is the total reflection of the Divine Names and Qualities, just as animals are the partial, but often more direct reflections. Humans, as central in the terrestrial environment, are better able to exercise responsibility for it.

The correspondence between microcosm and macrocosm, and the study of the gradation of beings, form the background for scrutinizing the various forms in nature. Humankind stands at the pinnacle of the hierarchy. But "man cannot gain an awareness of the sacred aspects of nature without discovering the sacred within himself or herself," Nasr once told an interfaith conference on "Spirit and Nature," which was recorded for a program produced by Bill Moyers. The perfect expression of the microcosm opening to the macrocosm lies in Sufism, which Nasr calls the inner dimension of Islam.

One should learn to contemplate the world of nature as a mirror reflecting the Divine God, who is both transcendent and immanent. Trees are not only necessary to maintain life, they are a recurring symbol. The Qur'an compares the cosmos to a tree whose roots are firm in the heavens and whose branches spread to the whole of the universe, symbolizing the participation of the whole cosmos in prayer. In Islamic tradition, it is a blessed act to plant a tree even one day before the end of the world. Water has a fundamental reality which symbolizes Divine Mercy. In Islamic law, to pollute the water is a sin, and according to certain jurists, the person who does so can even be called a kafir, a condemnatory term for someone outside the pale of religion.

Ranging through a broad spectrum of wisdom traditions, Nasr pays homage not only to the two other Abrahamic faiths, but also to the spiritual traditions of Native Americans and Shintoists, for whom revelation is directly related to natural forms. The American Indian, for example, sees the bear or eagle as a divine presence. All religious traditions, too, posit the hierarchical nature of reality — as in the orders of angels described by Dionysius, or intermediate worlds in the cosmologies of Mahayana Buddhism. Thus we have many traditions, yet one, the Primordial Tradition, which always is. This lessens neither the authenticity nor the complete originality of each, which emanates as a direct message from Heaven and conforms to a particular archetype. From interfaith dialogue we should not expect the conversion of participants. Rather, we can gain understanding of another world of sacred form and meaning through preservation of our own tradition.

The geometric patterns in Islamic art reflect the archetypal world. Traditional Islamic architecture and city planning never sought to convey a sense of defiant human power over nature. In the traditional Islamic pattern of life, work is not separated from life, but reflects natural rhythms. An artisan's workday, for example, may last from dawn until long after sunset, but the work is done in the bazaar, the bosom of the community, and is interrupted by coffee-drinking with friends, dining at home with family, prayers at the mosque, or quiet meditation.

Today, concern for a greater reality in the contemporary world can be observed, Nasr maintains, in the growing interest in ecology and a concomitant urge to rediscover the sacred. If the limitations imposed by a desacralized mode of knowing were removed, the sacred would manifest itself of its own accord, he tells us in Knowledge and the Sacred. "The light has not ceased to exist in itself. The cosmos seems to have become dark, spiritually speaking, only because of the veil of opacity surrounding that particular humanity called modern".

Contrasting Perspectives

The two modes of thought represented by Nasr and Berry are both so significant that they reach well beyond conventional boundaries of separate religious and cultural traditions. Comparing their ideas, not all of them mutually exclusive, may clarify their differing approaches and highlight basic intellectual choices that religious believers concerned with ecology will eventually have to make.

Berry's starting point is the natural world. For him, as St. Paul indicates in the Epistle to the Romans, the earth itself is divine Scripture, and the universe is the ultimate sacred community. Although Nasr has called Scripture and nature the two grand books of divine knowledge, he starts with the divine world. In another sense, his starting point is revelation, the only means by which the Source can, even partially, be known. It is revelation from a personal God who created the world, watches over the acts of all human beings, and intervenes in their affairs. Although Nasr acknowledges the mode of revelation in religions that center on a non-personal Supreme Reality rather than a personal God, and sometimes uses "revelation" simply to refer to the world of faith, he is most concerned with direct revelation, communicated to a human prophet.

For Berry, "revelation" is the awakening of the sense of ultimate mystery. The "revelatory import of the natural world" is a recurrent motif; he asks us to listen to the universe. More often, Berry speaks of "the divine," for it conveys better the ineffable/numinous presence in the world about us. For Nasr, "nature," a symbol of a transcendent reality, teaches human beings about God. His vision seems propelled by an urge to perceive patterns of unity, hierarchy, order. It might be called a mathematical vision; mathematics, an abstraction with respect to the world of the senses, is regarded by Muslims as the gateway leading from the sensible to the intelligible world. Nasr perceives reality through the lens of archetypes.

These contrasts seem related to a fundamental difference in emphasis between the religions that nurtured these men. Christianity tends to be a way of love, Islam a way of knowing through illumination. Like Hinduism, Buddhism, and Zoroastrianism, Islam has stressed sapiential doctrines. Mainstream Christian thought has tended, in Nasr's words, to limit the "function of intellection to that of a handmaid of faith rather than the means of sanctification, which of course would not exclude the element of faith" (Knowledge and the Sacred, 36). In Christianity caritas is more important. In Berry's vision, this theme extends to the earth, and he even speaks of "falling in love with the universe."

Metaphysics is a realm that Berry rarely discusses, while for Nasr it is the scientia sacra. For the latter it is a key to perceiving the hierarchy and humankind's elevated position in it as vicegerent of creation. Berry's perception is closer to the Native American view that we are one among many species, each with its own distinctive grandeur: for flying the birds are infinitely superior; for swimming, the fish.

The concept of "evolution" holds different meanings for Nasr and Berry. Nasr sees it as a vain attempt to prove that higher biological forms emerge out of lower ones. The idea violates the principle of hierarchy fundamental to Islam and is wrong in the strictly scientific sense, and in its influence on other modes of thought. Berry finds excitement in the idea that there was a time sequence in the very formation of the earth, that earlier life-forms were simpler than later ones, that the earth, especially its life forms, is in a state of continuing transformation. The universe has revealed itself as an emergent evolutionary process.

In Berry's perspective, the universe had a beginning; and time is irreversible. In Nasr's complex discussions of different conceptions of time, a recurring theme is that the movement we see in our environment is cyclical rather than evolutionary — witness the seasons. But for Berry this does not mean that the natural world moves only in eternal, unchanging cycles. In fact, the reason we are in trouble is that while the seasons do come round again every year, the life-systems are deteriorating, continually, bringing more dust storms, contaminated water, spoiled harvests, and extinction of species that once made this earth their home.

Berry focuses on cosmogenesis, understanding the universe not as "being" but as always in the process of becoming. We human beings also evolve and our vision evolves; our story and that of the earth are intertwined. We are truly of the earth; our sense of the divine reflects the outer world, and can alter as that world is altered. Such a view violates the very principle of the unchanging nature of sacred realities that is fundamental to Nasr's thought. For him, nature is a reflection of the paradise whose memories we still bear. The Way is the way back, through the revival of traditions as manifested in the great civilizations. Only thus can we rediscover the sacred and dissipate the loneliness of a world from which the spirit has been banished.

Each way — Nasr's and Berry's — contains wisdom. Although their perspectives differ radically, both philosophers locate the source of our plight less in external conditions than in the way we perceive and approach them. Both suggest that we humble ourselves before the mystery, the awesome forces of creation — and simplify our lives accordingly. Both remind us of the peril of hubris, forgetfulness of human limits.

7

Face of Islam in America

The 1990s may be the last decade in which Islam is viewed as a "non-mainstream" religious tradition in America. At its current rate of growth, by the year 2015 Islam will be the second largest religion in the United States, following Christianity. There are approximately four million Muslims in the United States and 650 mosques. Foreign-born Muslims and their descendants constitute about two thirds of those numbers; indigenous Americans (born in America), mostly African Americans, constitute the other third. Islam is already the world's second largest religion, with 900 million members—about one sixth of the world's population—living in geographic regions that include, but extend far beyond, the Middle East. Islam is either the major religion or has large populations in such diverse cultural environments as Africa, Malaysia, and Indonesia, the former Soviet Union, Turkey, India and Pakistan, northwestern China and Europe.

Yet there is surprisingly little awareness or understanding of Islam in the American consciousness. What Americans do think about Islam tends to be formed by media images, specifically by the presence of one-sided negative imagery on the one hand ("Arab terrorists," "Islamic fundamentalists"), and by the absence of positive, or even neutral images on the other. American Muslims often express frustration over a situation that seems to be the last bastion of tolerated stereotyping. Clearly, the poor relationship between Islam and the "Christian West" has its roots in the confrontational and competitive history which Christianity and Islam have shared since Islam arose as a religious and political challenge to Christianity in the seventh century. The roots of confrontation also lie in the remembered history of the Crusades, in the relationship established during the colonial and the post-colonial periods (including the loss of Palestinian lands to Israel) and, now, in the heightened rhetoric and mistrust created by Muslims and "Westerners" alike, who would present Islam and "secular democracy" as polar opposites. Ideologues on both sides would like to present an image of a monolithic "Islam" with a unified agenda and clear leaders.

The reality is that the situation of Islam worldwide and in the United States, in particular, is extremely complex and shifting. Islam developed its forms of orthodoxy in the early history of the community. There were, of course, different interpretations of basic principles derived from sacred scripture which led to a number of contending discourses in Islam (theological, juridical, philosophical, mystical, popular, political) as well as differing "styles" of Islam depending on the cultural milieu into which Islam was introduced. This complex reality is also the "process" of Islam in America. There have already been a number of stages in the development of an "American" Islam as well as a number of different groups and styles that constitute the Muslims of America.

There are three major constituents of Islam in America: immigrants, who bring Islam from their homelands; African-American converts to Islam; and the Sufi groups, the "spiritual confraternities" of Islam. The historical development of certain segments of the Islamic community in America namely, immigrant groups and African-American groups see themselves as members of traditional or "orthodox" Islam. Sufism will also be treated in a separate chapter in this volume. It will be evident that there are a number of important issues facing American Muslim communities and individuals at this time, but they all point to the overarching question of how to define and manifest what "Islam" means in the midst of a secular, pluralistic, contemporary American culture.

Beliefs and Practices

The Islamic religion had its historic origin in the figure of Muhammad ibn Abdullah. Muhammad was born in the Arabian city of Mecca in 570 C.E. and was a member of the Quraysh tribe. According to traditional accounts, Muhammad was in the trading business, Mecca being a crossroads for many of the overland trade routes of the day, and was married to Khadija, his former employer who was fifteen years his senior.

He was a reflective man and often meditated in a cave near Mt. Hira. From 610 through 632, when he died, Muhammad experienced a number of visions and "hearings," which he came to understand as true revelation (wahy) from the one God, Allah, which was communicated through the angel Gabriel. These "revelations" began as warnings directed at the Meccans for their forgetfulness of God, for their polytheism and idolatry, and for the social and economic injustices of Meccan society.

The revelations also warned of an inevitable judgment that all human beings would experience at the "Final Hour," an idea which was alien to the prevailing view of life and death in Arabian tribal culture. Muhammad understood his role to be that of the final prophet and messenger of God, and his message of submission (islam) to God's will as the same message that had been revealed to Abraham, Moses and all the other prophets of Jewish and Christian Scriptures as well as to the "prophets" of other peoples from the beginning of time. Jesus was seen as a prophet, born of the Virgin Mary, and a special model of sanctity; but

Christian claims of Jesus' divinity and "sonship" were rejected. The collection of Muhammad's revelations is the sacred book of Islam, the Quran. Muslims traditionally accept it as the authoritative word of God which "preexisted" eternally with God.

Muhammad began to preach in Mecca and, as a result of persecution, immigrated with a number of his followers to the city of Medina, where he established the paradigmatic "Islamic" community. The emigration (hijra) to Medina in 622 C.E. marks the beginning of the Islamic calendar. Muhammad eventually returned victorious to Mecca, clearing the Ka'ba—the pilgrimage site used by the many Arabian tribes of all idols in a symbolic act of reviving the original intention of the Ka'ba, which, according to tradition, had been built by Abraham and his son Ishmael to worship the One God, Allah.

The Quran and the example (sunna) of Muhammad became the main sources for the development of belief and practice in Islam. The Quran established the main articles of belief and practice, which are known as the Five Pillars of Islam. The first pillar is the shahada, the affirmation that "There is no God but God (La ilaha illa Allah), and Muhammad is His Prophet."

The shahada is normally understood as stressing the utter transcendence and distinction of God "above" all created orders, although the Sufis would traditionally interpret the shahada as affirming that ultimately only God can be called "the Real." The shahada is also seen as affirming the authenticity of God's prophets and holy books, the angels, the jinn (invisible creatures created out of "fire"), and the final judgment of one's deeds and consignment to heaven or hell. The five pillars also include the basic duties of Muslims.

Thus, the second pillar consists of the salat, the liturgical prayers said in Arabic five times daily, facing Mecca. On

Fridays, Muslims gather in mosques for congregational recitation of prayers. The salat prayers create the basic orientation of time and space for Muslims. Arabic became the sacred language of Islam and an important unifying element for Muslims throughout the world. With the third pillar, the zakat, or charity tax, Muslims are required to pay a yearly tax of 2.5 percent of one's holdings for the care of the society's poor. The fourth pillar is sawm, or fasting—refraining from all food and liquid—from sunrise to sunset each day during the lunar month of Ramadan.

It is a time of inner reflection and training of the nafs, the "lower self," as well as of experiencing something of the hunger of the poor. Finally, Muslims are required to make the hajj, the pilgrimage to Mecca once in their lives so long as it is not a financial burden. The primary ritual of the hajj is the circumambulation of the Ka'ba, which is seen as a reenactment of Muhammad's "clearing the idols" as well as symbolic of the ideal of the "unity of humankind" that has attracted so many marginalized peoples to Islam. Muslim men and women arrive in Mecca from virtually every race, class, and ethnic group, shedding their outer garments for a plain white shroud-a symbol of equality as well as the Muslim death shroud-and begin their common "journey to the center."

In principle, there is no division between religious and secular law in Islam. All of life is to be oriented toward the Divine Will. The shariah, or Islamic law, was developed to provide specific guidelines for all areas of life, from religious ritual (e.g., requirements in prayer) to sexuality (e.g., no premarital sex) to political principles (e.g., rules of war) to dietary restrictions (e.g., no pork, no alcohol). Of course, the shariah is based on interpretation of the Quran, the remembered history of Muhammad's actions, and the cultural customs of the geographic regions in which the shariah developed during the eighth and ninth centuries. It is not surprising that a major area of contemporary discussion among Muslims is the issue of reinterpreting the shariah in light of considerations of modernity. The variety of Islamic "revival" and "reform" movements that have emerged in the contemporary Islamic world (often inaccurately lumped together under such terms as "radical" or "fundamentalist") have tended to see the political, social, and economic ills of the Islamic world as indications that Muslims have fallen away-because of infatuation with the West or corruption of their own leaders from the moral and civic principles of the shariah, and that a return to an "Islamic" way of life, the shariah, would revitalize both Islamic society and, ultimately, the world community. However, it is this same activist spirit that has led to disagreement over "what," or "whose," version of Islam is correct, as well as how the shariah should be implemented.

The issue of interpretation is particularly crucial in the area of the rights and treatment of women. Muslim women writers, both in America and abroad, often point to the curtailed role of women in the post-Muhammadan community in comparison with the egalitarian thrust of the Quran itself and the more active participation of women in the early Muslim community. Thus, the issue of "women and the veil" is symbolic of discussions that have become particularly important for Muslims in America. In addition to the shariah, many customs have spread throughout the Islamic world which Muslims see as rooted in the example of Muhammad, and which they feel incumbent to cultivate-for example, modesty, hospitality, and respect for teachers and elders.

Two major branches of Islam developed early in the community's history in response to the question of succession of authority after Muhammad's death. Sunni Islam and Shi'ite Islam reflect two approaches to politics and rule. Shi'ites believes that Muhammad's charisma—and hence, political and spiritual guidance—was continued in the bloodline of Ali (Muhammad's cousin and son-in-law) and his descendants, the Shi'ite imams (leaders). Shi'ites believe in the continued guidance from the final imam (although different sects of Shi'ites disagree on whether that was the fifth, the seventh, or the twelfth in the line of succession), and tradition maintains that he will return as the mahdi to usher in the Day of Judgment. About 20 percent of all Muslims, mostly from Iran and southern Lebanon are Shi'ites. The other 80 percent, the majority of Muslims, are Sunnis, for whom selection of leaders is supposed to take place through representatives (originally the tribal elders) of the people. Both Sunnis and Shi'ites are considered "orthodox."

Within both Sunni and Shi'ite communities of Islam there emerged spiritual confraternities, the Sufi groups, or tariqas, which were centered on the teachings of certain pious individuals. These charismatic figures taught a "subtle wisdom" tradition of interpreting the Quran and the traditions of the Prophet. The Sufi groups developed a variety of approaches to Islamic spirituality—ecstatic, contemplative, devotional, poetic, musical, and chivalrous—the goal of which was both purity of devotion and attainment of a unitive experience of God. The Sufis contributed much to the development of the esoteric sciences of the medieval period (alchemy, subtle psychology), popular forms of piety, and the arts-literary, visual, musical, and poetic. While the Sufis at times strained the boundaries of "orthodoxy" with some of their teachings, their presence has been a historical constant in Islamic societies. They are recognized for their importance as transmitters of Islam to lands far from the original "heartland" of Islam. See "Sufism in America" in this volume.

The beliefs and practices of Sunnis and Shi'ites, of Sufis and non-Sufis, came to the shores of America with the arrival of immigrant populations, traditions brought by slaves, and popular Sufi teachers from "the East.

Muslims in America—Immigrant Communities

About two thirds of all Muslims in the United States are immigrants and their descendants. Muslim immigrants, both Sunnis and Shi'ites, arrived in waves beginning in the late 1800s, the first groups coming from what are now Syria, Lebanon, Jordan, and Palestine. Communities began to form in the industrial centers of the Midwest-Toledo, Cedar Rapids, Detroit, Michigan City, and Chicago. Most of these immigrants were uneducated and unskilled workers who sought economic opportunities in the United States. The extended families of these immigrants became the founders of the first mosques in North America. These first mosque communities functioned primarily to maintain social bonds, offer solidarity in this new land, and provide community space for rites of passage. Another wave of immigrants arrived between 1947 and 1960 and included Muslims from the Middle East as well as from India, Pakistan, Eastern Europe, and the Soviet Union. Some were children of ruling elites; some were refugees; many came solely for higher education.

The individuals comprising the last wave, from 1967 to the present, have come for both political and economic reasons. Many, especially Pakistanis and Arabs, are educated professionals. Substantial numbers of Iranians came prior to and after their country's revolution. A number of other countries are represented in this wave: Yemen, Lebanon, Egypt, Jordan, Turkistan-Turkey, Kuwait, Saudi Arabia, Iraq, and Afghanistan. The most recent arrivals are from the Sudan, Uganda, Guyana, Bermuda, and the former Yugoslavia.

Development of Islamic community life in America corresponded to the political and social concerns of particular immigrant groups. Earlier Muslim immigrants saw mosque life mostly in terms of social needs, and imams (leaders) of local congregations were not always trained as religious teachers. Thus, little emphasis was placed upon strict observance of traditional mosque functions. Adaptations were made to conform to American church patterns, such as scheduling congregational prayers on Sundays and allowing "mixed" (men and women) social functions, such as dances.

Later groups of immigrants brought the heightened religious and political self-consciousness that has been part of the legacy of the loss and occupation of Palestinian lands. These Muslims came with commitments to a variety of religio-political ideologies and with more religious training, usually more conservative, than their predecessors in America. Tension points developed in some of the earlier mosque communities as more recent and conservative Muslim arrivals attempted to correct their more Americanized brothers and sisters in areas of Islamic practice and custom.

In general, Muslims in America who have been raised in traditional Muslim cultures speak of the tension they experience in trying to remain close to linguistic, cultural, ethnic, and religious roots while trying to develop a sense of belonging in their adopted home. American societal patterns are often at odds with needs of Muslim life and practice: Work schedules do not easily allow for the five-times-daily salat prayers or Friday congregational prayers. Institutional eating facilities (schools, prisons, military) are not set up for Muslim dietary practices. The pervasiveness of alcohol in America and the cultural acceptance of sexual permissiveness and immodesty (in clothing and comportment) are seen as negative influences on the faith community, particularly on its young people. The shariah, however, continues to be held as the ideal pattern of life to be striven for, somehow, in the midst of contemporary American culture.

Mosque governance in America appears to be taking the pattern of some Protestant denominations, such as the Baptists, in which each community has autonomy in deciding its local leadership and ideological orientation, but in which each member and each community shares a commitment to sacred scripture as the ultimate source of guidance in areas of belief and practice. American mosques, unlike mosques in Islamic countries, are self-supporting, and therefore they must rely on membership contributions or fund-raising activities. The imam of the American mosque often finds himself in a role that goes beyond the traditional function of reciter of prayers. He may assume additional roles, common to American pastors, such as administrative and counseling responsibilities.

There are a variety of styles and emphases in mosque communities of the United States. Some mosques function in the way of America's small, urban ethnic churches, in which ethnic ties are emphasized, cultivated, and preserved. These communities function as centers for learning and sharing information about surviving in America as much as they function as centers for prayer. Other mosques, while being centers for prayer and social activities, also emphasize "outreach," utilizing the Islamic cultural tradition of hospitality in order to establish communication and goodwill with the surrounding community. Mosques in the Midwest, such as the Islamic Center of Toledo, Ohio, are known for this approach. More recently established mosque communities, such as the Islamic Society of Central Jersey, have taken this approach as well, particularly in light of escalating fears of Islam and Muslims. The focus of their work is in correcting misunderstandings about Islam by inviting non-Muslim groups to their facilities and by offering lectures and programs. Finally, a new trend has emerged in America: the large "mega-mosques" that serve the needs of large, rapidly growing, racially and ethnically diverse communities, such as in the Los Angeles area. These mosques most clearly reflect the historical pluralism within the Islamic community as well as the continually widening ethnic pluralism of the United States.

There are a number of active Islamic organizations that exist alongside the mosque communities. In the middle of this century, the Muslim population was still small and dispersed over the continent. The need for a unifying organization led second-generation Muslim immigrants to form a federation of mosques that would provide a pooling of resources and contact with other communities. It was originally called the Federation of Islamic Organizations; today it is the Federation of Islamic Associations in the United States and Canada, and its headquarters are in Detroit.

While the federation of mosques was taking shape within the earlier ethnic communities, Muslim student organizations were forming on college campuses. In 1963 the Muslim Student Association (MSA) was created to coordinate activities of the student groups. The MSA symbolized the international diversity of Islam as well as the ideological concerns of a more activist Islam worldwide. For these students, Islam was a way of life, a mission, and the organization's goal was to help create an ideal community and to serve Islam. The MSA is still one of the largest and most well-organized Islamic organizations, and it has led to the creation of a number of other service and professional organizations designed to meet the needs of Muslims beyond the student community. Among them are the Muslim Community Association, American Muslim Social Scientists, Muslim Youth of North America, American Muslim Scientists and Engineers, Islamic Teaching Center, Islamic Medical Association, and the American Muslim Mission. These and other groups are now under the umbrella organization of the Islamic Society of North America (ISNA). The groups have their own committees and boards, but their administrative, legal, and financial affairs are linked at the center by ISNA's legislative body, the Majlis al-Shura. ISNA groups sponsor national, zonal, and profession-specific congresses, where members engage in social, business, and intellectual exchange while maintaining connections with the larger international Islamic community.

One of the most important developments that characterize the current Islamic community in America is the movement in the direction of political activity in the United States. While ISNA's leadership always tended to be individuals with affiliation to or backing by politically minded "Islamist" groups, such as the Ikhwan al-Muslimin and the Jammati-Islami, there was never agreement on the appropriateness or the form of political action in the United States. Some of the more "ultraorthodox" movements (such as the Salafiyya, comprised mainly of Gulf Arabs and some African Americans) and some of the African-American "utopian separatists" felt reluctant to participate in the kufr ("unbelieving") American governmental system. Nevertheless, in trying to offer some balance to the influence of the many pro-Israel political action committees, a number of Muslim PACs have emerged since 1985, including ISNA's own ISNA-PAC. In addition, a number of Muslim groups, such as the United Muslims of America and the Islamic Society of Greater Houston have encouraged participation in such mainstream American activities as registering and voting in elections, actively supporting candidates, and even running for office.

One of the results of this public visibility in the political system is that Muslim candidates sometimes find criticism coming from conservative elements within the Muslim community for such things as not using an Islamic name, dressing in an "overly Western" manner, or making other concessions to American secular culture. (There are a number of Muslim organizations and activities which are not specifically political. Among them are da'wa (missionary, education, ministry) oriented groups, such as the Muslim World League and the Shi'ite-based Islamic Societies of Georgia and Virginia; the Muslim "think tanks," such as the

International Institute of Islamic Thought, formed in 1982 to promote "Islamic" scholarship and methodologies; and the National Committee on Islamic Affairs, which has begun to utilize the media as a forum for Muslim discussion on affairs in the Middle East.

There are also many Muslim "activist-scholars" in America who are engaged in critical examination of a wide variety of issues and assumptions related to "tradition" and "modernity" in Islam. These scholars often find themselves caught between cultures: they find it difficult to take scholarship back home to countries where ideological concerns rule the academic discourse; but they also find it difficult to challenge ideological assumptions that exist in American academia.

African-American Islam

Most of the "non-immigrant" Muslims in America is African-American converts to Islam. For many African Americans, Islam has become a means of self-definition and of "choosing" to identify with a religio-cultural system that was other than the one (the Christian West) that had failed in establishing a truly racially inclusive society. Certainly the phenomenal growth of Islam among African Americans, even the injection Of Islamic themes into black popular culture (such as rap music), is related to the meaning that "Islam" holds for many African Americans, namely, identifying with a religious faith that has affirmed their African heritage.

The roots of a "black Muslim" perspective can be traced back to Timothy Drew (Noble Drew Ali) and the founding of the Moorish American Science Temple in Newark in 1913, as well as to the emergence of the Elijah Muhammad and the Nation of Islam. Certainly the most well-known convert to the Nation of Islam was Malcolm X, whose expositions of Elijah Muhammad's teachings were most influential in bringing membership to the Nation. There were/ are some themes taught in the Nation of Islam that reflects traditional Islamic teachings: submission to Allah, the repudiation of such vices as alcohol, sex outside of marriage, the eating of pork, and gambling. However, such teachings as the "white man as devil" and the quasi-scientific theory of the origins of human history run counter to traditional Islamic accounts of human history and purpose. It was Malcolm X's pilgrimage to Mecca and his experience of a "universal brotherhood" in submission to Allah without color lines that helped make permanent his break with Elijah Muhammad and the Nation of Islam in favor of what he regarded as "true Islam." Malcolm X's teachings after his trip to Mecca became a major catalyst for moving many African Americans in the direction of "orthodox" Islam. Elijah Muhammad's own son, Warith Deen Muhammad, was one of these.

After the death of his father, Warith Deen Muhammad took over the Nation and formally brought the organization into mainstream Islamic belief and practice. He rejected the preaching of racial hatred, including the "white man as devil" idea. He instituted the use of traditional Islamic rituals, and he repudiated teachings that identified Elijah Muhammad as a prophet. The organization went through a number of name changes.

It had been the Lost-Found Nation of Islam in the Wilderness of North America, then the Nation of Islam. It then became the American Bilalian Community, then the World Community of Islam in the West, and, finally, the American Muslim Mission.

In 1985, Warith Deen Muhammad decentralized the organization, delegating the central responsibilities to local imams. He encouraged the merging of African-American Muslims into the worldwide Islamic community. These directives were not accepted by all members of the Nation. Louis Farrakhan is the best-known current spokesman for Elijah Muhammad's teachings, maintaining the name, the

Nation of Islam, and the centralized form of the organization. Farrakhan tends to draw more media attention than the American Muslim Mission, confirming the conviction of many Muslims, African American and immigrants alike, that normative Islam is rarely depicted in the U.S. media.

In reality, there are hints of an increased public awareness of African-American Muslim activity beyond Farrakhan's "Nation." There is increased reportage on mosques being built in American cities. Furthermore, the American Muslim Mission's nationwide system of schools, the Clara Muhammad Schools, has received media attention for the positive contribution to the quality of life and education they are providing in the larger urban areas where they are situated as alternatives to the public schools.

There are over sixty of these academically certified schools. Also of significance in the development of American Islamic communities is the fact that these schools are drawing children of recent immigrants into already established African-American communities, thereby fostering a sense of community across ethnic lines? The teachers tend to be immigrants themselves, often with advanced degrees in their native countries. Islamic studies are interwoven with subjects such as English, history, and science, and Arabic is taught from kinder-garden.

They espouse a philosophy that is racially inclusive and religiously tolerant. The Clara Muhammad Schools are an example of the growing ties emerging between indigenous and immigrant Muslims. As mentioned, tension does occur when new immigrants attempt to make changes in already established mosque communities, whether they are predominantly African American or immigrant, and this friction has become somewhat heightened in the present climate of growing emphasis on cultural self-affirmation of minority groups in America (mirroring the worldwide self-affirmation of ethnic identity).

However, the larger pattern that seems to be emerging is one of increased cooperation, interaction, and even intermarriage between indigenous and immigrant Muslims. Another important segment of the African-American Muslim population that must be mentioned in any consideration of current developments in America is the unprecedented numbers of African Americans who are converting to Islam while in prison.

For these (mostly) men, Islam is an important means of identity formation. Many mosques, including Sufi communities, are involved in ministry to prisons, forging community support systems for these prisoners. Furthermore, Muslims in prison are raising important legal questions with regard to freedom of expression of religion for "non-conventional faiths" within prison walls. Issues of whether Muslim prisoners should be entitled to consideration in terms of space and time for worship, dietary restrictions, and wearing beards are being argued in the courts presently. Certain accommodations in the area of religious expression are already permitted in the case of Christian and Jewish prisoners.

The Islamic community in America includes the many mosque communities which are attempting to find ways to accommodate both traditional religious norms and changing constituencies within the cultural context of American society. It includes Muslim "conservatives" and "traditionalists," whose ideologies put them at odds with American secular values, and Muslim "modernists" who wish to be transmitters of Islamic values while working within the framework of the American democratic tradition. The Islamic community includes individual Muslim women and men in every American mosque community who are struggling with the tension between traditional practices and modern secular Western views about the rights and role of women. American Muslims include African-American groups who have chosen to be integrated in the larger Islamic community, but who seek affirmation and respect for their African-American cultural identity. There are those African-American and immigrant Muslim communities that are combining their resources to improve the conditions of recent immigrants and the marginalized poor of the inner cities.

Finally, it is evident that the distinction between immigrant and indigenous Islam is rapidly becoming meaningless as "foreign-born" Muslims and their American-born children share mosque community life with growing numbers of American-born Muslims and their children. The Islamic community in America is becoming the major melting pot of the wide variety of racial and ethnic groups that constitute the "traditional" Islamic world. Islam has long been regarded by Westerners as the religion of "the other." Clearly, this perception of Islam will undergo revision in America as Muslim communities grow, and as America comes to re-define itself in terms of its increasingly multicultural and multi-religious nature.

The Modern American Muslim

The Muslim community in the United States is also facing a crisis of participation. Is it religiously legitimate for the believer to be politically active in a system of government which is not only non-Islamic but is potentially anti-Islamic from time to time? Should a Muslim agree to vote under the United States constitution and against the background of the role of the United States' controlling if not intimidating many Muslim countries?

In the 1990s alone American bombs and missiles have fallen on Iraq, Afghanistan, Sudan, and accidentally, Pakistan. We could use some of the categories of medieval Islamic jurists who divided the world between Dar el Islam (the Abode of Islam) and Dar el Harb (the Abode of War). Are Muslims in America an enclave of Dar el Islam lodged in the body politic of Dar el Harb? Where does the political participation of Dar el Islam fit into the political process of Dar el Harb? Or should we abandon altogether these medieval Islamic divisions of the world as being outdated?

Another dilemma concerns possible differences between Muslim minorities from one Western country to another. Are British Muslims in a different predicament from American Muslims? Is there a difference between Muslims voting in a Christian theocracy (like England) on one side, and Muslims voting in a secular state (like the United States), on the other?

The Head of State in England is also the Head of the Church of England. The Archbishop of Canterbury is chosen with the participation of the Prime Minister. And major doctrinal changes in the Church of England need the approval of the British Parliament either directly or by delegation through the Synod of the Church. The United States, on the other hand, is a secular state which constitutionally is supposed to favour no religion. Is it therefore more halal to participate in U.S. elections than in British elections?

In the world as it exists today, we have to allow non-Muslims to vote in every Muslim country. If non-Muslim minorities vote in Muslim societies, why should not Muslim minorities vote in non-Muslim countries? If Christians can vote in Egypt, why should not Muslims vote in the United States?

The most famous Egyptian of the 1990s was for a while Boutros Boutros-Ghali who would not have been eligible for the post of Secretary-General of the United Nations had he not had extensive political and diplomatic participation in Egypt before hand. Boutros-Ghali was and is of course a Christian.

The Deputy Prime Minister of Iraq is Tareq Aziz, another Christian. No Christian country in the West has as yet allowed a Muslim to rise to such a status. Should Muslims themselves in Christian countries prevent their own rise to power?

For 20 years Muslim Senegal had a Roman Catholic President (1960-1980) - Leopold Sedar Senghor. The percentage of Muslims in Senegal is 94% - higher than the percentage of Muslims in Egypt. Senegal is a remarkable illustration of Muslim ecumenicalism. If Muslim countries allow the participation and even empowerment of non-Muslim minorities, why should not Muslim minorities in non-Muslim countries seek participation and increasing empowerment for themselves?

On the other hand, it is possible for a Muslim to attain the highest office in the land in a country in which Muslims are a minority - provided the Muslim minority has not been politically inactive.

This happened in Malawi in May 1994 when, in the first internationally supervised election since independence thirty years earlier, the voters in Malawi elected Bakili Muluzi as their first Muslim president. According to most estimates, Muslims in Malawi are less than a third of the population. Could a Muslim president have been elected if the Muslim minority had declared themselves to be politically neutral? In Sierra Leone the numerical strength of Muslims is less clear. Are they a minority or are they over 50%? What is clear is that Sierra Leone elected its first Muslim President in 1996 - Ahmed Tejan Kabba. Once again the question arises whether Sierra Leone would have had its first elected Muslim president in 1996 if the Muslims of the country had declared themselves politically neutral? (President Kabba's fortunes have had ups and downs in that militarily troubled country).

The fourth largest concentration of Muslims in the world is a minority in a largely non-Muslim country in the world. This is the minority of some 100 million Muslims in the Republic of India. They are fourth numerically after the populations of Indonesia, Pakistan, and Bangladesh (others have argued that Indian Muslims are second numerically).

One of the factors which have influenced most political parties in India to be tolerant towards Muslims has been the voting leverage and participation of this 12% of the population. Had Indian Muslims opted out of politics completely Indian Muslims would have been more marginalized and perhaps even more victimized than ever.

The following distinctions need to be made concerning Muslims and U.S. laws:

Can Muslims live in the United States without obeying U.S. Laws? - Can they refuse to pay U.S. taxes, even if the taxes are not remotely Islamic?

Can Muslims become U.S. citizens without allegiance to the U.S. Constitution which is not Islamic?

Can Muslims insist that their money should not be used in wars against Muslim countries abroad?

Since Muslims in America cannot long endure without obeying U.S. laws, should they not try to influence the process of making those laws? Voting for Members of Congress and for the President constitutes part of the process of influencing the making of those laws - and not merely obeying the laws. Even those militant opponents of Muslim voting in U.S. elections do obey U.S. laws.

The Third domain is not merely Muslims voting but also Muslims running for office. This would be a process of Muslim empowerment.

If elected, Muslims would not only be more directly affecting the making of the laws. The Muslims would also be influencing the implementation of the laws and their enforcement. Overtime the judicial and legal system of the United States would become more sensitized to the Muslim experience and related issues.

The central underlying question is that once American Muslims have recognized that they have to obey the laws of the United States, almost all of which have nothing to do with the Shari'a, the next question is whether Muslims should strategize to help influence the making of those laws and their implementation in the hope of making those laws more sensitive to the multicultural and multi-religious nature of the population of the United States.

Fifthly, there is the nagging question: If Muslims cannot be voters in the United States; can they even be lawyers or legal consultants? Do opponents of Muslims voting in U.S. elections have sons or daughters training to become U.S. lawyers?

If it is haram to be a voter in a U.S. election, is it ten times haram to be trained as an expert in U.S. law and practicing it? Is a Muslim-American lawyer who is devoting his or her time defending Muslim clients committing at least a double haram?

On the other hand, if we concede that Muslims may become attorneys and lawyers in the United States, why should not Muslims become voters also? Voting is connected with law at many different stages and in many different respects.

What we have here is the complex inter-relationship between law-making (legislature), law interpretation (the judiciary), and law implementation (the executive). Voting is part of the process of choosing who makes these laws, who interprets them, and who implements them. The logic of the legal process is intertwined with the logic of the electoral process.

The logic of saying that it is haram to seek to influence law- making in the United States would make it haram to have Muslim lawyers practicing under U.S. law. It would also make it close to haram to obey the laws of the land. Such advice would be dangerous indeed for a Muslim minority living almost anywhere in a primarily non-Muslim country.

The conclusion to be drawn is that it is to the unmistakable advantage (maslaha) of a Muslim minority to seek ways of influencing governance in the direction of greater enlightenment.

Muslims located in the United States have additional obligations since they are geographically located in the most powerful country in the world - with an immense capacity to either harm or benefit the rest of the ummah world-wide.

The United States can either do such positive things as helping Afghanistan get rid of Soviet occupation or do such negative things as bombing Khartoum and Tripoli when there is suspicion of so-called Sudanese and Libyan "terrorism".

The United States can either look the other way or let Iran arm Bosnian Muslims against Serbian genocide or the United States can pass illegal legislation penalizing Third countries for trading with Iran and Libya.

American Muslims need to be active enough to monitor and influence American policy not only in domestic affairs but also in foreign affairs. The self-denial of voting power by some U.S. Muslims is an exercise in political castration.

Had the United States in the 20th century had very few Jewish citizens, the history of Israel and the Middle East would have been vastly different. Without a large and powerful Jewish lobby within the United States, U.S. generosity towards Israel would probably have substantially evaporated. At the very minimum the United States would have spent less money on arming Israel, used fewer vetoes to defend Israel at the United Nations, been more attentive to Palestinian and Arab concerns, and been more publicly critical of Israeli atrocities. Jewish activism in U.S. politics produced pro-Jewish results.

American Muslims may never equal the power of the Jews in the U.S. system, but the Muslims may one day help provide some counterbalance in policy-formation.

Muslim participation and empowerment within the U.S. political system is therefore vital not only for the sake of Muslims themselves but also for the sake of the wider ummah world wide, and for the sake of enriching the pluralism and global representative ness of American civilization.

Muslim Community Now

Islam in America is wider, deeper and more diverse than ever in its history, and Muslims are poised to bring their faith, politics and culture into the mainstream of national life, according to a new, comprehensive study, "The Mosque in America: A National Portrait."

The study, scheduled to be released today, is based on a scientific sampling of all 1,209 U.S. mosques — from lavish new suburban complexes to storefront and university student centers — and lengthy interviews with mosque leadership. It was conducted by a consortium of academic and Islamic groups, coordinated by Hartford Seminary Institute for Religious Research.

Researchers have compared the new portrait of mosques with a similar study in 1994. Some key findings:

- The number of mosques has increased 25%, from 962 in 1994 to 1,209 in 2000.
- Average mosque attendance at Friday prayers has nearly doubled, up 94% from 150 to 292.
- Most have an ethnic diversity unmatched in Christian and Jewish congregations, with 90% of mosques reporting a mix of South Asian, African-American, Arab and other groups born in the USA and abroad worshiping together.

- There may be more than 6 million Muslims in America today, researchers calculate, based on 2 million people who are formally affiliated with mosques, up from 500,000. They attribute the growth primarily to immigration.

But the most newsworthy finding is the determination of Muslims to make mosques "the platform for full participation in American life," says Ihsan Bagby, co-chairman of the research committee. "The Muslim community is maturing and coming into its own."

"We found that 90% of mosque leaders said yes, Muslims should become involved in American society and in the political process. I thought they would be more reticent. Because mosque leadership is still primarily based on immigrants, I thought they would be more socially and politically conservative than the general public," says Bagby, of Shaw University in Raleigh, N.C.

"Mosques today are not only centers for spirituality, they are also bases for political and social mobilization, focal points for Muslim life in a way they may not have been in more traditional Islamic societies," says Nihad Awad, executive director of the Council on American-Islamic Relations, one of the study sponsors with Hartford, the Islamic Society of North America and the Muslim American Society.

"Muslims believe that by involvement with the larger society, they can do service to America," Awad says, citing last year, when mosques conducted their biggest and most visible voter registration drive.

"We have a local face now. We can begin to break down animosity and fear as people see this is a godly religion, a comprehensive way of life and a diverse community committed to equality," Awad says.

Look for new voices in schools, workplaces and voting booths, says David Roozen of Hartford Seminary, which led an overview study on American congregations, "Faith Communities Today."

"Increasingly, they are going to be claiming a place in the public square. They still see themselves as an 'out' group rather than a 'core' group in American life right now, but that is going to change as they move into positions where they can assert their heritage."

It's a red-white-and-blue pattern in American history as each immigrant group has developed a congregational, organizational life different from their home countries, Roozen says. Their houses of worship are "more than just houses of prayer, but centers for a whole range of fellowship and community programs just as the German Lutherans, the Irish and Italian Catholics and the Dutch Reform did in centuries before."

The Rev. Eileen Lindner, editor of the Yearbook of American & Canadian Churches, says the integration of Muslims in the mainstream will help break down stereotypes that she calls "ruinous and silly." As American perceptions of Islam change, "we are heading toward true religious pluralism."

8

Emergence of Islam in the African-American Community

Many African-Americans view Christianity as the White man's religion and associate conversion to Islam with recovering their ethnic heritage. Thus, to effectively evangelize African-American Muslims, it is crucial to understand the development of the American Muslim movement. The following study examines the rise of the movement and traces its history and theological development. Muslims make up about 6% of the population in the United States. The majority of conversions to this growing religion are occurring within the African-American community (a little over 11% of America's population).

Theological Vacuum

Like the struggle for freedom and dignity, historic African-American theology developed along two streams, northern and southern. In both cases an over-arching Biblical pattern and theme (paradigm) developed for doing ministry. Of course, like all other Bible-believing communities, the historic African-American church preached Christ crucified and risen, as well as the doctrine of salvation by grace through faith. The ministry paradigm came in the way the church worked out and applied its faith to the surrounding community.

In the ante-bellum South where slavery was king, the theological paradigm was 'Exodus'. The slaves identified with the children of Israel in Egyptian bondage and saw the hand of God at work in terms of their hope in deliverance from slavery. This theology addressed the issues of survival, refuge and resistance to oppression. In the ante-bellum North where slavery died out, the theological paradigm was the 'Exile'. The freedmen saw the hand of God at work in terms of a special calling they sensed to bring the gospel of Christ to the rest of the 'African Diaspora', people of African descent living in the South, Canada, the Caribbean, and Africa. Had it fully developed, this would have been a theology addressing the issues of dignity, African identity, and global significance.

With the official end of slavery in 1865, the former slaves were devastated and confused about their identity in the economy of God. Yet the indigenous African-American church experienced explosive growth. A major contributing factor was the fact that the church in the North and the South adequately addressed the need for a true identity. This was achieved when the church adopted the Northern 'exilic' theological paradigm. They called it 'Pan-Africanism'. Under this banner the African-American church became actively involved in cultural and economic development in the United States and in missions, especially in Africa.

However, three events radically altered the theological direction of the African-American church. They were 1) the end of the post-Civil War Reconstruction in the South in 1877, 2) the Industrial Revolution in the North, and 3) the consolidation of European colonialism in Africa as the result of the Congress of Berlin (1878) and the Conference of Berlin (1884-85).

With the end of Reconstruction in the South, the former slaves were subject to racist terrorism and intimidation as White supremacy was re-established. Concurrent with the industrial revolution in the North was a massive wave of European immigration. This led to the rise of the White-only trade unions. The result was the elimination of African-Americans from the skilled labor force.

The consolidation of colonialism in Africa decimated the missions' movement of the African-American church. These traumas forced the church to abandon the Pan-African approach to ministry and revert to the old survival approach which had emerged in the context of slavery. This created a theological vacuum in the areas of dignity, African identity, and global significance.

Several non-Christian attempts were made to fill this vacuum. Among them was 1. W. E. B. Dubois and his advocacy of solidarity through education 2. A few Black Jewish sects 3. Marcus Garvey and the United Negro Improvement Association (U.N.I.A.) and 4. Several Black Nationalist oriented Islamic sects.

A Religion of Separatism

The first actual African-American Muslim sect was the Moorish Science Temple Divine and National Movement of North America, founded in Newark, New Jersey by Timothy Drew (Noble Drew Ali) in 1913. In 1925, the name of the sect was changed to the Moorish Temple of Science. Drew Ali developed the 'Koran of the Moorish Holy Temple of Science' and taught that Allah had ordained him as his prophet to the dark people of America. Ali stated that Negro and Black signified death and Colored signified something painted. Therefore, the terms Asiatic, Moor or Moorish-American must be used. Ali taught that salvation was found by discovering national origin and refusing to be called Negro, Black, Colored, Ethiopian, etc.

Noble Drew Ali died in 1929, and two of his disciples claimed to be his reincarnation and heir to the leadership of the sect. The first of these disciples was Sheik Timothy

Givins El who established a faction called Moorish Temple of Science headquartered in Chicago, Illinois. In 1975, Grand Sheik Richardson Dingle-El founded a splinter group and reverted to the original name.

The second of these disciples was Wali D. Fard, a mysterious White man of Turkish origins, also known as Aka Wali Fard Muhammad. Fard established the Temple of Islam headquartered in Detroit, Michigan. He appeared in the Paradise Valley of Detroit, declaring him to be the leader of the Nation of Islam. He claimed to have remedies for the social and economic problems facing Americans of African descent. He asserted that he had come to gain freedom, justice, and equality for them.

Fard made his living peddling silks and other artifacts door to door, presenting them as African. In this way, Fard gained access to African-American homes and began propagating his doctrine. Since his audience was familiar with the Bible, he used it as a springboard for his teachings. He then slowly introduced them to the text of the Quran. Fard's message was this Christianity is a tool in the hands of the White slave masters to control the minds of Black people. White people are devils, the embodiment of evil. The only hope for Black people in America is total separation and self-reliance. Between 1930 and 1933, Fard recruited 8,000 followers among Detroit Blacks. As a result of the organization's rapid growth, Fard found it necessary to train several ministers to help him. Among these was an unemployed auto worker named Robert Poole.

As the son of a Baptist minister, Poole knew the Bible quite well. Poole, later known as Elijah Muhammad, became the chief minister of the Temple of Islam and Fard's eventual successor. In 1932, Elijah Muhammad moved to Chicago and founded Temple #2. However, he returned to Detroit to aid Fard, who had been imprisoned. Later, Fard joined Elijah Muhammad at Temple #2 in Chicago, but he was soon arrested there as well. Under the pressure of continued conflict with police, Fard eventually mysteriously disappeared.

Later, the Temple of Islam divided into two factions. One faction, led by Abdul Muhammad, believed that Fard was a prophet of Allah and kept the name Temple of Islam. The most prominent faction was the Chicago-based Nation of Islam led by Elijah Muhammad. He believed that Fard was Allah in person. Eventually, Abdul Muhammad's faction was reabsorbed into the Nation of Islam.

Elijah Muhammad expounded his doctrine in the book Message to the Black Man in America. Fard's disappearance made his image as a Christ-figure more marketable. Also, Muhammad used his familiarity with the Scriptures to present Fard as the fulfillment of prophecy. 'You must forget about ever seeing the return of Jesus who was here 2000 years ago. Set your heart on seeing the one that he said would come at the end of the present world's time (the White race's time). He is called the 'Son of Man', the 'Christ', the 'Comforter.'' Muhammad argued that Jesus did not know the day or the hour of the coming of the Son of Man (Matthew 2436), thus he could not have been predicting his own return. Muhammad asserted that Fard was the Mahdi spoken of in the Quran.

Elijah Muhammad taught that the ultimate solution to the problem facing the African-American community was total separation from White society and the establishment of a Black Muslim state somewhere in North America or elsewhere. Furthermore, Muhammad taught that integration was a hypocritical and deceptive offer. Its intention was to deceive Black people into believing the opponents of freedom, justice, and equality were now their friends. Elijah Muhammad despised the Christian doctrine of loving one's enemy. In fact, his thinking concurred with W. D. Fard's hostile view of Christianity. Moreover, he saw the Black preacher as the greatest impediment to the progress of the Black race.

The allegation that 'Christianity' had been used to subjugate Black people is undeniable. Although the Quakers opposed slavery early on, staging the first anti-slavery demonstration in 1688, most churches either defended slavery, ignored it, or were divided over the issue. In light of this fact, the teachings of Elijah Muhammad fell upon eager ears. He was preaching to people who were waiting for a claim to dignity and self-sufficiency, as well as for spiritual fulfillment. He convinced them that the answers to their problems were found only in Islam.

A New Theology

Elijah Muhammad's teachings were by no means orthodox Islam. He taught that Allah was a man, W. D. Fard, whom he knew personally. He taught that Black people created and owned the universe and founded the city of Mecca. He also taught that a mad scientist named Yacub created the White race 6000 years ago.

According to Muhammad, Yacub was an exile from Mecca. He determined to take revenge on Allah and on those who exiled him and his 59,999 followers to the island of Patmos. Hence, through crude genetic engineering, he created a race of white devils. After Yacub's death, this devil race returned to Arabia. They began to turn the peaceful society into a hell torn by quarreling and fighting. They were eventually exiled to Europe and penned in to keep them from spreading.

Muhammad also asserted that there are 24 scientists who rule the universe and write a prophetic book of history prior to each 25,000 years. They predicted Yacub would create this race of devils, who would rule the earth for 6000 years. According to Elijah Muhammad, those 6000 years are over. The battle of Armageddon between Blacks and

Whites, Muslims and Christians is about to occur.

For the most part, Elijah Muhammad was preaching to uneducated people, unfamiliar with Islam. Just as he twisted passages of the Bible to suit his purpose, he concocted a version of Islam to address what he saw were the needs of Black Americans. The appeal of his new religion was its emphasis on Black self-awareness, self-sufficiency, and the promise that God was on the side of African-Americans in their struggle against racial oppression in America.

The Appeal of the Movement

A demographic study of Black Muslims by C. Eric Lincoln revealed some startling insights into who responded to Elijah Muhammad's message. The majority of those who joined the Nation of Islam were young, economically disadvantaged, African-American males from Christian backgrounds. Up to 80% of a typical congregation was between the ages of 17 and 35. Traditionally, the church in the Black community has had difficulty attracting young males. In an article entitled, 'Why Most Black Men Won't Go to Church,' Reverend William Harris attributes the primary reason to economics.

'Many Black males won't go to church because today's church does not address their needs. The Black male needs money, job opportunities, business resources, and relevant skills training. The church collects money, but does little to create opportunities through which he can make more money. Jesus understood the need to feed people before preaching to them. Today's church must likewise set the table for the Black man before asking him to pay to have the dishes done.

Elijah Muhammad's program for economic development played a crucial role in the rapid growth of the Nation of Islam. With the money donated by members,

Muhammad purchased land for farms, store fronts, bakeries, apartment buildings and schools. The economic base of the organization grew in proportion to numerical growth. By owning businesses and land, Elijah Muhammad was able to provide both housing and employment for needy followers. Furthermore, the members had the added pride of sharing in the ownership of these various enterprises and being, to a great extent, independent of the broader society. Scarcity of employment for young Black males offers one explanation of why they were drawn to the Nation of Islam in such large numbers.

Men were also drawn to the Nation of Islam because of the emphasis placed on male leadership. African-American churches tend to be dominated by women, with one central male figure, the pastor in the pulpit. As a result, many men do not feel affirmed in the church environment. They see the pastor as a threat and even a rival. Elijah Muhammad was able to criticize the Black male while affirming his role. Thus he challenged men to take the lead, and they responded. 'Unlike the typical Christian church, the Muslim temples attract many more men than women, and men assume the full management of temple affairs. Women are honored and they perform important functions within a defined role.'

The role of women consists of teaching other women and managing the affairs of the home. Ironically, women were also attracted to the Nation of Islam because they appreciated the strength of the men and the protective posture they took towards Black women. As C. Eric Lincoln noted in his research, the Nation of Islam appeals to the young regardless of gender.

'A surprising number of young people are attracted by the Muslims' redefinition of the roles men and women should play in the home and in the religious life of the sect. There is a strong emphasis on the equality of individuals irrespective of sex, but each sex is assigned a role considered proper for it. The trend in our larger society seems to be towards blurring the distinct line between the traditional social roles of men and women. The Muslims, on the other hand, claim to have restored the women to a place of dignity and respect...Muslim women seem to welcome the security and protection implicit in this arrangement....Children seem to profit most, for among Muslim children, delinquency is unheard of.'

Among people who were not accustomed to the security of a strong nuclear family with well-defined roles, the Nation of Islam provided welcomed structure. The underlying message of the Nation was that the disorder they had experienced up until then had been caused by outside forces beyond their control, evil influences they were now to avoid at all cost.

'Muslim women particularly are forbidden contact with either sex of the White race, on the theory that, 1) 'no White man has honorable intentions toward any Black women', and 2) White women are immoral by nature. White women are said to corrupt the minds of Black women, who then try to imitate them by 'displaying their bodies, neglecting their children and abandoning their men'.

Just as Adolf Hitler salved the consciences of the Germans by blaming the Jews for all their economic and political woes, Elijah Muhammad found in the White race the source of every ill within the Black community, especially with regard to the family. Thus the causes for the growth of the movement were both economic and psychological.

Dynamic Young Spokesman

The greatest period of growth in the Nation of Islam cannot be directly attributed to Elijah Muhammad. In 1948, while serving a prison sentence in Massachusetts, a young man by the name of Malcolm Little became acquainted with the teachings of Elijah Muhammad and was converted. Upon release from prison, Malcolm Little, a former pimp, drug pusher, armed robber, and numbers man, returned to Detroit and began aggressively recruiting for Detroit Temple #1. He received recognition for his efforts from Elijah Muhammad, who changed his name to Malcolm X. 'X' symbolized his original African name, which he never knew, and replaced the slave master's name, Little. This individual bearing the name 'X' would soon make both the name and organization it represented a symbol of freedom for some and fear for others.

Malcolm X frequently visited Elijah Muhammad in his home in Chicago to talk for hours. Because of his aggressive recruiting, new ideas and unyielding devotion to Elijah Muhammad, Malcolm was appointed as national spokesman. 'He was crisscrossing North America, sometimes as often as four times a week. From Detroit, Malcolm was sent to organize Temple #11. In March 1954, Malcolm moved from Boston to Philadelphia, and in three months Temple #12 was opened....From Philadelphia, Malcolm moved to New York City and became minister of Temple #7. In fact, Malcolm X was instrumental in the establishment of most of the temples in North America, and he took credit for the increase in membership from 400 to 40,000 that occurred within a few years after he joined the Nation of Islam.

Even today, Malcolm X looms larger than life in the African-American quest for the elusive prize of freedom and dignity. He attracted tens of thousands with his emphasis on cultural concerns, discipline, solidarity of the brotherhood, and African identity. It seems these factors will continue to be a strong draw for young African-American males in the foreseeable future. It is also unlikely that the church will make any significant headway among these young men until it addresses these concerns. The Bible more than adequately addresses these issues, and it is time for Christians to apply God's word.

The Hanafis

In 1950, Khalifa Hamaas Abdul Khaalis (Ernest T. McGee) joined the Nation of Islam in an attempt to bring the sect into line with orthodox Sunni Islam. By 1956, he had become national secretary. His efforts proved unsuccessful, so in 1958, he broke with Elijah Muhammad and founded the Al-Hanif, Hanafi, Madh-Hob Center, Islam Faith, United States of America, and American Mussulmans. Based in Washington DC, the Hanafis still adhere to the basic tenets of Sunni Islam.

The Hanafi Muslims gained notoriety in 1973 when five members of the Philadelphia Nation of Islam brutally murdered seven Hanafis, including five members of Khalifa Hamaas Abdul Khaalis' immediate family. Again in 1977, the Hanafis captured national headlines when they tried to stop the screening of the movie Mohammed Messenger of God. They did this by seizing three buildings in Washington, D.C., the District Building (City Hall), the B'nai B'rith Building and the Islamic Center. They took several hostages. Several were injured and one was killed. Khalifa Hamaas Abdul Khaalis was sentenced to 21 to 120 years for his role in these seizures.

The Five Percenters

Clarence 13X was a member in the Nation of Islam's Temple #7. He began to teach that the Black man was the god of the universe and had his origins in Mecca. His iconoclastic teachings resulted in his suspension from the Nation of Islam. In 1964, he founded the 'Five Percent Nation of Islam'. In 1969, Clarence 13X died of suspicious causes. Those who followed him referred to him as 'Father Allah'.

The Five Percenters agree with Elijah Muhammad's teaching that the White man is the devil. However, they also include all unscrupulous and deceitful people in this category, regardless of color. They believe that the Black race was the original race and the creator of civilization. For the Five Percenters, the demographics of the African-American community break down as follows:

Eighty-five percent- the masses who are ignorant of true 'divine self', 10% - the corrupt rulers over the 85% and 5% - the truly righteous followers of Father Allah

The Five Percenters are very influential in today's youth pop culture. Many of the most influential 'Rap' artists today are Five Percenters. Among the rappers who propagate the doctrine of the Five Percenters are King Sun, The Supreme Team, Lakim Shabazz, Rakim Allah, Brand Nubian and The Poor Righteous Teachers.

Malcolm on His Own

With his platform as national spokesman, Malcolm X became an international figure. He was a coveted lecturer at universities, mosques and churches throughout the country. He recruited new leaders to the Nation. He even had a profound influence upon Elijah Muhammad's son, Wallace D. Muhammad (also known as Warith D. Muhammad). For many other leaders of the movement, however, Malcolm was gaining too much prominence too quickly. Many began to view him as a threat to Elijah Muhammad's leadership. He frequently made statements that went beyond the teachings of Elijah Muhammad and was often reprimanded.

There were those within the Nation of Islam who believed that Malcolm was trying to build a financial empire for himself. They began to leave him out of every edition of Muhammad Speaks, the organization's newspaper. Ironically, it was Malcolm who was instrumental in creating the paper. Aware of the controversy surrounding him, Malcolm began refusing interviews. He frequently told reporters, 'Please use Mr. Muhammad's picture instead of mine'.

The tension reached its apex when Elijah Muhammad was implicated by two former secretaries in a paternity suit. Disillusioned, Malcolm X began searching the Bible and Quran for some prophetic explanation for what was happening. This he did with the help of Warith D. Muhammad. He then conducted his own investigation into the allegations, and finally questioned Elijah Muhammad himself. 'I'm David', Elijah Muhammad replied. 'When you read in the Bible how David took another man's wife, I'm David....You read about Lot who went and laid up with his own daughter. I have fulfilled all those things. Malcolm's directness in questioning the 'messenger of Allah' was perceived as overstepping his bounds.

Shortly after that incident, President Kennedy was assassinated. Elijah Muhammad commanded all ministers of the Nation of Islam to refrain from commenting on Kennedy's death. However, when asked his opinion of the assassination, Malcolm X replied, 'I saw it as a case of the chickens coming home to roost'. Warith D. Muhammad and Malcolm X were subsequently suspended from the Nation of Islam. Reflecting upon that time, Warith remarked, 'I was charged with trying to influence Malcolm's theological thinking. I was also charged with giving him personal, private knowledge of the Honorable Elijah Muhammad's living, which was a lie'.

Actually, Warith D. Muhammad did have an effect on Malcolm X's theological views. Both men began to lean more toward orthodox Islam. The more Warith read the writings of W. D. Fard, the more he questioned his father's claim to be the 'messenger of Allah'. Warith and Malcolm both concluded that Fard could not have been Allah himself.

Malcolm's ideas were further broadened by his travels. He went on the Hajj and changed his name to El-Hajj Malik El Shabazz. He met with various African leaders and discussed the conditions in their respective countries. Malcolm's ideological shift was drastic. His intention was to broaden his scope from American Black nationalism to global human rights. He intended to take the case of racism in the United States before the United Nations for action.

On March 8, 1964, while still on suspension, Malcolm X announced that he was leaving the Nation of Islam and forming his own organization. Actually, he started two organizations, Muslim Mosque Incorporated (MMI) and the Organization of Afro-American Unity (OAAU). MMI was based upon the principles of orthodox Islam. OAAU was an all Black, non-sectarian organization dedicated to creating a society where Blacks and Whites could live in brotherhood. Malcolm contended that Black/White brotherhood could not occur until Black people themselves were united. At that stage Black and White coalitions would be possible. He encouraged Whites to fight racism and was willing to accept aid from White donors.

However, Malcolm's new vision didn't have a chance to take root. On February 21, 1965, Malcolm X was assassinated. He was speaking to a group of about 500 people in the Audubon Ballroom in New York City. Several gunmen opened fire on him from the third row. Three former members of the Nation of Islam were convicted of the crime. One of them, Talmadge Hayer, confessed and implicated the other two. Later he claimed that these two men were innocent, but that four active members of the Nation of Islam had actually helped him.

New Leader with New Ideas

After a series of suspensions, Warith D. Muhammad was restored to the Nation of Islam in 1969. His father, Elijah Muhammad, restored him to ministry in 1974, giving him freedom to preach what he pleased. On February 25, 1975, Elijah Muhammad died of congestive heart failure. The following day the Nation held its annual Savior's Day Rally in honor of Elijah Muhammad. There they pronounced Warith D. Muhammad as the new leader. W. D. Fard had actually chosen Warith before he was born, by predicting that Elijah Muhammad's next child would be a boy and would succeed his father.

Under the leadership of Warith D. Muhammad, the former Nation of Islam has become an orthodox community of Sunni Muslims. From the moment he took over as leader, he sought to align the doctrine of the organization with the Quran. He did away with Elijah Muhammad's doctrine of racial separation. He struggled to dismantle the cult-like structure. He also restored Malcolm X to a position of honor, naming a mosque after him. Warith began honoring the Constitution and encouraging participation in the political process. Most of the real estate holdings were quickly sold off. He redefined W.D. Fard as a 'wise man', and began to teach the five pillars of orthodox Islam. The name of the organization was changed to the Bilillian Community and later to the World Community Al-Islam in the West (WCIW). Although Warith opened the WCIW to people of all races, its membership remained predominantly Black. They continue to be known as Bilillians. Billal was an Ethiopian Muslim who was born in circa in 600 AD. Billal was so firm in his convictions that when punished by his slave master after refusing to denounce Islam, he cried, 'Ahad, Ahad' (One, only one God).

Imam Warith D. Muhammad made greater attempts to foster better relations with the United States government and foreign Islamic governments. His most comprehensive changes were in the realm of the family and the roles of women. In a 1979 interview with Clifton Marsh, Warith D. Muhammad explained some of his views on women in Islam. 'Women in the Nation of Islam had a subordinate role to men. Warith D. Muhammad has changed that role, and in many cases, women are placed over men in administrative roles'. The new structure in the WCIW does not make distinctions based on sex. In the mind of the imam, there was no religious justification for such rigid divisions between men and women. Imam Muhammad studied the role of women in Arabia during the time of the prophet Muhammad. He concluded that the right of women to equal education was protected under Islamic law. He justified the new status of women in the WCIW by saying, 'We cannot make any distinction between men and women in terms of intelligence, spirituality or moral nature. Women are equal to men and they are not to be treated any differently'.

Girls' training courses were changed from home economics to general intellectual development. Women were free to seek employment outside of the home. 'I have looked at the role of women...in the light of what the prophet Muhammad did, to give more freedom, more equality to women'. He noted that women at the time of the prophet owned businesses, employed men, and had equal rights to education. He added that if women pursue higher education, 'how can we expect them to stay home? What is all this education for? You can't keep her at home nursing babies'. This new teaching was a radical departure from the teachings of the Nation of Islam. It also deviated from the traditional expression of Islam in the Middle East.

When asked where he saw the WCIW in the year 2000, Imam Muhammad replied, 'I hope Muslims will be so comfortable in America that they won't have to introduce any structure or anything, just be American Muslims'. This vision has been fulfilled. The structure of the WCIW continued to diminish in scope. The name of the sect was changed to the American Muslim Mission. Their publication The American Muslim Journal was discontinued in 1984. The group was decentralized and absorbed into a larger body of Muslims in 1985, and Warith D. Muhammad became recognized as an Islamic leader by Muslim people of all national origins.

The Old Time Religion

In 1970, toward the closing years of Elijah Muhammad's leadership, a splinter group broke with the Nation of Islam and founded Calistron. This first group saw the need to be more nationalistic than the parent group. However, by 1980, Calistron had disintegrated.

In spite of the restructuring which took place under Warith Muhammad, four reactionary factions within the Bilillian Community remained. They resisted the changes and held to the doctrine of Elijah Muhammad, 'the old time religion'.

The leader of the second splinter group was Silas Muhammad. In 1976 he broke with Warith Muhammad and founded the Lost, Found Nation of Islam. He restored all of Elijah Muhammad's myths and teachings.

The leader of the third splinter group was a former national spokesman for the WCIW, Louis Adul Farrakhan. Farrakhan broke with Warith Muhammad in December of 1977. He now refers to himself as the national spokesman for the Honorable Elijah Muhammad. His Black separatist organization first used the name Original Nation of Islam, but is now also known as the Nation of Islam. Minister Farrakhan has received a great deal of media attention for his inflammatory statements. Reporters continue to ask Mr. Farrakhan about his alleged anti-Semitism. In reality, the doctrine to which Farrakhan subscribes classifies all White people, Jews and Gentiles, as devils.

The leader of the fourth splinter group was John Muhammad. In 1978 he broke with Warith Muhammad and founded another Nation of Islam. The leader of the fifth splinter group was Caliph Emanuel. In 1978 he broke with Warith Muhammad and founded yet another Nation of Islam.

Other Islamic Groups

Some Islamic groups sprang up without growing out of the Moorish Temple of Science. Among them are the Ahmadiyya Movement in Islam, USA and the Nubian Islamic Hebrews. The Nubians generally address themselves to issues of African-American identity, while the Ahmadiyya generally do not.

The Ahmadiyya Movement itself started in India in 1889. Its founder, Mirza Ghulam Ahmad, saw himself as the Madhi (the Messianic savior of Islam). His aim was to bring reformation and revival to Islam. Ahmad's beliefs were expressed in his book Barahim-i-Ahmadtah. Dr. Mufti Muhammad Sadiq brought the Ahmadiyya movement to the United States in 1921.

Muhammad's original intention was to convert Islamic immigrants to the movement, but he experienced great success among African-Americans. In terms of evangelism, the Ahmadiyyas are among the most aggressive Islamic denomination. Because of Mirza Ghulam Ahmad's claim to be the Madhi, the Ahmadiyyas are not regarded as truly Islamic by orthodox sects. The Nubian Islamic Hebrews were founded in New York City in 1970 by Muhammad Ahmed ibn Abd'ullah. He was Sudanese and his followers believed him to be the Khaliyfa, the expected successor to the prophet Muhammad.

The Nubian Islamic Hebrews believe that the origin of the Nubian [Black] race goes back to Adam and Eve [Hawwah]. They have developed their own twist on 'the curse of Ham myth'. For them, Ham tried to commit sodomy with his drunk and naked father, Noah. The result was Noah's curse upon Canaan, which turned his skin pale. Thus the Canaanites became the father of all pale-skinned races. Some Nubians intermarried with the outcast children of Canaan and produced the Chinese, East Indians, Eskimos, Indonesians, Japanese, Koreans, Malayans, Pakistanis, and Sicilians. Though these races are mixed, they are regarded as Black.

The Nubian Islamic Hebrews also believe that two additional nations came from Ibraahiym [Abraham]. They were the descendants of Ishmael (the Ishmaelites) and the decedents of Isaac (the Israelites). Like the Israelites who were in Egyptian bondage, the Ishmaelites were held in American bondage for over 400 years. Out of this experience came the Nubians [Black people] of North America and the Caribbean. Because of their parallel experience with the Israelites, the American Nubians consider themselves to be Hebrews.

They believe that the beginning of their sect in 1970 was the opening of the seventh seal in Revelation 81. Basically the theology of the Nubian Islamic Hebrews is a mix of Christian, Islamic, and Jewish beliefs. Their current leader is As Siddid Al Imaan, Isa Al Haahi Al Madhi, the great-grandson of the founder Muhammad Ahmed ibn Abd'ullah.

The Present Situation

Today the Islamic sects are all challenging the African-American church for the minds of the next generation. Because of Islam's emphasis on external religious practices, African-American adherents tend to operate on their internal instincts, which are essentially Christian. If the church takes the Muslim challenge seriously and theologically addresses the issues of dignity, African identity and global significance, then there is the potential of a great harvest among these Muslims. If the church fails to take the challenge seriously, then the Muslim presence will become a Muslim dominance and this will be a scourge upon the church.

9

The Islamic Movement in Israel

On the eve of the High Holidays in Israel in September 1999, just days after the Sharm al-Sheikh accord was signed by Israel and the Palestinians to relaunch the peace process between them, two car-bombs exploded in the northern cities of Haifa and Tiberias, injuring innocent passers-by. Within days, the Israeli security authorities had arrested six Israeli Arabs, all affiliated with the northern faction of the Islamic Movement in Israel, who were apparently recruited by Hamas in the West Bank for the purpose of wrecking both the accord and the Jewish holidays.

Tensions in Nazareth

The radicalization of Muslims in Israel may also be seen in the tensions making headlines in the Arab city of Nazareth in the Galilee. On December 21, 1997, just four days before Christmas, Muslim zealots in Nazareth invaded the plaza at the foot of the Basilica of the Annunciation, the major Christian shrine in the city. They fenced off an area, declared the land to be a holy Muslim endowment (wakf), and began to erect a mammoth tent as a provisional mosque prior to the construction of a permanent mosque with a planned 86-meter-tall minaret which would tower above the adjacent Christian shrine. Israeli authorities have sought to resolve the controversy by peaceful means, thus unwittingly consecrating the Muslim claim and complicating the resolution of the issue.

In November 1998, the local elections in Nazareth brought into office a city council dominated by the Islamic movement. The campaign had revolved around the controversy over the mosque, whose supporters won a majority of the vote. In addition, the present mayor, Ramez Jeraysi, is likely to be the last Christian mayor of the city. Jeraysi is a represen-ztative of the former communist Hadash party, and the Islamists are, by definition, anti-communist. Fur-thermore, as a result of the tensions surrounding the mosque, Jeraysi was physically attacked by assailants in mid-October 1999.

Just prior to the attack, the Israeli government approved the construction of a mosque of more modest size at the site, outraging Christians who warned that in response the pope may cancel his visit to Nazareth scheduled for Spring 2000.

In Nazareth, a Christian city during most of its history, the now outnumbered Christians appear to have lost confidence in their ability to maintain their long-standing coexistence with their Muslim neighbors, and many have left the city for neighboring Christian villages or other mixed Israeli cities where they can escape from Muslim hegemony. Others have immigrated from the country altogether, much like the Christians of Lebanon, Bethlehem, and other locations in the Muslim world. This is a sign that the Christian minority living in Israel believes that the Jewish state is either unable or unwilling to protect them any longer, or that the Israeli authorities, themselves menaced by mounting fundamentalist Islam, are more concerned with their own protection than they are with the plight of the Christians.

The trend is clear; Nazareth will soon become a Muslim city. Though it is part of Israel, and the government in

Jerusalem still wields some influence through its funding of the local government, major decisions are being made within an intensely Muslim ambiance with regard to the Christian holy places, urban priorities, city planning, and the position of non-Muslims in the community, casting a long shadow on the future of the remaining Christians. Perhaps now that the events of Nazareth, Haifa, and Tiberias have converged to illustrate the dangers that lay ahead, new measures will be required to meet the challenge of the Islamic movement in Israel.

A Million Muslim Israelis

While the Muslim population within Israel is now approaching one million, it is difficult to gauge the sentiments of this community. Most of its members embrace a quietist attitude toward Israel, enjoying the benefits they draw from their Israeli citizenship, and refraining from overt acts of disloyalty.

They are indeed on record as condemning the recent acts of violence by the Islamists, and are wary not to wreck the rather comfortable boat in which they find themselves. However, in contrast to the current misconception that they are "loyal" to their country, one should recall the near-consensus among them that shuns Independence Day celebrations in Israel and terms that day the nakbah (disaster).

They also side automatically with their Palestinian brethren in any confrontation with Israel, and express a growing desire for practical steps toward autonomy. The quietist majority among Muslims also identifies itself as Palestinian rather than Israeli, and regards itself as a national rather than an ethnic, linguistic, or religious minority in Israel. All of these perceptions and self-perceptions are pregnant with the potential for dissent, unrest, disobedience, and hostility, though they generally do not yet transcend the boundaries of legality.

The Worldview of Radical Islam

The range of cleavages between the Jewish majority and the Arab minority in Israel is often bridgeable by common language, economic interest, and neighborly relations. But Islamic fundamentalism, which has injected massive doses of Islamic symbolism into the Arab-Israeli dispute, has often lent to it a religio-cultural nature, thus turning it into a qualitatively insoluble dispute. In turn, Muslim fundamentalists in Israel, who would otherwise accept their minority status and adjust to the vagaries of life under a Jewish authority, once imbued with the general mode of thinking of other Muslim radicals, tend also to exacerbate their anti-Israeli rhetoric and attitudes.

The Arabs of Israel, even more than other Muslims who may feel resentment and frustration at their inability to retrieve the Holy Land of the Muslims with Jerusalem at its heart, sense in a more immediate fashion the humiliation of being ruled by an erstwhile dhimmi (inferior) people which had itself submitted to Islamic rule, and which had projected a questionable reputation and status in Islamic tradition. As pious Muslims, these Arabs cannot disregard the vehement anti-Israeli arguments advanced by masters of radical Islam all around them.

The Israeli Arabs felt thrust aside by Israeli society, which relegated them to something less than the accepted norms of equality in the country, and they also felt that they were looked upon suspiciously by other Palestinians because they were Israelis. For some, Islamization was the way out, not only in order to escape the margins and set themselves in the center stage, but also to signal to both the Israeli and Palestinian societies which had alienated them that they, together with other Palestinian fundamentalists in the West Bank and Gaza, constitute the core and the vanguard of the future. Indeed, after 1967, Arab Muslims in Israel began inviting renowned Palestinian clerics from those areas to deliver sermons in mosques, schools, and social gatherings. Thus, the ideologies of the Muslim Brothers and the Islamic Liberation Party of old were propagated among Israeli Arabs. Conversely, Israeli Muslims who attended Islamic institutions of higher learning in the territories went back to their communities in Israel imbued with the new Islamic revivalist spirit. These processes had an immediate impact on the Muslims in Israel: a massive return to Islam among the young in tandem with a similar trend in the West Bank and Gaza.

The Islamic movement among the Muslims in Israel has grown by leaps and bounds since the 1980s, and has by now imposed its presence not only culturally but also politically, both in intra-Arab and in Israeli national politics. Prior to the local elections of November 1998, the Islamic movement split between the southern faction headed by Sheikh Abdallah Darwish, the founder of the movement, who has opted for joining Israeli national politics, and the more radical northern faction led by Sheikh Ra'id Salah, the Mayor of Umm al-Fahm, who has chosen the course of isolating his constituents in Islamic enclaves within Israel and remains adamant in his support of Hamas and other fundamentalist Muslim movements. It is the northern faction which engendered the recent acts of terror, but one fears that the general atmosphere of violence created by those acts, and the high prestige which the perpetrators enjoy among their peers, might encourage others to join the circle of terror.

The recognized founder and spiritual leader of the movement is Sheikh Abdallah Nimr Darwish of Kafr Qassem. Outwardly, he and his disciples adopted the slogan of activity and change by peaceful means within the framework of law. Sheikh Ra'id Salah of Umm al-Fahm leads the more radical Islamists, who have split from the mainstream which remains under the aegis of Sheikh Abdallah.

A New Generation of Leaders

Umm al-Fahm, the hub of Muslim fundamentalism in Israel, owes its status to Sheikh Ra'id, a local youth who attended the Islamic College in Hebron in 1976, and after graduating in 1979 began roaming the country and preaching a return to Islamic values.

An Islamic organization was set up locally, as in other places, complemented by voluntary welfare associations which sought to step into the social and cultural vacuum left by the lack of involvement of the Israeli government in the township. The Islamic message had a tremendous appeal to unskilled laborers who worked in Tel Aviv and other Israeli urban centers, and underwent daily humiliation in their encounter with Israeli prosperity and cultural assertiveness. It also appealed to the youth who were seeking new avenues and new answers, and to professionals who were in search of new channels for their nationalism and new definitions for their identity. The movement also appealed to the rank and file who observed with admiration and pride the welfare, development, and cultural projects undertaken by the Muslim movement, led by Sheikh Ra'id.

Sheikh Abdallah, who appeared to represent the more conciliatory trend towards Israel, came to be upstaged by the younger and more militant sheikhs who now lent much more primacy to the hard-line Islamic position and came dangerously close to the Hamas line of argument, calling to substitute an Islamic state in the entire expanse of Palestine for the existing State of Israel. No longer confined to the three regional hubs of Umm al-Fahm, Kafr Qassem and Kafr Kanna, the Islamic movement has now also taken root in the mixed cities of Nazareth (with its sizable Christian population), Jaffa, and Acre (with a sizable Arab minority). Most spectacular were the gains of the movement among the Bedouins in the Negev, where an Islamist mayor was elected in Rahat in 1989.

It was precisely the young leaders of the movement, who were dipped in Western principles, studied in Israeli universities, and knew Israeli society, language, and culture well, who became the most radically opposed to it and veered toward an uncompromising Islamic fundamentalism. In the local elections of 1993, the Islamic movement further consolidated its position.

In addition to the six mayor ships gained previously by the movement, it added Islamist local councilors in many other villages and towns, including mixed councils where the Muslim population coexisted with non-Muslims.

Participation in Israeli National Elections

After the younger leaders were catapulted to power in the elections, they no longer depended for their status and reputation on the backing and confirmation of Abdallah Darwish. Therefore, the young and militant mayors led by Ra'id Salah, who drew their power and popularity directly from their electorate, could afford to bring to the fore their differences with the founder.

For example, before the Israeli national elections of 1992, Abdallah advocated participation of the movement in the Knesset race, while Ra'id was strictly opposed.

The ideological stakes were enormous. Unlike the local elections, in which the Muslim movement came to take control of several mayoralties, thus contributing to self-reliance and reinforcing the separateness of their communities from the Israeli mainstream, contesting in the national elections entailed three major doctrinal breaches. First, participation in the elections means acknowledging an acceptance of the rule of the non-Muslim majority; second, it entails a respect for the laws of Israel which every elected member of the Knesset swears to uphold in his inaugural oath; and third, it means recognition of Israel's sovereignty.

Furthermore, a Muslim is not supposed to respect and act according to secular laws made by humans, but follow the Shari'a, the law which emanates from Allah himself. Thus, when the Muslim movement in Israel participates in local elections and elects Islamic mayors, they do not need to swear allegiance to the State of Israel. Moreover, under Israeli law, local councils are entitled to adopt bylaws, for example, governing the separation of sexes at school or forbidding the sale and consumption of alcohol. From the fundamentalist point of view, this is not an enactment of law but merely an application of the law of Allah. However, participation in government at the national level would require acceptance of the secular laws of the Jewish state and behaving in accordance with them instead of cultivating a separate patrimony in isolation and segregation. Despite these convictions that are shared by all fundamentalists as a matter of principle, pragmatists like Sheikh Abdallah Darwish and some of his followers argued consistently for participation in national elections as the only way to bring pressure to bear on Israeli governments to respond to their particular needs.

This issue came to the fore on the eve of the national elections of 1996 and, coupled with personal ambition and other matters of contention, contributed to the split within the Islamic movement when the organs of the organization, controlled by Sheikh Abdallah, overwhelmingly supported the resolution to run for the Knesset. Sheikh Ra'id, and his fellow radical Sheikh Kamal Khatib from Kafr Kanna, rejected the resolution and, taking advantage of Abdallah's absence abroad, published a communique stating that the resolution did not apply to them. Many attempts to reconcile between the parties were made, but all in vain. Then, Sheikh Ra'id gathered his forces and declared the establishment of his own "Islamic movement," with an identical name as the mother-movement but evidently much more radical. Or is it?

The Question of Coexistence

The segregated environment that the fundamentalists have been creating around them in Israel is, by definition, a temporary step. With regard to the long-term solution to their plight, the Islamic movement entertains in its midst various points of view, some of which translated into a rift and then a schism. Some of these expressed views are ambiguous and sometimes they even consist of explicit statements of coexistence with and within the Jewish state. Others amount to veiled or even open threats of revolt and visions of establishing a Muslim state over all of Palestine.

To the pragmatists, coexistence permits the movement to organize, participate in the elections (local and national), inculcate their norms into their constituencies, champion Islamic causes, and at the same time maintain their segregation. By exploiting the means afforded to them by Israeli society, they are willing to play by the rules of democracy as long as this serves their purposes. Ultimately, at some undefined point in the future, they entertain the hope to replace the existing system with a new Islamic order. Those among them who speak about an "Islamic state in Palestine" seldom specify its boundaries, leaving open the possibility that it might encompass the entire territory, including Israel.

The pragmatists, who specifically prescribe a "Palestinian state alongside Israel," claim that in such a case they would prefer to continue to dwell in Israel as a Muslim minority. This has been, incidentally, the prevailing position among most Arabs in Israel, and it is not surprising that it should be so. For both the pragmatists and the radicals, and for that matter for all Israeli Arabs, the realization prevails that they are much freer in the Jewish state to express their views and implement them than in any neighboring Arab country. In most Arab countries, indeed, including "moderate" and "liberal" Egypt and Jordan,

Islamic parties as such cannot run for elections while in Israel they can and do. At any rate, an element of Palestinian-Muslim nationalism is implicitly enmeshed in the demand for a Palestinian state, although both currents officially negate nationalism as a matter of principle and view the ultimate solution in merging into the future revived caliphate of the universal Muslim umma (the community of all Muslims).

In the real world, however, like Hamas and other Muslim fundamentalists elsewhere, the Islamic movement in Israel has also been tinged with nationalist tendencies, except that in Israel, "nationalism" for the Arab minority does not mean Israeli nationalism but Arab nationalism, thereby raising the unresolved contradictions discussed above.

The radicals among the fundamentalists have little patience to wait in indolence, and they prefer to embrace the road of militant activism which, they believe, might hasten the attainment of those goals.

Demography of the Islamic Movement Sheikh Abdallah, who has recently distanced himself from the daily management of the Islamic movement but continues to command the respect of his followers as the supreme spiritual guide, enjoys the support of his own town, Kafr Qassem, whose mayor, Ibrahim Sarsur, is the spokesman for the movement; the neighboring village of Kafr Bara, with Mayor Kamal Rayan who began the political revolution of local Islamic rule in Israel; the Bedouins of Rahat in the Negev; the towns of Jaljulya and Kafr Qara; and the Islamists of the mixed cities of Lod, Ramle, Jaffa, Nazareth, and Acre. When this group ran in the national elections in 1996, it counted among its leadership two Knesset members - abd-al-Malek Dahamsheh of Kafr Kanna and Tawfiq Khatib of Jaljulya - who were reelected in 1999. To this group of leaders also belong Tayasir Masri, the mayor of Kafr Qara'; Jum'a Qasasi, a former mayor of Rahat;

and Suleyman abu-Ahmad, a member of the Nazareth city council.

The more radical group, founded and headed by Sheikh Ra'id, consists primarily of Umm al-Fahm, the largest Muslim town in Israel (with a population of some 30,000 as of 1997), some satellite villages around that town, and part of Kafr Kama under the leadership of Sheikh Kamal Khatib.

Nothing is more indicative of the thinking and ambitions of the two groups than their respective modus operandi. Abdallah Darwish focuses on parliamentary activity via the movement's Knesset members, and tirelessly labors for a rapprochement between Arabs and Jews in Israel. He also mediates in local conflicts and rifts between Israeli Arabs and has gained prestige in doing so as a man of peace and conciliation.

Yet the schism within the movement deprived Abdallah of the hub of Umm al-Fahm, where the printing house, the editorial offices of the weekly Sawt al-Haqq wal-Huriyya, the Islamic College, the Islamic Sports Association, the Islamic Association, and the Zakat welfare committees are located. He had to set up his own parallel organizations to make up for the lost ones, and founded a new journal, Al-Mithaq (the Covenant), which reflects his outlook.

Targets of Islamic Activism

Ra'id's group, which took command of all the institutions in Umm al-Fahm, has turned to activism of another sort, which can be summed up in two main domains: First, they undertook to rehabilitate physically and restore to Islamic control old waqf and Muslim holy sites, especially the destroyed mosques and cemeteries in the multitude of Arab villages that had been ravaged and abandoned during the 1948 war. This was particularly significant as part of the mood in which Israeli Arabs recognized the fiftieth anniversary of Israeli independence as commemorating the nakbah, the disaster of the loss of Palestine to the Israelis. Their signal was clear: while other Arabs were commemorating, parading, and demonstrating, they were rehabilitating, reconstructing, and taking the lead in recovering their lost patrimony. They scan and monitor all national construction projects in order to oppose and raise the level of awareness among the Arabs of Israel toward any attempt by the Israelis to desecrate or destroy what they consider to be a religious site.

One prominent example of this is the Istiqlal cemetery near Haifa where Izz a-Din al-Qassam is buried. The memory of this Islamic hero of the 1930s who had fought against both the British and the Zionists until he was killed in battle in 1935 was revived by Hamas, and his name adopted by the military arm of the movement. When the Nesher municipality planned to widen the highway at the expense of the cemetery, the Islamists posted a round-the-clock guard at the newly renovated tomb and warned the authorities against touching the spot. The movement also strives to restore to Islamic control old mosques which had either been destroyed or turned into entertainment and tourist sites. They demand that the revenues from the property be put under their exclusive control.

A second major target of activism involves Arab claims in Jerusalem. Although most Israeli Arabs toe the PLO and Hamas line that eastern Jerusalem should be under Palestinian rule, no element has committed itself more deeply and acted upon its commitment more insistently than the Ra'id group. Sheikh Ra'id has become the chief bearer of the banner of the struggle for Jerusalem. He warns against the "impending menace to al-Aqsa" mosque, and attempts to mobilize local and world Islamic public opinion to his side in order to "rescue the mosque." He virulently condemns the Israeli archeological digs near the Temple Mount and invites delegations of Muslims from Israel and other Islamic countries to come and see for them the works which, he claims, are calculated to undermine the foundations of the Holy Shrine of Aqsa in the Haram a-Sharif compound.

To counter the perceived Israeli threat, Ra'id initiated the takeover and refurbishing of the underground floor of the Aqsa mosque, known to Israelis as "Solomon's Stables," and by Muslims as "al-Musallah and Marwani" (the Prayer Grounds of Marwan, one of the Umayyad Caliphs), thus adding more praying space during the peak flow of worshippers during Muslim holidays. He also organized a meeting of Muslim Brothers in which he lamented the state of affairs of the Jewish occupation of a holy Islamic site, and ran a Jerusalem festival for the same purpose, which attracted some 40,000 believers. All this frenzy of activity, which followed the controversial opening by Israel of an exit to the Hasmonean tunnel next to Temple Mount, has won Sheikh Ra'id support from the Muslim Brothers everywhere. He is perceived as a man of action with an unswerving commitment to the Islamic cause, as he had shown back in 1992 when he mobilized assistance and whipped up support for the 415 Hamas leaders who had been deported by Israel to southern Lebanon.

Sheikh Ra'id travels often to Islamic countries, especially to Egypt and Turkey, which was at the top of his preoccupations and hopes during the brief tenure of the Erbakan government in the mid-1990s, which championed world Islamic causes in the name of the ruling fundamentalist Welfare Party in Ankara. At the time he even sought recognition for his Islamic College by Turkish Muslim authorities. Ra'id has also maintained close relationships with the political branch of Hamas. When Hamas spiritual leader Sheikh Yasin was jailed in Israel, Ra'id built up a close partnership with Dr. al-Zahar, one of the top leaders of the movement in Gaza, and after Yasin was released in late 1997, Ra'id inched closer to him. His activities in support of Hamas, which have apparently included material aid to the families of suicide bombers and subventions to the needy, have won him much scorn from Israeli authorities and public opinion.

When Sheikh Yasin was released from Israeli captivity following the failed Israeli Mossad attempt against the life of the Hamas leader Mash'al in Jordan, Ra'id headed a delegation to Amman to welcome the venerated Hamas hero. The Jordanian authorities, who had become wary of the zealous young sheikh who had attempted to intercede in favor of the Muslim candidates in Jordan's parliamentary elections, had to yield to popular demand and allow him in for the occasion.

When Yasin arrived in Gaza, Ra'id and his crowd were there to greet him, and the contacts between the two have not abated despite Yasin's continued incitement against Israel. Abdallah Darwish, by contrast, has refrained from all these gestures, and his stature among Hamas supporters has greatly declined as a consequence.

Ra'id and his group neither sympathize with nor are supported by the Palestinian Authority. The distribution of Sawt al-Haqq has been prohibited in the territory of the PA. In turn, Ra'id and his supporters do not hide their criticism of the Oslo process in which, they claim, the Palestinians have been short-changed. This did not prevent Ra'id from trying to organize a meeting between the Israeli Chief Rabbi and Sheikh Yasin, something that did not materialize due to Yasin's venomous stand against Israel, but a discussion did take place in Gaza with Israeli Rabbi Menachem Fruman of Tekoa. Ra'id's strategy is crystal-clear: he tries to circumvent the political establishments in both Israel and the Palestinian Authority and channel the contacts into religious matters so as to short-circuit the intergovernmental Oslo mechanism.

When the Persian Gulf crisis was rekindled in April 1998, both factions of the Islamic movement like the rest of the Arab and Islamic world, condemned American interference and sided with the Iraqi people. Ra'id's group in particular abhors the godless Saddam, and so does Abdallah; therefore, they refrained from showing any sympathy to him personally or to his rule. If they had, they might also have endangered the generous support received from the Muslim Brothers and other Muslim fundamentalists disbursed by Saudi Arabia and Kuwait.

The Fundamentalists and Israel

The two splinter groups of the Islamic movement in Israel have become so deeply entrenched in the landscape of the country that they are likely to maintain their separate institutions, their mutual bickering, and ideological differences, which are mainly a question of nuances and tactics, not of doctrine or long-term strategy.

Abdallah's group may grow on the national level due to its participation in national politics through its Knesset members and the likelihood of its providing a better and more updated leadership than the defunct communists. Ra'id's faction, which is stronger at the local level, may pursue its policy of capitalizing on the frustrations of the young Arabs in Israel who cannot identify with the Israeli establishment, though they continue to tap its grants and services, and who are happy with the growing segregation of their Islamic enclaves from the Israeli mainstream. Both factions have enough cadres, vested interests, institutions, leaders, and popular support to last. Within a general atmosphere of dissatisfaction with and alienation from the Israeli polity, which has so far failed to reconcile the contradictions between its nature as a Jewish-Zionist state and its democratic aspirations for equal rights and duties for all its citizenry, the prognosis cannot be optimistic.

Admittedly, the processes that the Arab population in Israel has been undergoing are complicated and diverse, and no blanket statements can justly apply to all. For while

Israelization is proceeding apace in the internalization of values of democracy, human rights, and freedom of speech; higher standards of living; high-technology education; and the substitution of meritocracy and personal politics for the old machinations of the traditional patriarchal hierarchies, elements of alienation and nationalism are also noticeable.

Viewed merely through the focus of the general success story of Islamic fundamentalism in the world today, it is conceivable that many more Muslims in Israel will regroup around their religio-cultural heritage in the years to come. If they do so, and regardless of the Islamic faction they will elect to follow (if by then the two groups have not merged), their common doctrinal and cultural heritage, and the joint ideological infrastructure they have cultivated over the years, will provide them with a common denominator to rally around. This common denominator is made up of two components: one negative regarding the Jews, and the other positive, reflecting the vision of an Islamic state.

The Muslim movement in Israel, especially Sheikh Ra'id's faction, has been professing institutional and political self-reliance in their own enclaves within Israel, much like the Arabs in Israel in general who have also been vying for their own institutional and cultural autonomy. The difference is that Ra'id's supporters often voice the dream of an Islamic state that might replace Israel, while Abdallah's group has not come that close to denying the existence of Israel. Nevertheless, even during its period of unity under Sheikh Abdallah, the Islamic movement did not mince words, recognizing the intifada as a jihad (holy war) against Israel and openly urging the Palestinians to raise the banner in order to "die for Allah."

Since the Oslo process began in late 1993, a tone of pragmatic realism seems to have struck Muslim fundamentalists in Israel. The radicals still pursue their rhetoric as in the past, but the mainstream pragmatists seem to have adopted a more realistic approach to their status and dreams, especially since they participated in the national elections and sent their representatives to the Knesset. During the local elections of 1998, the balance of forces between the two groups remained basically unchanged, while permitting the parties to sharpen their messages and to crystallize and update their views.

There are observers in Israel who regard the process of moderation of the Islamic movement in Israel as irreversible, and they predict that even the radicals will ultimately come around. They find indications of this trend in the fact that the mainstream has joined the fray of Israeli politics and has made itself not much different from prevailing views of Israeli Arabs, something that was manifested in the alliance of the Islamists with the Arab Democratic Party to run together in the 1996 national elections, and thereafter to operate in the Knesset as one faction.

The line-up of the two groups following the 1998 local elections showed mixed results. Sheikh Ra'id ran for the third time for mayor in Umm al-Fahm, received 70 percent of the vote, and took 7 out of the 11 seats on the council. In Nazareth, Salman abu-Ahmed, who was identified with the Abdallah Darwish faction, lost the mayoral elections but his group won 10 of the 19 seats on the city council.

Yet, as is the case in Israel in general, these results show that municipal politics shun ideologies, and that worthy men and able administrators are valued over ideologues and preachers. This explains the recurring victory of Sheikh Ra'id as well as the failure of some of his supporters in other places. Conversely, many of Abdallah's candidates did win in their villages, something which will certainly prop up the prestige of that group. Ra'id's more radical group may have to moderate its conduct if it wishes to retain its constituency, when it recognizes the gains of its rivals made through moderation and joining in national politics. What happens between Israel and the Palestinians, which naturally relates to what happens between Hamas and the Palestinian Authority, will also either facilitate or obstruct that metamorphosis.

10

Islam's First Contacts with the Balkan Nations

Islamic civilization is the dominant force over a great number of nations, from the Atlantic Ocean in the West to Indochina in the East, and from the West and North Africa in the South to the Central Asia in the North, encompassing the Balkan Peninsula in the South-Eastern Europe. It has faced and absorbed various "small" civilizations of the many different nations around the world and presented them with new moral and spiritual alternatives.

It is very difficult to exactly point out the nation that has done the most in forming, developing, and spreading this civilization around the world. However, the Arabs have the honor to be the first in spreading the God's revelation—the Koran—but, they were not alone. The Persians, Berbers, Mongols, and the Ottomans have given great contribution to this end.

Insofar as the people of the Balkan Peninsula are concerned, the Ottomans were crucial in spreading Islam. However, it would be a great error to qualify the Islamic civilization in the Balkan Peninsula as "Turkish," because the whole material and cultural development was achieved through Islam—the complete way of life—together with the other Balkan nations, especially the Albanians and Bosnians.

It is very important to note here that the Balkan nations had extensive trade, political, and military relations with their Muslim counterparts. Exchanging officials and migrations of individuals, or groups of people, are other important features of their strong relations. But, the relations of the Balkan nations with the Ottomans were much longer and more intensive compare to those with other Muslims, and lasted from the end of the 15th century to the Balkan Wars in 1912.

The relations between the Balkan nations (especially the Albanians) and Arabs have existed for a very long time (even before the Christian era), and the Arab world was of great importance for the emergence of the Albanian and Bosnian phenomenon (read the quick acceptance of Islam). However, in spite of these facts, this point was never made the subject of a thorough research from any institution or individual.

The problem is very complex in nature because its sociological, ethnic and cultural, political, ideological, and religious aspects are very much intervened. Political prejudices and mistaken assumptions were considered as "true historic facts" and became part of the official stance towards Islam.

Thus, a new study was needed to shed light on the truth. A new historic approach, free of any prejudice in dealing with the religious, political, economic, and cultural aspects of the pre-Islamic feudal life of the Balkan nations, especially of the Albanians, had to be undertaken.

Historians and Muslim scholars who have seriously approached and studied the pre-Ottoman period are very few in number. Among the Albanians are M. Tërnava, S. Rizaj, M. Mufaku, H. Kaleshi, E. Çabej, etc., and among the Bosnians we have M. Handi or M. Hadijahi, etc. But, it is a pity that some very important literature of the oriental history has yet to be considered by our scholars simply because it is mainly written in Arabic, Turkish, or Persian. A translation of those works has to be urgently done.

In this "small" book, which is an elaborated version of an article of mine in Takvin some ten years ago, I have presented some recently published new facts from the history of the Balkan nations (especially of the Albanians) taken from various writings and put them together in a constructive and objective manner.

I do not pretend to have included everything, thus the research remains open. I have not been able to consult some very important literature and crucial to this book that I had collected between 1987 and 1992 because they were confiscated by the Serb police and never returned.

However, I only look at this book as the first sparkle that is going to give a strong impetus to future and much more thorough works. The existence of Islam and Muslims in the Balkan Peninsula for not less than thirteen centuries must be understood justly and without any prejudice.

Historical and Social Conditions of the Balkan Nations

The time period studied in this book spans from the beginning of the Christianization of the people living in the Balkan Peninsula until the Ottomans conquered it at the end of the 14th century. The events that took place during this period were very important and would subsequently influence the developments during the 14th and 15th centuries, and later, that is, the quick acceptance of Islam by the Albanians and later by other nations. Thus, in order to better understand such a quick acceptance of Islam by the Balkan nations, it is very important to give an exposé of the historical, social, and religious conditions of the people living in the Balkan Peninsula, firstly the Illyrians and later the Slav tribes.

The Illyrians, who were settled in between the Danube River and Adriatic Sea, were polytheists; however, Christianity was gaining ground slowly. In 313, by virtue of the Edict of Milan, the Roman Empire adopted Christianity as its official religion and the people of the Balkan Peninsula were under strong pressure to give in.

The Romans entered Illyria mainly through Salonika in the South, the coasts of the Adriatic Sea in the West, and through Dalmatia in the North-West. It was during this time that the first Christian communities appeared among the Illyrians.

The invasion of the Germanic tribes that occurred from the 4th until the 6th century (the Ostrogoths, Visigoths, Huns, etc.) brought the collapse of the Roman Empire in 476. The end of the 5th and the beginning of the 6th century saw the Bulgars and many Slav tribes attacking and plundering the borders of the Byzantine Empire. The invasion of the Slav tribes that lasted from the end of the 6th until the 7th century resulted in them settling permanently in the territories between the Danube River and Aegean Sea.

According to some research done by E. Petrovi?, the autochthonous population (the Illyrians) found by the Slav tribes in the present-day Eastern Serbia were not Romanized (read Christianized), and he gives the names of places and peoples as an evidence.

This period was characterized by the institutionalization of the Christian religion and its emerging strong connections with the ruling feudal. The difficult social and economic conditions that followed brought about strong resurgences.

During this time in Illyria, as well as in many other places, the difficult economic situation and the spiritual discontention paved the way for many new doctrines to emerge, and some of them went against the institutionalized Christian religion. Small sects, such as Manichaeism, Arianism, etc., were to be found everywhere, something that was not to the liking of the Church and they took stern action against them. Even the later periods were characterized by the same conditions.

In the 9th century, the Byzantine Empire took some interest in the Balkan Peninsula and it was able to again control most of the present-day Albania. However, the invasion of Slav tribes, especially the Serbs, proved to be a big problem for the empire.

S. Hill notes that, in the end of the 9th century, the Bulgars had gained controll over the Eastern Albania and they were very near to the port-city of Durazzo, whereas S. Demiraj says that the Bulgars ruled much of the present-day Albania between 815 and 1018.

The Bulgars had their "golden period" when Simeon was reigning (893-927), when even Kosova was ruled by them. Thus, in the beginning of the 11th century, Albania was the battlefield for the Byzantine Empire fighting against the Bulgars. In 1018, the Bulgars were defeated in the battle near Berati and the Byzantine Empire, then ruled by the feared Vasil II, again took control of Albania. But, throughout the 11th century there were numerous resur-gences, those of 1040, 1043, 1070, 1078, 1080, etc.

In 1054, because of inter-Christian skirmishes, Kosova was divided into two parts: the Eastern Kosova fell under the influence of the Orthodox Christians, and the Western Kosova under the influence of the Catholic Christians.

Such chaotic situation lasted until 1347 when the Serbs under Stefan Dushan invaded the whole of Albania and drove out the Roman and Byzantine Empires. However, Kosova had been under the Serb rule earlier than that. All the historians agree that the Serbs settled in Kosova from the 12th until the 14th century when they invaded Zveçani, Gjakova, Peja, Drenica, Llapi, etc., but there had been no sings of them prior to that time.

The different invadors, religious contradictions between the Christians and others, religious contradictions between the Catholic Christians and Orthodox Christians, etc., enormously aggravated the situation of the Illyro-Albanians.

When Stefan Dushan died, the Serb kingdom was doomed and the feudals founded small independent principalities. The Albanian feudals sized the opportunity and formed three independent principalities: the Principality of Arta in Southern Albania, Principality of Durazzo in Central Albania, and the Principality of Shkodra in Northern Albania which was the largest.

On the other hand, when it came to strongly rejecting the institutionalized Christian religion, the Bogumils (the predecessors of the present-day Bosnians) stood out. They migrated towards the Balkan Peninsula around the 10th century and settled in the eastern parts of it (Rumelia, the present-day Romania). Their religious beliefs were strongly influenced by Hebrew and Manichaeism. This was the very reason that, when they were ruled by the Serbs from the 12th until the 14th century, the Bogumils were persecuted and, in the 13th century, forced to move to the Western parts of the peninsula (in what today is Bosnia). They were labeled as heretics by both the Catholic Christians and Orthodox Christians.

Factors that made Islam a Reality in the Balkans

The first traces of the Islamic civilization in the Balkan Peninsula go back as far as before the Medieval Period. The first Muslims among the Balkan nations date back to the time of the first invasions by the Slav tribes who were not Christians (they had their own Slavic beliefs).

The strategic geographic position of the Balkan Peninsula has made its people (especially the Albanians) to venture and establish contacts with many other nations, especially those in the Aegean Sea and Near East. The historians and archeologists have concluded that the Balkan people conducted extensive trade relations with others.

The Balkan nations had access to the Silk Road that connected Europe with China and Persia. Apart from travelling overland, they also used to travel by sea, and established mutual political, economic, and military relations.

Religious Factor

In the history of Albanians and in that of other Balkan nations as well, this factor has been generally overlooked when it came to analyzing how Islam penetrated the Balkan Peninsula. But, in spite of the difficulties, it is necessary to see what Islam offered in the face of Christianity, Manichaeism, or polytheism that made the Illyro-Albanians embrace it very early.

Islam made people to clearly understand what God is all about and what the humankind's mission on Earth was. Islam, apart from the spiritual aspect, regulates the daily life of the people as well—every single action of ours must be in accordance with the God's laws of harmony. Islam, through the Koran, offered new spiritual and material alternatives. Islam offered monotheism and the timeless law (shariah), and its main objectives were helping and enriching humankind as the God's vicegerent on Earth.

A European historian, Stavrianos, observes that "the religion itself was the main factor for the quick and large acceptance of Islam." Christianity presents only some restricted spiritual dogma, whereas Islam is a complete way of life incorporating spirituality to many other rules of the daily life.

Islam strongly preaches monotheism through its many prophets. However, in the course of time, the monotheistic concepts had degraded. Islam sought to reverse this process by propagating the oneness of God through the many injunctions in the Koran referring to this point.

A controversial element of the Christian religion that has made people think is the divinity of Jesus Christ. It is a historic fact that the divinity of Christ is a "product" of later periods. The notion of Christ as "God-human" was included in the Christian dogma in 451; however, some Christian sects still refuse to accept it. The example of Prophet Mohammed was of great importance in influencing people. Those who long to be the perfect son or daughter, husband or wife, father or mother, or long to be the perfect rulers, should follow his example. The Koran itself takes Prophet Mohammed to be the best model. And this was in contrast to the personality of Christ who, during his short life, was unable to provide people with the needed path to follow.

Many other aspects of the Christian dogma, the likes of original sin, celibacy, etc., go against the human nature. These aspects, together with the incompetent and ignorant Christian clerics, made people to behave indifferently towards Christianity and subsequently embrace Islam.

Moral Factor

Moral values play an important role in the development of a society, and Islam puts great emphasis on them. Moral values of a Muslim are founded in the loyalty towards God, and they are expressed in all daily actions.

The altruistic motto of Muslims—cares for your brother first and then yourself—gave a whole new meaning to human relations. Everything was based on love, harmony, justice, etc. The Koran totally refutes barriers of race, color, or language.

Islam puts into reality the timeless rule of "encouraging the good and prohibiting the evil." The Koran and Prophet Mohammed provide many injunctions in this aspect. This new element made the life of Muslims more complete, creative, and meaningful. Every action a Muslim does is part of the Islamic framework and God does not only encourage belief through prayers, but belief through actions as well. The stories of the great Muslim traveler, Ibn Batuta, are an example. In 1333, he visited the Asia Minor, and has only praise for the hospitality of the Muslims living there.

On the other hand, the Christian dogma was restricted only to the personal spiritual aspects of life—Christianity never preached moral rules applying to the society as a whole. This made the Christian religion loose ground to the emerging Islam.

Cultural and Intellectual Factor

Islam is a religion that does not recognize mythology and superstitions. Indeed, it is a very simple and rational religion that gives great emphasis on knowledge and learning. God has made learning the foremost obligation of the humankind, and because of this fundamental principle, the Islamic civilization has seen fourteen centuries of successful development.

The Muslims never destroyed like the Mongols did in Baghdad, or the Christians in Spain, or the crusaders in the Middle East, or the Romans in Illyria and Greece, but they absorbed and defended whatever positive the previous civilizations had. M. Asad, a well known Muslim scholar, said that Islam was "a new refined civilization full of life, using the cultural heritage Europe had forgotten."

Never in the history of Islam there were episodes like those of G. Bruno, N. Copernicus, G. Galilei, etc. Astronomy, chemistry, medicine, physics, etc., were not labeled as evil knowledge, but as a treasure to be enriched every day. Islam has never recognized the division of knowledge into religious and non-religious disciplines. Prophet Mohammed himself has encouraged people to do the utmost in seeking knowledge. This great affinity between Islam and knowledge made people to take a positive stand and eventually embrace it.

Political and Economic Factor

Many people have tried to represent Islam as a religion without any political and economic principles of its own. This was done to somehow put Islam in the same footing with Christianity, or other religions for that matter. However, Islam preaches a whole new concept of human relations with no place for nationalism, class divisions, clergy, etc. The sole aim of Islam is founding of theocracy concerning humankind's relations with God, and founding democracy concerning relations among humans themselves.

In the basis of the political system of Islam is the concept of vicegerency—the supreme power rests with God. Equality before the law is another strong principle of the political system of Islam and even the state's highest official, the caliph, cannot dodge this obligation. Another principle of the political system of Islam are the guidelines adopted to carry out state affairs, i.e., the God's timeless law—shariah. Everything must go accordingly to the God's law and some practices of Prophet Mohammed. Furthermore, the principle of democracy is crucial. All the state affairs are to be carried out through consultation (shura).

All the human rights (the right of expression, right of movement, right to elect and be elected, right to education, etc.) have their roots at those above principles. On the other hand, the political repression exercised by the Byzantine Empire over the Balkan nations, something that was elaborated in the first chapter, was important for the emergence of Islam. The victories the Muslims achieved against the Byzantine and Persian Empires were of great psychological influence and helped in the spread of Islam.

But, apart from the political aspect, Islam gives great emphasis to the economic aspect of life—the just ways to make a profit, the ways to the just possession, and moderate spending. In the economic framework of Islam, everybody must earn his living through honest means.

The concept of vicegerency applies to the economic life of Muslims as well. Everything that exists on Earth belongs to God, and the humankind constitutes only the "user." Islam strives for equality among the people, and this does not mean equal possession, but equal opportunity. In order to achieve this, Islam has prescribed some mecha-nisms: zakat, obligatory and voluntary sadaqah, inheritance laws, institution of waqf, jizya, etc. All these mechanisms have an important role in the consolidation of the economic system of Islam.

Many injunctions from the Koran that prohibit exploitation, monopolization, interests on loans, etc., and some traditions (hadith) of Prophet Mohammed form the basis of the economic system of Islam that has appealed to many people.

Social Factor

When establishing contacts with the Balkan nations, Christians or polytheists, the Muslims saw them living in very difficult social conditions. The many different rulers—the Roman Empire, the Byzantine Empire, the Bulgarians, and the Serbs—had created some kind of social chaos. It was the Muslims who brought a completely new approach to the social life of the Balkan nations.

God created the humankind from a single couple (one man and one woman), and this is the foundation of the Islamic approach to the society as a whole. In contrast to other religious and philosophical principles, Islam is not based on a particular birthplace, or nationality, or language. Islam recognizes these diversities and tries to establish itself as the uniting force above them all. Prophet Mohammed himself, in his address he made during his last pilgrimage to Mecca (hajj), advised people to establish just social relations without any prejudice.

Islam refutes unjust artificial criterions, and through the obligatory pillars of belief, i.e., proclaiming the oneness of God, the five daily prayers, fasting, zakat, etc., establishes a new feeling of social equality. In order to further elaborate the social aspect of Islam, and illustrate it as well, the role of women is a good example. It is well accepted that women play a crucial part in the institution of family.

Woman, whether she is a daughter, a wife, or a mother, is given a prominent role and considered equal in every aspect to her male counterpart. In the family, she is the first to instill love, kindness, sincerity, and educate the young generation. There are many injunctions from the Koran and many traditions (hadith) from Prophet Mohammed as well, concerning this point. But, the treatment given to women by other beliefs, Christianity for that matter, leaves much to be desired. They treat women as the devil's instruments to ruin people.

Slavery was another aspect that the new social order of Islam tried to regulate, and possibly totally vanish. Neither Christianity, which actually blessed slavery, nor have other philosophical doctrines spoken against it. But, Islam sanctions better conditions for the slaves, and even encourages the prohibition of slavery. The Koran has many injunctions, and Prophet Mohammed has many traditions (hadith) as well, concerning the possible prohibition of slavery.

Taking in consideration all these factors, i.e., the religious, moral, cultural and intellectual, political and economic, and social factors, and most importantly the changes that Islam had brought about, it was simple to understand the easiness with which Islam was accepted by the Balkan nations.

Islamic Civilization Inroad into Balkan Peninsula

How the Islamic civilization emerged in the Balkan Peninsula is one of the most complex problems and requires a multi-dimensional research. Unfortunately, a lot of historic facts concerning Islam and the Balkan Peninsula have been "forgotten," or even distorted. This has been because of centuries of pressure from the Serb and European historians and their political establishments.

Almost every book written on the history of Islam will somehow underline this point. One good example would be an article of R. Doçi where he calls the Christianization of the Albanians during the Medieval Period as "prosperity," forgetting the destruction and barbarisms that the many invaders inflicted for centuries. On the other hand, the emergence of Islam, which he ties to the Ottoman invasion, is called the "doom's day" of the Albanians.

There is place for subjectivism among the Muslim scholars, too. They often see the emergence of Islam from a very narrow "Islamic" angle. This has made the scholarship to be divided into two opposite poles: those who blacken everything Islamic, and those who idealize everything Islamic. That is why an objective study, free of any national sympathies, and free of any religious fundamentalism, is crucial so that we can learn the true history, and not the history we would like it to have been.

Looking at the relevant literature, we would conclude that the two ways that enabled the spread of Islam were:

1. The military expeditions sent to extend the borders of the state of Islam, and
2. The persuasive powers of the Islamic teachings themselves made people ultimately embrace it.

Insofar as the nations of the Balkan Peninsula are concerned, the overwhelming historic evidence points out that the military expeditions were of very little importance to the spread of Islam. Thus, the teachings of Islam themselves were crucial in wining people over. The Koran itself declares that "there is compulsion in religion," and this gave people the feeling of freedom for the first time in centuries. The very famous Albanian writer, S. Frashëri, observes: "Apart from the usage of military might to spread Islam, there does exist another way without turning to invasion or the force of arms, a way that is often not mentioned by the historians." T. Arnold considers this a major point and mentions it in his book, too.

Looking back in history, it is easy to understand which way was the most influential in spreading Islam, the force of arms or its teachings. In most of the times, the Muslim armies only opened the "door" for the Islamic civilization to present itself, and ultimately the people would see the difference.

Islamic civilization entered the Balkan Peninsula mainly from the West through the contacts with Andalusia in Spain, from South through Mediterranean Sea and Sicily, and from North-East through Hungary. However, this book does not tend to answer the question of where Islam came from, but it is more concerned with the question of how it came.

Even though the evidence is short, after a serious analysis, the answer to the above question—how did Islam come to the Balkan Peninsula—would be finally achieved.

After all the research, three are the ways through which the Islamic civilization gained its foothold in the Balkan Peninsula, and a further elaboration of them will follow.

Trade Relations

The development of Islamic civilization and of the Muslims themselves conditioned the expansion of trade. The goods produced were mainly traded with the neighbor nations, however, the traders often ventured even further to far and unknown places. This is why that since the 9th century the trade relations between Europe and Middle East through the Mediterranean Sea were booming. In these trade relations, the most daring Europeans were those from

Florence, Venice, Pizza, Genoa, followed by the French, and Catalonians. The European merchants through Egypt and Syria ventured far away to the Far East.

The Illyro-Albanians had established trade relations with the Arab and Turkish nations, and not only the port-cities of the Adriatic Sea, but the rural parts of the Balkan Peninsula inhabited by them as well. Such strong trade relations were established since the ancient times, and went on into the pre-Ottoman and Ottoman periods.The Arab gold and silver coins excavated in Potoci, near Mostar of the present-day Bosnia-Hercegovina, date back to the time of Marwan II (744-750) which tells of the extensive trade relations the Muslims had with the Balkan nations, first the Albanians and later the Slavs.

Port-cities along the Adriatic Sea like Dubrovnik, Tivari, Ulqini, Durazzo, Valona, Himara, etc., and other Greek and Southern Italian cities were centers of trade. During the 12th century, the well known Muslim historians and travelers, Al-Idris and Ibn Hawkali, tell in fine details the social and political situation of those places. They also describe the road going through the Balkan Peninsula, from the Aegean Sea along the valley of the Vardar River to the coasts of Adriatic Sea.

Usually the Italian merchants traveled by sea, whereas the Muslims mostly traveled overland. The merchants from Venice and Florence used to trade regularly and exchanged their goods mostly in Istanbul and Gallata. Well known are also the caravans from Dubrovnik to Istanbul, and vice versa.

Such strong trade relations have had a great impact on the Balkan nations. Apart from buying and selling, which was the primary intention, the merchants brought a lot of new ideas and changes. This was intensified further when the Muslim merchants started to establish themselves in some fortified and secured coastal cities. The first Muslim colonies appeared. Though they were very small in the beginning, they became larger, and even stronger.

Military and Political Relations

The quick development of the Muslim community (ummah) resulted in its expansion in all directions. By 634, the Muslims had started to attack the borders of the Byzantine Empire, and made the first attempt to conquer Constantinople (now Istanbul). Some years later, in 717-718, the Muslim army under the command of Maslama surrounded Constantinople; however, they could not conquer it. In this expedition, the Muslim army penetrated as far as Adrianople (now Edirne) and Salonika, and this is known as the first contact of the Balkan nations with the Muslim armies. They also built a mosque near Gallata, known as the Arab Mosque. This led the Arabs (read Muslims) to establish their first colonies in Constantinople and Salonika.

Apart from the Muslim colonies, the Slavs built their own small colonies inside the Byzantine Empire. In the battle of Sevastopol in 664, a group of 2000 Slav soldiers were fighting together with the Muslim army against the Byzantine Empire.

In 717-741, a very bloody conflict was going on between two Orthodox Christian sects: those who were against worshiping the paintings, frescos, sculptures, etc., and those who were for them. Often those who were against worshiping paintings, frescos, and sculptures asked the assistance of Muslims, thus, they were well aware that Islamic teachings were against worshiping idols. In the 9th century, the Arabs were more direct in their intentions towards the Balkan Peninsula. This was simple to under-stand because they conquered Crete in 823, Sicily in 827, and some parts of the Southern Italy as well, and the Balkan Peninsula was next in the line.

During 840-841, the Muslims conquered Taranto, Italy, and undertook incursions into the Balkan Peninsula invading Budva, Kotor, Rosi, and Rijeka. They even surrounded Dubrovnik for fifteen years, but without any success. This was the time when the Illyro-Albanians had their first contacts with the Muslim armies. They kept attacking the Balkan Peninsula until 1023 when they lost control of the Southern Italy.

The traces of this new civilization are to be found everywhere. Nearby the cathedral of Trogir there is a relief of an Arab man wearing turban which is a sign of well established relationships. There also are the tombs of two Arabs, which is a fact that they must have been living there for some time.

By the beginning of the 14th century, the Arabs ceased intervening directly into the Balkan Peninsula; however, other Muslim tribes from the Asia Minor were keen on the peninsula. In 1307, those Turkish-originated tribes under the leadership of Malik and Halil entered the peninsula as part of a Catalonian division and went as far as Sveta Gora.

The invasion of the Peceneg tribes had a great impact. There are contradicting views as to when they first appeared: some say they came in the 8th century, and some others say they came in the 9th and 10th centuries. It seems that the former view is more accurate because they appeared at the same time when the independent feudal states did so, i.e., the 8th century. T. Arnold observes that the Peceneg tribes migrated from the coasts of the Ural River and settled in the present-day Macedonia.

But, the most important point is that the Peceneg tribes were Muslims, and were also known as "Ismailites." However, many authors observe that the Peceneg tribes were real "barbarians" who attacked and looted all over the peninsula. But, this should not let us oversee the fact that they were Muslims.

On the other hand, Spain's invasion by the Muslims opened a new chapter in their relations with the Balkan nations. Some of the Slav tribes, especially the Slovenians and Croats, had good relations with the Muslim Spain. In the royal court of Hakemi I (791-822) there were 2000 guards of Croatian origin. Such a big number of guards indicates of extensive relations between them.

This variety of military relations was extended to the politics, too. The Muslim countries had cordial relationship with their Balkan counterparts. In 856, the Serb king, Mikhail III, sent his envoy to the caliph Mutawakil b. Rashid of the Abbasid dynasty to arrange a form of debate on the religious matters.

In 922, the Bulgarian king sent an envoy to caliph Al-Muktadir of the Abbasid dynasty to convey his family's decision to embrace Islam. In this point, well known are the contacts that Caliph Harun Al-Rashid had established with the European rulers. He had sent his envoy to the Serb king, Carl the Great, in order to establish cordial and reciprocal relations.

The Croat ruler, prince Tomislav, had good relations with caliph Abdurahman III and used to even exchange gifts. Abdurahman III had sent envoys to all the Slav kingdoms to discuss and charter their future relations.

The Europeans, the Balkan nations included, kept continuous contacts with the Muslims—the Fatimids (969-1171), the Eyubids (1171-1250) and the Mamelukes (1250-1517)—because of various interests, trade being one of them.

In general, we see the Slavs as allied to the Muslims against the Roman and Byzantine Empires. However, their relations with the Illyro-Albanians will define the future military and political actors of the Balkan Peninsula. At the beginning, those relations were cordial, but changed rapidly.

It looks like there were no military and political contacts between Illyro-Albanians and the Muslims, but that is not true. There were various contacts between them, however, the fact that Illyro-Albanians were ruled by the foreigners—the Roman and Byzantine Empires, the Serbs, etc.—mean that they were almost never identified as an independent political entity.

Missionaries and Migrations

Maybe the most important factor that influenced the rapid spread of Islam among the Illyro-Albanians was the missionaries and migrations of different groups of people. There are indications that travelers and theologists visited almost every part of the peninsula centuries before the Ottomans appeared and played an important role in preaching Islam. This was in some way assisted by the fact that the Muslims controlled many territories around the Balkan Peninsula (Southern Italy, some Greek islands, the Asia Minor, etc.), and by the incursions of the Muslim armies as well.

Maybe the most important among the migrations was a group of Turkish Muslims who settled in Southern Hungary (near the border with the Byzantine Empire) and somewhere near the Ohrid Lake as well (almost in the center of the peninsula).

This is the time when the first concentrated Muslim dwellings are seen in the peninsula. These Turkish tribes who migrated to the Balkan Peninsula were adhering to a breakaway sect of Islam known as dervish. They were persecuted by the mainstream Islamic sect, the Sunnis, and thus forced to live. They came prior to the Ottoman invasions and their leader was Sari Sallteku.

The well known historian, H. Inalcik, says that after much hardship, forty dervish Turkish families migrated to the Balkan Peninsula in 1261. However, they were alone. In 1291, a Muslim family from the Haleb of Syria migrated and settled in Mlik, a village in Kosova. They were known as the Al-Aga family and had a mosque built. This mosque is maybe the oldest in Kosova and still has the inscription of who built it and when.

The Russian Czar Theofil, while fighting in the Asia Minor, forced many Muslims to migrate. They settled in the Balkan Peninsula in the valley of the Vardar River. They came to be known the "Turks of Vardar."

But, the presence of the Muslims in the Balkan Peninsula was so great that the Christian kingdoms could no longer tolerate them. Thus, the many crusades directed for the Middle East passed through the peninsula and literally exterminated the Muslims living there. This happened in 13th century, and the Bulgarians and Serbs took great "pride" in defending Christianity. Hence, the great hate of the Slav against Muslims, and vice versa.

11

Islam and Globalisation

Islamic Universality

The *Quran* states that Islam is the universal religion and is a mercy to all creatures. Islam is a religion of peace. As a universal faith that has been subject to diverse interpretations Islam offers a living demonstration of qualities to which all human beings can relate: compassion, mercy, tolerance, and love. Bearing the label "Muslim" is no guarantee of living by its teaching since Muslims are not a single, homogeneous entity. Grave risks arise from thinking that they are. Islam is more than a system of theology, it's a complete civilization. The classical history of Islam proved the Islamic universality: Islam rejects discrimination, racism, and teaches men and women to disperse within the land and seek the bounty of God.

More clearly the tradition of the Prophet Muhammad instructs his followers to seek knowledge, even to China. Indeed, this Hadith calls for Globalisation at doctrinal and practical levels. Islam became the global power when the peoples of Arabia, Africa, Europe and Asia admired and followed the Islamic civilization and culture. The presence of Islam has contributed to the welfare and the prosperity of the peoples. The civilized peoples closely related to the basics of Islamic doctrine, ethics, values, morals, law, and their customs. Islam and its history have taught Globalisation at the most general level that refers to a process of change which affects all regions of the world in a variety of sectors including the economy, science and technology and to some extent – politics, the media, culture and the environment.

The characterization of Globalisation may be thought of initially as the widening, deepening and speeding up of worldwide interconnectedness in all aspects of social life, from the cultural to the criminal, the financial to the spiritual. The 12th Century was "The Golden Age of Islamic Globalisation". The majority of Muslims are not located in the motherland of Islam, but Indonesia, India and Pakistan. The faces of Islam in these geopolitical locations are more moderate than what has developed in the Middle East. However, the global interaction among the people of Muslim countries does not only introduce moderate Islam, but also militant ideas and practices as the resistance to the common enemy, namely the West.

With this in mind, this chapter attempts to explain the nature of Islam, its interaction with the West and its responses to the Western global economy and military as part of the triggering factors of how global resistance towards the West is expressed in the most inhumane form, such as terrorism. This is not to say that terrorism is acceptable in Islam and to Muslims. Terrorism is not Islamic at all and will never become part of the Islamic teaching.

Unity in Diversity

Although Muslims maintain that there is one divinely revealed and mandated Islam, there are many Muslim interpretations of Islam. There are two major branches of opinion about political and religious leadership after the death of Muhammad: Sunnis (85 percent of the World's Muslims) and Shi'is (15%). There are diverse school of theology, law and mystical tradition that includes many Sufi orders or brotherhoods. Islam represents a basic unity of beliefs within rich cultural diversity. Islam practices itself in different ways within a vast array of cultures that extend from North Africa to Southeast Asia, as well as Europe and America.

As a world religion, Islam is practiced in diverse cultures in Africa, the Middle East, Asia, Europe, and America. Differences in religious and cultural practices are therefore wide-raging. Like all faiths, Islam has developed divisions, sects, and school of thought over various issues. Islamic law provides one of the clearest and most important examples of diversities of opinion. While many law schools existed, only a few endured and were recognized as authoritative. While all Muslims share certain beliefs and practices, such as a belief in God, the *Quran,* Muhammad, and the Five Pillars of Islam, divisions have arisen over questions of political and religious leadership, theology, interpretations of Islamic law, and responses to modernity and the West.

Perhaps nowhere are differences in Islam more visible than in responses to modernity. Since the nineteenth century, Muslims have struggled with the relationship of their religious tradition developed in pre-modern time to the new demands of the modern world (viz. religious, political, economic, and social demands). The issues are not only about Islam's accommodation to change but also about the relationship of Islam to the West, since much of modern change is associated with Western ideas, institutions, and values. Muslim responses to the issues of reform and modernization have spanned the spectrum from secularists and Islamic modernists to religious conservatives or traditionalists, "fundamentalists", and Islamic reformists. The other groups are more "Islamically" oriented but have different opinions as to the role Islam should play in public life.

Islam and the West

The highest tide of Islamic culture, 800-1100A.D., was coincident with the lowest ebb of European culture. While the Muslims enjoyed general standards of living equal to, if not surpassing those of the proceeding Graeco-Roman civilization, the Europeans were living in the semi-barbarous squalor and restricted regime of feudalism – a pattern unalleviated by comforts and luxuries. One of the strangest dramas of history is that at the very moment when Europe, prodded by contacts with the Islamic culture in Sicily and Spain and by the Crusades, began to recover from its prolonged descent towards darkness, Islam entered a decline that was to carry it down into the very fog of obscurantism from which it had helped to rescue Europe. "The spirit" of Islamic civilization developed more rapidly in the West synergized by the philosophy of capitalism in economy and secularism in the politics. Both capitalism and secularism supported by sciences, technology and the military had created the Superpower State, especially after the Cold War.

The Islamic civilization has a significant contribution to drive the Enlightenment in the West and the modern world. The immenseness of the Arab-Islam contribution can best realized by recapitulating the most significant of her activities, considering at the same time their impact to a Europe struggling upward through the barbarism of the Dark Ages. The Arabic-Islamic science and technology, reaching Europe via Sicily and Spain, awoke her from the Dark Ages in which she was slumbering. The detailed elaboration of the actual routes by which this transference took place has only recently been outlined by historians. A hundred years ago a statement of the full influence of the Arabic culture on Europe would have been incredible. But modern research has firmly established its incontestability.

The principles of Western political systems typically are democracy and the rule of law. Together democracy and the rule of law save people from arbitrary whims of dictators and tyrants, and make all people politically equal. Democracy was pioneered by ancient Athens. The rule of law is to a great degree a product of Islam. Democracy in the words of Abraham Lincoln is similar to the syura' in the Islamic concept derived from the Quran by Fuqaha. The West learned the scientific method from Islam and has used that method to develop, amongst many other things, technologies for communication that have shrunk the world. The global civilization may be regarded as the joint legacy of Islam and the West.

The three most influential thinkers of the Western civilization represented the three Abrahamic faiths: Ibn Rusyd (Averroes) the Muslim, Maimonides the Jew, and Thomas Aquinas the Christian. Rationalism initiated the new modern world and ignited the secularism that only takes the Christian's ethic; meanwhile, ethics are a changeable point of view on what is good or bad. Conceptually, Islam and the West were born within the tradition of monotheistic religion, - Jews and Christianity - referred to the Abrahamic faith. In the spheres of politics and economics Islam and the West are often in conflict, where as in knowledge and ideas they are often in harmony. When there is a rivalry between Islam and the West (Christianity) or between capitalism and Islam, one of the solutions is military power and war. Therefore, there is a significant relationship between the economy and politics on one side and belief and religion on the other.

The only super power State nowadays is the United States (U.S.) that has become the "World Cop" who always monitors and unashamedly forces the other State or States to be under its control. This condition is Globalisation or hegemony. The Western world as a whole previously clashed with other civilisations long before the Cold War of Ideology. Firstly, there was genocide against the native ancient civilization of the Americans. Secondly, there was later enslavement of millions of Africans for use in the so-called New World. Thirdly, there was the phase of European imperialism and colonialisation of most of the world. Is the fourth phase the United States as an imperial superpower?

America has now become a new form of empire, controlling millions of people through a variety of inducements and intimidations. In addition, the global development that began after the Cold War left a vacuum from the influence of the two Super Powers or West and East Block represented by the USSR and the U.S. This area is well-known as the Middle East. The victory of the West pioneered by the USA, soon followed by founding the Israel State in the middle of the Middle East countries. The State, in the eyes of the world, inflicts injustice on the Palestinians. Muslims around the world consider the invasion of the Palestinian land as the core problem that creates the rebellion of the oppressed people (Palestinians) by the powerful and unjust state institution and government (Israel). Such rebellion is called "terrorism".

War on Terrorism

The lack of information and deeper misunderstanding of Islam may lead some to think that the war on terrorism is a war on Islam. That's why most Americans and Europeans think of Muslims as strange, foreign, and frightening, inevitably linked to headlines of terrorist events. This is not true since the war on terrorism is not a war on Islam. Islam and Islamic law have consistently condemned terrorism (the killing of non-combatants). Like the members of all religious faiths, Muslims have had to deal with religious extremism and terrorism from their earliest days.

The responses of the mainstream majority to groups like the Kharijites and the Assassins and more contemporary groups like Islamic Jihad in Egypt or al-Qaeda have been to condemn, combat, and marginalize them. From the origins, the Islamic community faced rebellion and civil wars, violence and terrorism, epitomized by groups like the Kharijites and Assassins. The Kharijites were a pious but puritanical and militant extremist group that broke with the Calip Ali and later assassinated him.

The Assassins lived apart in secret communities from which they were guided by a series of Grand Masters, who ruled from the mountain fortress of Alamut in northern Persia. The Assassins' jihad against the Seljuk Dynasty terrorized the princes, generals, and ulama (scholars), whom they murdered in the name of the Hidden Imam. They struck such terror in the hearts of their Muslim and Crusader enemies that their exploits in Persia and Syria earned them a name and memory in history long after they were overrun and the Mongols executed their last Grand Master in 1256.

The response of Sunni Islam and Islamic law was to marginalize extremist and develop a political theory that emphasized stability over chaos and anarchy. This, of course, did not dissuade all from the extremist path. In more recent decades, alongside mainstream Islamic political opposition, terrorist groups have risen up to challenge the regime and terrorize their populations and attack foreign interests. Often they portray themselves as the "true believers" struggling against repressive regimes and in the midst of a "pagan" society of unbelief.

They attempt to impose their ideological brand of Islam and "hijack" Islamic doctrines such as jihad, claiming to be defending true Islam, to legitimate their illegitimate use of violence and acts of terrorism. In Egypt, groups like Egypt's Islamic Jihad and other extremist groups assassinated President Anwar Sadat and government officials, slaughtered tourists in Luxor, burned churches, and killed Christians. In Algeria, the Armed Islamic Group has engaged in a campaign of terror against the Algerian government. Osama bin Laden and al-Qaeda undertook a global war of terror against Muslim governments and America, distorting Islam and countering Islamic law in issuing their own fatwas (legal opinions) in an attempt to legitimate their war and call for an attack on civilians (non-combatants).

The Suicide Bombing in Jakarta, Bali and Poso by Indonesians terrorists under their commander of Malaysian citizenship "the late Dr. Azahari" and his close companion and successor Nordin Top. They have distorted the true Islam and seemed to endorse the mistaken view so common in the West that Islam is essentially a fanatical and violent faith. Terrorism has multiple faces and may be hiding under the name of a religion, philosophy, politics, or any other name. Terrorism is a way of life. It may be a part of the history of human civilization and culture. Defining terrorism is most important in order not to be changeable between "terrorism" and "the warrior of freedom".

The scholars have their own definition of terrorism based on their point of view and field, or they define it as the ruler's outlook. Anyway, how divers those definitions, but the might is the rulers' definition that enforce their definition to be accepted by the people either using military, political, and economic, technology or cultural power. Terrorism may be derived from religious doctrine or motivated by any other beliefs. Terrorism may be come to the true when the terrorists regard themselves as the victim of a repressive and hypocritical regime that never takes care of them, for instance: the IRA, EPTA, and some groups of terrorists in Latin America, and the intifada movement of the Palestinians.

The beginning of the terrorist's movement seems to be Hassan Bin Sabbah (1057 AD), the leader of the impressive movement in the Middle East, Hashashiyyin or Assassins as mentioned above. Meanwhile, Maximilien Robespierre of France was the father of modern terrorism, as claimed by the scholars. Vladimir Lenin (b.1870-1924) is the modern terrorist. His ideas and theories of terrorism are followed by his successor as Vladimir Lenin said. Joseph Stalin (d. 1953) is the master executive of terror. Furthermore, the greatest terrorist of the East was Mao Tse-Tung. Mao led a world class of terror. Mao believed that the government needed to be a dictatorship to remain in control; using terrorism as a means to oppress the people to obey all the governments will.

Mao modernized terrorism and made it more effective, more powerful and more horrific than before. America has been described as "conceived and born in violence". Noam Chomsky has stated that the USA is a rich and powerful country that practices international terrorism on smaller States. Noam Chomsky stated that Osama bin Laden has caused the USA to bomb poor countries, such as Afghanistan and Osama bin Laden is the creation of the USA and for Kuwait, the USA is the savouir and the defender against Saddam' aggression.

For Egypt, the U.S. is the donor of millions of dollars in order to take Egypt out of alignment with countries against Israel. For Saddam Hussein, the U.S. is the big enemy who removed him from his crown. For many countries of the world, the U.S. is a never ending Superpower State.

There is no state in history that has made more progress in economics, the military, science, technology and politics, than the U.S. In both good and bad, the U.S. is an incomparable State. Globalisation or hegemony is a new phase of the U.S. as an imperial having global power, including economic power and power over, information such as the internet. After the Cold War, the U.S. was the winner. Recently this State successfully brought freedom and democracy for peace. The U.S. seems to pull the rest of the world to follow its system. Unfortunately, the U.S. is trapped in imperializing other States. It represented the Jew-Christian ethic that created the capitalist system in economics and secularism system in politics.

Anti-Americanism (along with anti-Europeanism) is a broad based phenomenon that cuts across Arab and Muslim societies. It is driven not only by blind hatred of religious zealotry of extremists but also by frustration and anger with U.S. foreign policy among the mainstream in the Muslim world. The West's espousal of self-determination, democratization and human rights is often seen as a hypocritical "double standard" when compared to its policies, what is actually does – for instance, imposing sanctions upon Pakistan for its development of nuclear weapons while failing to press Israel and India on their nuclear development.

The moral is so evident in America's helping Kosovo is seen by many Muslims totally absent in the U.S. policy of permissive neglect in the Chechnyan and Kashmiri conflicts. The impact of sanctions on more than a half million Iraqi children does not seem to have been considered when they were imposed. Another inflammatory issue involves the significant presence of U.S. military and arms in the Gulf, which critics perceive as a neo-colonialist military influence. The American presence is equated with support for unpopular authoritarian regimes and pressure of Arab governments to comply with U.S. foreign policy objectives, especially with respect to Israel and Palestine. This long litany of grievances stretching over many years feed the anger of many mainstream Arabs and Muslims, as well as extremists.

Globalisation of communications has created a situation in which Arabs (Muslims and Christians) and Muslims around the world often see more than before. Unlike the past, today international Arab and Muslim media are no longer solely dependent on Western reporters and channels. While America's overseas media presence (reporters and overseas posts) and coverage have waned over the past decade, television stations like al-Jazeera and others provide daily coverage of the violence in many Muslim countries. They show, for example, the violence and acts of terror committed by both sides as well as the disproportionate firepower used against Palestinians by Israelis armed with American-supplied weapons, F-16s, and Apache helicopters. America's record of overwhelming support of

Israel-witnessed in its levels of aid to Israel, the U.S. voting record in the United Nations, and official statements by the administration and State Department – has proved to be a powerful lightning rod for Muslim anger over injustice.

Terrorism and Misconsception of Jihad

Osama Bin Laden is the only terrorist leader to have formally declared a jihad- holy war – against the United States. This declaration of holy war is not an empty gesture. Laden's objective was the establishment of a "true" Islamic State under the Sharia. The realization of his objective would require confrontation with the United States because Saudi Arabia had been turned into "an American colony". Asked if he was declaring war on the West, he replied, "It is not a declaration of war – it's a real description of the situation. This doesn't mean declaring war against the West and Western people – but against the American regime which is against every Muslim". He hates the United States passionately and considers it his principle enemy. He accuses the U.S. – the locus of Westernization and modernity – of being the source of all crises and trouble afflicting the Muslim world.

Bin Laden is convinced that U.S. presence in the Muslim world, particularly in his home country of Saudi Arabia, prevents the establishment of real Islamic governments and the realization of the Islamic revivalism to which he and other Islamists aspire. Since a frontal assault is out of the question, the U.S. must be terrorized into withdrawing from the Muslim world. While the atrocities and acts of terrorism committed by violent extremists have connected Islam with terrorism, the Islamic tradition places limits on the use of violence and rejects terrorism, hijacking, and hostage taking.

As with other faiths, mainstream and normative doctrines and laws are ignored, distorted, or hijacked by a radical fringe. Islamic law, drawing on the *Quran*, sets out clear guidelines for the conduct of war and rejects acts of terrorism. Islam, like all world religions, neither supports nor requires illegitimate violence. The *Quran* does not advocate or condone terrorism. However, Quranic verses also underscore that peace and warfare are the norm. Permission to fight the enemy is balanced by a strong mandate for making peace. The root of terrorism within the Muslim community refers to the misconception and misinterpretation of the jihad as the Quran's command. Jihad (to strive or struggle) is sometimes referred to as the Sixth Pillar of Islam.

The Quranic teaching of jihad have been of essential significance of Muslim self-understanding, piety, mobilization, expansion, and defence. Jihad as struggle pertains to the difficulty and complexity of living a good life; struggling against the evil in oneself-to be virtuous and moral, making a serious effort to do good works and to help to reform society. Depending on the circumstances which one lives, it also can mean fighting injustice and oppression, spreading and defending Islam, and creating a just society through preaching, teaching, and if necessary, armed struggle or holy war. The two broad meanings of jihad, non-violent and violent, are contrasted in a well-known Prophetic tradition. It's said that when Muhammad returned from battle he told his followers: "We return from the lesser jihad (warfare) to the greater jihad".

The greater jihad is the more difficult and more important struggle against one's ego, selfness, greed, and evil. Jihad is a concept with multiple meanings, used and abused throughout Islamic history. Although jihad has always been an important part of the Islamic tradition, in recent years some have maintained that it is a universal religious obligation for all true Muslims to join the jihad to promote Islamic reform or revolution. Some look around them and see a world dominated by corrupt authoritarian regimes and a wealthy elite minority concerned solely with its own economic prosperity and awash in Western culture and values. Western governments are perceived as propping up oppressive regimes and exploiting the region's human and natural resources, robbing Muslims of their culture and their option to be governed according to their own choice and to live in a more just society.

Better understanding and a comprehensive study of Islamic teaching in respect of relations between Islam and the West, both by Muslims and the others (Westerners) will eliminate the misconception of a jihad in one side; and misconception of Islam and the Muslims in the other one. Understanding Islam and Muslim peoples will be one of eliminating terrorism. But the most importance is how Muslims all over the world have a good understanding of how the Prophet explained what really jihad is. Jihad is not "holy war", but "struggle" and "effort". This is a very important religious principle. The term jihad reminds all Muslims that Islam as a religion (al-din) is never something achieved or finished. The revelation is given, but those who follow it have to make an effort, day by day, year after year, to put it into practice in a flawed and tragic world.

Islam Post 9/11

Within hours of the planes hurtling into the World Trade Center of New York and Pentagon on 9/11, Americans were crying out in anguish: "Why do they hate us"? The question was echoed throughout Europe, since no doubt the attack was directed not just at America, but at the whole of Western civilization. However, the tragic events of 9/11 and the fear and paranoia they have generated have set Muslims back. America before 9/11 was on the verge of accepting Islam as one of it own, but after the attack of 911 it has paused to once again reassess Islam and Muslims. What happened on 9/11 and afterward has had significant and mostly negative consequences for the Muslim communities in Europe, and has set back the process of mutual accommodation between

Muslims and European populations and the integration of both Islam and Muslims into Europe's social, cultural and political landscape.

In the aftermath of 9/11, people of goodwill on both sides of the divide between the Judeo-Christian and Muslim worlds were filled with deep anxieties. For Westerners, it seemed that a dreadful clash of civilizations had become imminent and unavoidable. For Muslims, it was clear that serious injury had been done to the most powerful nation on earth – a wound that could only call for terrible retaliation. Many Jews and Christians seized on the belief that something feral and evil in the faith of Muhammad had made 9/11 inevitable. Many Muslims feared that a new "crusade" against Islam would ensue, expressing deeply ingrained impulses in the West. Indonesia has the biggest Muslim population in the world. Some Western educated or Western civilized leaders (Prime Ministers or Presidents) regarded Indonesia as a heaven and paradise for terrorists.

They saw Baasyir as an example of the Indonesian terrorist and that this was proven by some of the Islamic doctrines taught at Pondok Pesantren Ngruki where Baasyir typically teaches his students. The popular words of wisdom among the Santri that says "be alive honourable or die as a martyr" are regarded by Westerners as the doctrine of Islamic extremism and terrorism. Meanwhile, the well-known words of wisdom among Indonesian Muslims are just a motivation of achievement and teach the students how to live in dignity. This prejudice was supported by the fact that some actors involved in suicide bombings were the alumni of Pesantren or Islamic institutions. Suicide bombing was introduced as a new type of warfare in the Palestinian-Israeli conflict as a response to the brutal aggression by the Israelis.

On February 25, 1994, Dr. Baruch Goldstein, a Jewish settler who immigrated to Israel from the United States, walked into the Mosque of the Patriach in Hebron and opened fire, killing twenty-nine Muslim worshipers during their Friday congregational prayer. In response, Hamas (Islamic Resistance Movement) introduced suicide bombing promising swift revenge for the Hebron massacre.

The Hamas militia, the Qassem Brigade, undertook operations within Israel itself, in Galilee, Jerusalem, and Tel Aviv. In Israel-Palestine, the use of suicide bombing increased exponentially during the second (al-Aqsha) intifada (uprising), which began in September 2000? The most horrific example of suicide bombings or attacks was seen in the attacks of 911. Traditionally, Muslims are unconditionally forbidden to commit suicide, because only God has the right to take the life he has granted. There is only one verse that appears relevant to suicide in the Holy *Quran*.

The Validity of the Approach

The purpose of study of culture in relation to human rights education and implementation is not "to legitimize such values on the basis of cultural continuity from the past as part of a specific way of life or culture." To regard such a study of culture as purely a legitimization exercise is to reduce it to a selection exercise, i.e. selecting quotes from important texts regarded as basic sources of a particular religion or any other cultural source. This may be extended to selections from favorable episodes from history. Such an exercise belongs mostly to the propaganda sphere. The promotion and protection of human rights by way of implementation requires much more than propaganda.

Legal formulations of human rights (international as well as local) only constitute an initial stage in the achievement of these rights. The gap between law and its implementation needs to be bridged if human rights formulations are not to remain mere illusions. Bridging this gap is an exercise in social transformation and such transformation can only take place within a living cultural context, which needs to be addressed. The essence of the pursuit of human rights is to establish the dignity of the human being as the most central concern of society. This end cannot be pursued without at the same time making efforts to understand the indignities that are meted out to human beings in that society and the cultural forms by which such indignities are constantly reinforced.

For such a purpose, what is required is not selective use of quotes from religious texts or other sources of culture. For example, to select quotes from Buddhist texts which are supportive of freedom of thought and expression or on the rights of women may be an interesting exercise but hardly enough to meet the needs for achieving a proper implementation of these rights. An example of the study of culture from a human rights perspective is the work of Dr. B.R. Ambedkar on the issue of untouchability and his promotion of the notions of equality and fraternity in the cultural context of Hindu India.

The fear that cultural studies may lead to complications is hardly a serious objection. All attempts to move from ignorance to understanding creates complications and this is especially so in such issues as implementation of human rights norms and standards.

The search for uncomplicated means of modernization is not a new one. It is shared by leaders from differing political perspectives. Pol Pot believed in wiping out the past as a fundamental tenet of his modernization philosophy and experimented with it ruthlessly within the four years he was in power. This was his way of doing away with the cultural complications involved in dealing with local culture. A less sincere attempt in this direction was the cultural revolution of Chairman Mao.

The political perspective of avoiding cultural complications has been articulated most clearly in Singapore by Lee Kuan Yew and in Malaysia by Mahathir. It was particularly stressed that possible ethnic confrontations need to be avoided to achieve rapid modernization. The end result was either to restrict freedom of expression and human rights altogether as in the case of Singapore or to a very great degree as in the case of Malaysia.

It is quite natural that for a country like Sri Lanka, which is bedeviled by ethnic violence, to admire a seemingly less complicated model of development. What is implied in such a proposition, however, is to accept an authoritarian model of development as a way out of ethnic conflict. In fact minority parties and many liberal intellectuals preferred a strong Head of State capable of settling ethnic issues as against a democratic government which was perceived as too weak to deal with the views of the majority on the ethnic issue.

In fact, authoritarianism of some sort was seen in Sri Lanka as a short cut to modernization from the late sixties. The "limited dictatorship", as advocated by Felix Dias Bandaranayake is well known. The attempt at a full authoritarianism was attempted by J.R. Jayawardene and Ranasinghe Premadasa, the first and second executive Presidents of Sri Lanka. Such authoritarianism was seen as an imperative for economic modernization of the country and received support from the powerful economic lobbies in the country and outside. Many intellectuals gave theoretical and moral support to this political venture.

This authoritarian model was less complicated in that it believed in the use of violence against dissenters and was expected to be able to carry out modernization rapidly. The resulting displacement of democracy is well documented. The ethnic issue grew into civil war and the country, instead of achieving modernization, descended to unprecedented chaos. This very chaos in turn can create a desire for simple methods of getting over such chaos and achieving some form of prosperity as some countries have achieved in Southeast Asia. However, the experience of the last two decades has distanced most people from the belief that such a result could be achieved through authoritarianism.

Modernization in the West was accompanied by a fundamental transformation of culture achieved through religious reformation. Perhaps this process contributed to the evolution of democracy and its accompanying modernization. Thus modernization in the West included the replacement of the feudal culture with a democratic culture. Such transformation was not an automatic process following economic modernization but a conscious process achieved by the critical examination of the cultural foundations of the feudal society in different countries. The feudal lords as well as the feudal clerics came under scrutiny as a part of this transformation.

In a country like Sri Lanka, is it possible to protect and promote human rights without a thorough scrutiny of society and culture? If one answers this affirmatively, then it is quite understandable to divorce human rights issues from issues relating to culture. However, the experience in Sri Lanka shows that despite increase in the number of legal enactments on human rights and quite a lot of programs for education on such rights, the country's human rights problems are increasing. There have not been significant improvements either in the civil or the economic rights spheres. Any serious attempt at promotion and protection of human rights must be accompanied by an effort to understand the root causes for the existence of such a situation.

A short examination of some of the basic human rights problems may be useful at this stage. Equality remains a basic issue that the Sri Lankan psyche does not easily accept despite the Constitutional recognition of the concept as a fundamental aspect of the legal system. Sri Lanka has a very deeply rooted caste system both among the Sinhalese as well as among the Tamils. To regard the Sinhala Buddhists who constitute over 69.30% of the population, as a homogenous community, is to overlook the deeply-rooted caste system that exists among the Buddhists even more than in non-Buddhist Sinhala communities. In India, Buddhism rose as a social movement that radically rejected and replaced the caste-entrenched Hinduism. Buddha went so far as to exhort the rejection of Hindu sacred texts (Shastras) as a part of radical rejection of caste.

Centuries afterwards it took a ruthless Hindu counter-revolution to oust Buddhism from India and to re-enforce a rigid caste system. However, when Buddhism was introduced to Sri Lanka and was accepted by the Royalty of the time it incorporated unto itself the existing caste hierarchy of the country. Later, even the organization of Sanga attained a caste character. This continues to the present. Thus in Sri Lanka Buddhism - the world's most egalitarian philosophy popularly regarded as a religion - lost its capacity to contain the concept of equality within its body of thought.

The opposite of original teaching - the caste system-was accommodated within itself. As a result, a deep religious barrier exists in the country reproducing discriminatory practices among the Sinhala Buddhists themselves. In provinces such as Kandy, Ratnapura and Matara, where the population is overwhelmingly Sinhala Buddhist caste-based discrimination exists to appalling degree. It is the caste character of Sinhalese that prevents the acceptance of the Tamils on an equal basis. A race that does not accept equality among them is not likely to accept equality with other races. Buddhism as is practiced in Sri Lanka has been psychically transformed to accept and justify caste and is unable to generate social energy to accept racial equality.

While some intellectuals have tried to create the notion called Sinhala Buddhism, as an important component on the contribution to anti-Tamil racism, they have failed to raise the issue of caste which deeply divides the Sinhalese. Lack of familiarity with equality as a human experience among the majority community itself is more responsible for the present ethnic crisis than any other factor. Caste discrimination exists in the Tamil community too. The caste system of Tamils in Sri Lanka is even more rigid than the Sinhala caste system. There have been many Tamil movements fighting for such rights attending to Kovils (Hindu Temples).

At the early phase of militant organizations of Tamils in the middle part of this century, their violence was directed towards "higher" castes of the Tamils themselves (this was so in southern rebellions of the South in 1971 and afterwards also). Perhaps the continuing violence in Tamil communities has leveled down caste barriers among the Tamils living in these areas. The study of cultural factors relating to lack of familiarity of the concept of equality in Sri Lankan culture can contribute greatly to understanding the present situation of the country and will help towards finding ways to cultivate a culture of equality.

A doctrinal basis for this exists in Buddhism as taught by Buddha, though the actual Buddhism as found in Sri Lanka has assimilated local caste prejudices. Another important human rights problem in the country is the general tolerance of violence. The use of torture by the police is endemic. Psychological forms of torture are so common that no one even cares to challenge them in a court of law. As far as law goes, the Constitution of Sri Lanka has incorporated the provisions of the International Covenant of Civil and Political Rights against torture and cruel and inhuman punishment. The Supreme Court of Sri Lanka has given several laudable judgments protecting these rights as absolute rights which know no limit.

However, torture and inhuman treatment remain quite an accepted cultural habit, so that anyone who has some connection with the police gets its support to punish their less influential opponents. During the times of instability, use of such violence reaches unimaginable proportions. In the South, such occasions were the periods around 1971 and 1988-1993. And in the Tamil areas it has continued from early 1980 up to date. The extra-judicial killings have now become quite a part of the stuff the Sri Lankan psyche has learned to put up with. There were a considerable number of such deaths in 1971 in the South and between 1988-1992 the conservative estimate of such deaths is twelve thousand (NGOs have claimed the number to be sixty thousand.)

The bodies were exhibited on the roads and were thrown into rivers. The attempt to prosecute offenders is almost negligible. Even the horrific cases such as the killing of over thirty school children have not ended in the prosecution of all the suspects. While there have been protests, these have not been in proportion to the massive violations. An old psychic habit has asserted itself and there has been the willingness to adjust to the situation as if fearing that the pursuit of justice may lead to further trouble. Among the weaker sections of the population, tolerance of such violence may be a way of expressing their weakness. Among the socially strong it can be a way of asserting their power and authority.

In case, promotion and protection of human rights implies understanding of such human behavior. Houtart analyzed the statistics of the participants in 1971 and claimed that there was a clear indication of a link between heavily discriminated castes and the participation in rebellion. After the rebellion, when thousands of youth surrendered answering a call of the government for amnesty, interviews were conducted to find the extent of each person's involvement. One question was about the caste of these persons. Belonging to a particular caste was regarded as prima facie evidence of possible participation in the rebellion. In the suppression in 1988-1993, some of the worst police violence was directed towards some "low" castes.

A further important human rights issue is the seeming indifference towards the weakest in society. This is a very important aspect in a country where over 40 percent of the people live below the poverty line. (It must be noted that the category below poverty line in a third world country like Sri Lanka is very different from a similar category in the first world where it is implied that poverty is relative poverty. In a third world context this means lack of basic food, shelter and clothing.) Still, most businesses including those providing professional services rely on the exploitation of the poorest.

In the agricultural sphere which is the largest economic sphere, the traders rely on the purchase of products below the cost price. Many attempts by the state and other agencies to regulate price mechanism have not been resolute enough to be successes. Suicides among peasantry are high. In fact, the suicide rate in the country ranks among the highest in the world. Recent published statistics showed 70,000, suicides from 1983 to 1997, a number higher than the accounted for deaths in ethnic warfare during the same period. Vast numbers of these suicides have taken place among the poorest. Those who have died in the ethnic war on both sides also, for most part, belong to poorest sections of society.

The professionals have a long-standing cultural habit of exploiting the ignorance and the backwardness of the poorest sections of society. A frank relationship where professionals inform their clients of the things that these clients have as a right to know is not yet a part of the local culture. While there is some improvement in the right to information as against the state, there is hardly any improvement in the area of scrutiny of professional behavior. Enforcement of the right to health implies scrutiny of practices of the medical profession: due process rights require an examination of the legal profession. The poor can have the benefit of such scrutiny only if the guardians of rights such as the press and the human rights community take a serious attempt.

The indifference to the poor is related to the caste-based character of the society where "lower caste" by definition is the socially weak. The social consciousness in Sri Lanka has been determined by the land distribution of the feudal society. The landless were dependent on the land owners, usually referred to as "Radalayas". Radalayas were arrogant and trampled on the people with impunity. The impunity of the "upper caste" and people who belonged to a higher status than those known as "Sananya Minissu" (ordinary people) is a deeply imbedded cultural concept. Recently, (June 1997), a senior judge who has been presiding over some serious human rights cases said," independence of judiciary in this country is a myth where even getting a warrant executed is impossible if the suspect does not happen to be a "Haramanis" (small person).

While legally no one is immune from prosecution, in reality, many are. Thus medieval conceptions still continue in the practical application of laws. Radalayas treated "Samanaya Minissu" with contempt and use of violence against such people was a common practice. One example is a criminal case which happened in the seventies in a town in the south called Akurassa. One Radala family occupied positions in town such as posts in town council and the cooperatives. One male youth, who was a son of a woman who worked for this family, joined the local communist party and at one cooperative meeting challenged the Radala master on some points.

Such a question was too much for this man to bear. He stabbed the young man to death with a huge knife and surrendered to the police with the knife in his hand. According to a close relative he never regretted this act. A farmer from Tabutthegama, Anuraddhapura summed up what human rights means to poor people in the country-side: "When the officer-in-charge of the police station shoots our cow and takes it to a party at his home, my mother prepares chillies and sends it through my father to the police officer's house. This is the way my father tells the officer that he bears no grudge for the police officer killing his cow. If the officer feels that there is some ill-will my father may face other problems."

The cruelty that "upper castes" have perpetrated in the past centuries on the "ordinary people" is immense. It may well be the psychic patterns of this behavior that gets repeated during times of disturbances by way of crude killings, humiliating forms of the disposal of bodies, and other forms of violence.

Is it not the same psychic pattern that creates in the victims inhuman and cruel forms of revenge? With more people from "low castes" getting educated due to free education, resentment grew in rural "upper" castes and much violence developed on this basis. In the promotion and protection of human rights it is very necessary to study and understand the patterns of violations in the country.

The Sinhala language in its grammatical form still retains a distinction of addressing people on the basis of status. In the colloquial form such distinctions are expressed in even a harsher manner. Another important area concerns rights to information and freedom of expression and besides the limitations imposed by the state there are limitations which are culturally imposed. A close scrutiny of patterns of corruption and a pattern of violence is not generally pursued consistently.

Even the pressure to expose the extra-judicial killings did not reach anywhere near to similar investigations in Argentina. To hide things under the carpet continues as a cultural habit. The cultural habit is re-imposed by the use of violence against those who break the taboo. This violence is often initiated privately.

Creating a human rights culture involves much more than legalistic approach. As against the Indian Marxists of the pre-independence period who ignored social and cultural aspects Dr. B.R. Ambedkar argued, "History bears out the proposition that political revolutions have always been preceded by social and religious revolutions." The sensitivity the conservative elements show against examination of religion from a religious point of view was demonstrated by the ex-communication of Fr. Tissa Balasuriya, a Sri Lankan priest, for his attempts to look into the rights of women from a theological point of view.

The literature relating to this debate is a rich source on the issue of Religion, Culture and Human Rights.

Bibliography

Ali, Syed Ameer. *The Spirit of Islam: A History of the Evolution and Ideals of Islam*, with *a Life of the Prophet*. London: Chatto & Windus, 1978.

Bloom, Jonathan and Sheila Blair. *Islam: A Thousand Years of Faith and Power*. New Haven, CT: Yale University Press, 2002.

Burrell, D. *Knowing the Unknowable God: Ibn Sina, Maimonides, Aquinas* (Notre Dame: 1986).

Cook, Michael. *The Koran: A Very Short Introduction*. Oxford, UK: Oxford University Press, 2000.

Davidson, H.A. *Proofs for Eternity, Creation and the Existence of God in Medieval Islamic and Jewish Philosophy*. Oxford, 1987.

Elias, Jamal J. *Islam*. Upper Saddle River, NJ: Prentice Hall, 1999.

Esposito, John L. and John Obert Voll. *Makers of Contemporary Islam*. UK, Oxford University Press, 2001.

Fakhry, M. *A History of Islamic Philosophy* , 2nd ed. New York, 1983.

Gilsenan, Michael. *Recognising Islam: an anthropologist's introduction*. London: Croom Helm, 1982.

Gutas, D. *Greek Philosophers in the Arabic Tradition*. Aldershot, 2000.

Hodgson, Marshall G.S. *The Venture of Islam*, 3 Vols. Chicago, IL: University of Chicago Press, 1974.

Hourani, G. (ed.), *Essays on Islamic Philosophy and Science.* Albany, 1978.

Keller, Nuh Ha Mim, trans. *Al-Nawawi's Manual of Islam.* Cambridge, UK: The Islamic Texts Society, 1996.

Marmura , M.E. (ed.), *Islamic Theology and Philosophy.* Albany, 1984.

Murata, Sachiko and William C. Chittick. *The Vision of Islam.* New York: Paragon House, 1994.

Nasr, Seyyed Hossein. *The Heart of Islam: Enduring Values for Humanity.* San Francisco, CA, Harper San Francisco, 2002.

Peters, F.E. *A Reader on Classical Islam.* Princeton, NJ: Princeton University Press, 1994.

Qadir , C.A. *Philosophy and Science in the Islamic World.* London, 1990.

Rippin, Andrew and Jan Knappert, eds. *Textual Sources for the Study of Islam.* Chicago, IL: University of Chicago Press, 1986.

Rippin, Andrew. *Muslims: Their Religious Beliefs and Practices.* London: Routledge, 2nd ed., 2001.

Robinson, Francis. *Atlas of the Islamic World since 1500.* New York: Facts on File, 1982.

Rosenthal, F. *Greek Philosophy in the Arab World.* Aldershot, 1990.

Ruthven, Malise. *Islam in the World.* New York: Oxford University Press, 2nd ed., 2000.

Savory, R.M., ed. *Introduction to Islamic Civilization.* Cambridge, UK: Cambridge University Press, 1976.

Schimmel, Annemarie. *Islam: An Introduction.* Albany, NY: State University of New York Press, 1992.

Schulze, Reinhard. *A Modern History of the Islamic World.* Washington Square, NY: New York University Press, 2000.

Schuon, Frithjof (D.M. Matheson, trans.). *Understanding Islam.* London: George Allen &

Schuon, Frithjof. *Islam and the Perennial Philosophy.* London: World of Islam Festival Publ. Co., 1976.

Sharif, M.M. *A History of Muslim Philosophy,* 2 vols. (Wiesbaden: 1963-6).

Stern, S.M. *Medieval Arabic and Hebrew Thought* , ed. F. Zimmermann, London, 1983.

Stern, S.M., Hourani, H. and Brown, V. (eds.), *Islamic Philosophy and the Classical Tradition.* Oxford, 1972.

Tayob, Abdulkader. *Islam: A Short Introduction.* Oxford, England: Oneworld, 1999. University of Chicago Press, 1986.

Waines, David. *An Introduction to Islam.* Cambridge, UK: Cambridge University Press, 1995.

Watt, M.W. Islamic Philosophy and Theology. Edinburgh, 1962, revised ed. 1985.

Watt, William Montgomery. *The Formative Period of Islamic Thought.* Oxford, UK: Oneworld,1998.

Watt, William Montgomery. *What is Islam?* London: Longman, 1970.

Williams, John Alden, ed. *The Word of Islam.* Austin, TX: University of Texas Press, 1994.

Wolfson, H.A. *Studies in the History of Philosophy and Religion* , ed. I. Twersky, G.H. Williams, in 2 vols. Cambridge, MA, 1973, 1977.

Wolfson, H.A. *The Philosophy of the Kalam.* Cambridge, MA, 1976.

Ziai, H. "Islamic Philosophy," in *The Oxford Companion to Philosophy,* ed. T. Honderich. Oxford , 1955.

Index